The Iconography of Independence

This book explores the phenomenon of Independence Days. These rituals had complex meanings both in the territories concerned and in Britain as the imperial metropole, where they were extensively reported in the press. The book is concerned with the political management, associated rhetoric and iconography of these seminal celebrations. The focus is therefore very much on political culture in a broad sense, and changing perceptions and presentations over time. Highlights of the book include an overview by Sir David Cannadine relating the topic to ornamentalism, invented tradition and transitions in British culture. Although the book is mainly concerned with the British Empire, Martin Shipway – a leading historian and cultural analyst of French decolonization – contributes an acute summary of how the same 'moment' was handled differently in the other great European empires. There are detailed and lively studies by noted specialists of the onset of Independence in India/Pakistan, Malaya, Ghana, Zimbabwe, and Guyana. The book includes a thematic focus on the role of representatives of the British monarchy in legitimating transfers of sovereignty at their point of climax.

This book was previously published as a special issue of *The Round Table*.

Robert Holland is Professor of Imperial and Commonwealth History at the Institute of Commonwealth Studies, School of Advanced Study, University of London.

Susan Williams is Senior Research Fellow at the Institute of Commonwealth Studies, School of Advanced Study, University of London.

Terry Barringer is the Assistant Editor of *The Round Table: The Commonwealth Journal of International Affairs*.

The Iconography of Independence

'Freedoms at Midnight'

Edited by Robert Holland, Susan Williams
and Terry Barringer

LONDON AND NEW YORK

First published 2010 by Routledge
2 Park Square, Milton Park, Abingdon, Oxon, OX14 4RN

Simultaneously published in the USA and Canada
by Routledge
711 Third Avenue, New York, NY 10017

Routledge is an imprint of the Taylor & Francis Group, an informa business

© 2010 The Round Table
First issued in paperback 2013

Typeset in Times by Value Chain, India

All rights reserved. No part of this book may be reprinted or reproduced or utilised in any form or by any electronic, mechanical, or other means, now known or hereafter invented, including photocopying and recording, or in any information storage or retrieval system, without permission in writing from the publishers.

British Library Cataloguing in Publication Data
A catalogue record for this book is available from the British Library

ISBN13: 978-0-415-55145-8 (hbk)
ISBN13: 978-0-415-85374-3 (pbk)

Contents

	Abstracts	vii
	Preface *Susan Williams, Robert Holland* and *Terry A. Barringer*	ix
1.	Introduction: Independence Day Ceremonials in Historical Perspective *David Cannadine*	1
2.	Independence Day and the Crown *Philip Murphy*	19
3.	"At the Stroke of the Midnight Hour": Lord Mountbatten and the British Media at Indian Independence *Chandrika Kaul*	29
4.	The Ending of an Empire: From Imagined Communities to Nation States in India and Pakistan *Yasmin Khan*	47
5.	Casting "the Kingdome into another mold": Ghana's Troubled Transition to Independence *Richard Rathbone*	57
6.	Whose Freedom at Midnight? Machinations towards Guyana's Independence, May 1966 *Clem Seecharan*	71
7.	Freedom at Midnight: A Microcosm of Zimbabwe's Hopes and Dreams at Independence, April 1980 *Sue Onslow*	89
8.	'Transfer of Destinies', or Business as Usual? Republican Invented Tradition and the Problem of 'Independence' at the End of the French Empire *Martin Shipway*	99
9.	*Merdeka!* Looking Back at Independence Day in Malaya, 31 August 1957 *A.J. Stockwell*	113
10.	The Pattern of Independence: A Postwar Chronology	131
	Index	135

Abstracts

Introduction: Independence Day Ceremonials in Historical Perspective
DAVID CANNADINE

Independence Day ceremonies deserve serious scholarly attention and should be set in a longer historical time-frame and broader geographical perspective. There was more variation in practice than is generally recognized but common characteristics and general themes emerge. The ceremonies marking India's independence in 1947 provided a prototype and model. The consensus displayed at Independence was in many ways superficial and the pomp and partying concealed continuing tensions and paradoxes. This chapter also considers observances in the metropolis, including the elaborate funerals of Churchill, Mountbatten and the Queen Mother, with their sense of recessional and retreat.

Independence Day and the Crown
PHILIP MURPHY

The role of members of the royal family at independence ceremonies deserves more attention. There was a widely accepted hierarchy of royals. The aspirations of new states, the fears and concerns of the Palace and the Colonial Office and gender issues all affected decisions and arrangements. This study reinforces David Cannadine's ornamentalist view of empire.

"At the Stroke of the Midnight Hour": Lord Mountbatten and the British Media at Indian Independence
CHANDRIKA KAUL

This chapter examines the portrayal of Indian Independence in the British media with particular attention to the orchestration of official publicity by Lord Mountbatten and his press attaché, Alan Campbell-Johnson. The British press managed to portray Independence as a British achievement, arising almost organically out of its long-term policy and vindicating British rule. The chapter also explores press portrayal of Indian leaders, the Princely States, the role of the Commonwealth and communal violence.

The Ending of an Empire: From Imagined Communities to Nation States in India and Pakistan
YASMIN KHAN

The ritual and rhetoric of Independence Day celebrations in New Delhi and Karachi masked confusion about the kinds of state coming into existence and complex new questions about nationality and citizenship that would take a long time to resolve.

Casting "the Kingdome into another mold": Ghana's Troubled Transition to Independence
RICHARD RATHBONE

The pomp and partying of Ghana's Independence Day in March 1957 obscured some messy politics. The triumphalist story, widely accepted outside Ghana, of a heroic Nkrumah and the Convention Peoples' Party eclipsed alternative stories from the North, the rural areas and those who opposed Nkrumah. This chapter also considers the ironies and iconography of Ghana's 50th anniversary celebrations.

Whose Freedom at Midnight? Machinations towards Guyana's Independence, May 1966
CLEM SEECHARAN

This chapter explores the tactics and rhetoric of Cheddi Jagan of the People's Progressive Party and Forbes Burnham of the People's National Congress in the negotiations and events leading to the independence of Guyana. It looks at the role of the colonial government and of President Kennedy, the CIA and American intervention. Burnham out-manoeuvred his rival to win the 'prize' of independence. Guyana remains a poor and racially polarized country.

Freedom at Midnight: A Microcosm of Zimbabwe's Hopes and Dreams at Independence, April 1980
SUE ONSLOW

This chapter recounts the events leading up to Independence Day in Zimbabwe in April 1980, the celebrations on the day and the hopes, fears and dreams around them.

'Transfer of Destinies', or Business as Usual? Republican Invented Tradition and the Problem of 'Independence' at the End of the French Empire
MARTIN SHIPWAY

Details of independence ceremonies in French sub-Saharan Africa in 1960 are sparse. Republican France had no place for monarchist pageantry and ornamentalism, although there was some borrowing from the British rhetoric and iconography of the end of Empire. This chapter explores differences between French and British decolonization with particular attention to the French experience in Vietnam and French West and Equatorial Africa 1958–60.

Merdeka! Looking Back at Independence Day in Malaya, 31 August 1957
A.J. STOCKWELL

This chapter starts by examining the ceremonies in which the transfer of power from Britain was celebrated and legitimated half a century ago. It discusses Malay traditional rites which accompanied the birth of the nation-state and the rituals which the British devised to cover their retreat from empire. Both sides worked for a cordial hand-over in order to demonstrate to the world that the process was both right and effective. The transition appeared almost too smooth to some, suggesting that the realities of power had scarcely changed and that the independence of the Federation was being compromised. In fact, the records show that Malaya advanced to independence much faster than the British had expected and that, notwithstanding their anxieties about Malaya's prospects, they had no practical alternative to falling in with Tunku Abdul Rahman's timetable.

Preface: 'The Midnight Hour'[1]

SUSAN WILLIAMS, ROBERT HOLLAND AND
TERRY A. BARRINGER
Institute of Commonwealth Studies, University of London

Tryst with Destiny

"At the stroke of the midnight hour, when the world sleeps," declared Prime Minister Jawaharlal Nehru to the Constituent Assembly in New Delhi, just before the moment of independence on 15 August 1947, "India will awake to life and freedom." Long years before, he said, the people of India had made a "tryst with destiny", which they would now redeem:

> A moment comes, which comes but rarely in history, when we step out from the old to the new, when an age ends, and when the soul of a nation, long suppressed, finds utterance.[2]

This image of "the stroke of the midnight hour"—on the cusp between the old and the new—captured the imagination of India and the world.

In fact, though, the reason for choosing midnight had been a pragmatic one: a compromise over dates. The Viceroy, Lord Louis Mountbatten, had set 15 August as Independence Day, but Hindu astrologers argued that the day before was more auspicious. Nehru solved the problem by arranging for India's Constituent Assembly to convene on 14 August and continue in session until his speech at midnight—when independent India would be born.[3]

Over the next half century, as the process of decolonization from Britain ran its course and more than 50 colonies achieved self-rule, the marking of 'freedom at midnight' became a tradition at independence celebrations, endorsed by an assumption that its embryonic enactment in India had been deliberate. As symbol and image, it developed a powerful meaning that entered art, poetry and fiction. In 1981, when Salman Rushdie published *Midnight's Children*, the resonance of the title was instantly understood. It was underscored in the opening paragraph, where the protagonist and narrator is born at the exact moment of India's birth:

I was born in Doctor Narlikar's Nursing Home on August 15th, 1947. And the time? The time matters, too. Well then: at night. No, it's important to be more ... On the stroke of midnight, as a matter of fact. Clock-hands joined palms in respectful greeting as I came. Oh, spell it out, spell it out: at the precise instant of India's arrival at independence, I tumbled forth into the world.[4]

By the time of the final transition from Britain—the handover of Hong Kong to China in 1997—a countdown to midnight was the inevitable centre of the ceremonies.

The year 2007 saw the 60th anniversary of the independence of India and Pakistan, the 50th anniversary of the independence of Ghana and Malaya, and the 10th anniversary of the Hong Kong handover. This was an appropriate moment to hold a conference on the iconography of independence days, looking at their meanings as beginnings (to the nascent state) and endings (to the imperial power). This conference, *'Freedoms at Midnight': The Iconography of Independence*, took place on 28 June 2007 at the Institute of Commonwealth Studies, University of London. The results of that conference are published in this book.

Earlier Prototypes

At the outset, it is worth recalling that the phenomenon with which this book is concerned—with all its sensitivities, requirement for the careful management of delicate circumstances, and divergent perceptions—was not without prototypes from an earlier era. On 2 June 1864, the Ionian Islands obtained their 'freedom', though the freedom the local inhabitants wanted then was not independence, but union with Greece. For weeks and months beforehand the British governor (or Lord High Commissioner), Sir Henry Storks, had fretted that the day in question would spill over into the violence and ill-feeling that had always bedevilled Anglo-Ionian relations, instead of 'signing off' British rule with images of fraternity and a mission well accomplished. To ensure stability, the British naval and military presence in the capital, Corfu Town, was increased in the period leading to the climax of withdrawal. When the moment of transfer arrived, no Greek troops were allowed to disembark until the last British soldier had already boarded the waiting transports. Storks admitted afterwards that he was overcome with emotion when, departing himself from the famous Venetian Esplanade, he was met not by hostility, but by acclamation and goodwill on the part of a vast local crowd gathered for the occasion. Whether, as he surmised, this was because the Ionians were sad to see the British depart, was, however, another matter entirely.

What this earlier prototype underlines are the very powerful emotions and anxieties permeating the arrival of 'freedom' in colonized societies, and the razor's edge between order and chaos on which it was sometimes positioned. In the Ionian case, Storks had in advance written to the Colonial Secretary in London

> At Corfu especially, it is very important that so great an event as the spontaneous cession ... of the Ionian states to Greece, and the withdrawal of the British Protectorate after a period of fifty years, should be marked by such a display as will not lead the people of these countries to suppose that we have

been driven away or have yielded to any pressure which the Ionians have been able to impose upon us.[5]

In truth, the cession was not 'spontaneous' at all, and the British were leaving because they could no longer summon the will to maintain their domination. This was how the matter was instantly framed in Greek political folklore, and indeed, interpreted in the rest of Europe. But for domestic British consumption at least, another 'narrative' was essential, one in which the day of departure encapsulated not British weakness and defeat, but strength, magnanimity and determination to ensure an ordered process. From the iconography of this departure, we can see that the complex political and psychological currents of 'freedoms at midnight' in the later 20th century were not so unique as contemporaries at the time might have supposed.

Endings—Image and Reality

Just as the British always sought to dignify and ritualize the fact of running an empire, finding ways of reconciling it to long-standing self-perceptions as a liberal and democratic culture, so they sought to do the same when getting out. Independence Day celebrations may have signified a defeat for Britain, in some cases the outcome of long years of bitter conflict. But the defeat was dressed up as a victory, giving the impression of ongoing power and importance. This led at times to confusion. When Bechuanaland and Basutoland in 1966 were preparing to become Botswana and Lesotho, respectively, the British Embassy in Paris wrote to the Foreign Office in Whitehall to report an inquiry from the Quai d'Orsay, which wanted to know how to address the letters introducing their delegates to the Independence celebrations: "Should the letters be addressed to the governments of these two countries or to the Queen?"[6]

On occasion, British administrators overreached themselves. In Botswana, in the hours leading up to 'freedom at midnight' on 30 September 1966, the officials minding Princess Marina of Kent grew anxious about a gathering sandstorm. When it was time for the party of dignitaries to leave for Gaborone's newly erected independence stadium, they suggested to Sir Seretse Khama, the first President, the possibility of postponing the ceremony. "You cannot postpone independence!" admonished Seretse. Princess Marina agreed, pulling a headscarf over her tiara.[7]

In his book, *Ornamentalism* (2001), David Cannadine looks at how the British saw their empire—beginnings, localities, generalities, and endings. In his introduction to this volume, he develops his analysis of endings—specifically, the iconography of independence day ceremonials, from the point of view of the departing British. There is now sufficient distance from these episodes and events, he believes, "to see them in a historical perspective which, as so often in imperial and post imperial matters, is simultaneously global and general, yet also place-bound and particular". The spectacles were carefully choreographed but also, he shows, different from each other—"no two independence observances were ever wholly alike".

Although it took the British half a century to wind up their empire, it was during the 1960s that the process of imperial withdrawal was at it most intense. So frequent were these imperial departures between 1960 and 1970, records Cannadine, that a retired British army officer, one Colonial Eric Hefford, took on the role of organising the events that proclaimed 'freedom at midnight':

> in one guise he was the undertaker of the British Empire, orchestrating valedictory colonial observances, in the other he was the impresario of freedom, planning the independence day celebrations by which new nations came to birth.

Colonel Hefford claimed that the valedictory rituals were "plucked from the book of ancient British traditions"; but, argues Cannadine, this was not so. It was rather the case that they were "deliberately made up and self-consciously invented". The invented tradition generated new mythologies. For example, in neither India nor Pakistan was the British flag actually hauled down at midnight; but in the subsequent ceremonies, based on the Indian model, this is what happened. Another mythology has included the idea that every independence celebration involved a member of the British royal family; but on a quarter of these occasions, observes Cannadine, "no member of the House of Windsor was present".

This means, of course, that at three quarters of these occasions, a British royal *was* present. Philip Murphy, in 'Independence Day and the Crown', explains that a great deal of energy and anxiety was devoted to the role of the British royal family at independence ceremonies by Whitehall, by the Palace and by the independence leaders themselves. He picks up on Cannadine's notion that hierarchy was at the heart of the British empire, suggesting that the royal presence on Independence Day was a symbolic reassertion of the pecking order, just as formal imperial control was ending. This notion of hierarchy extended to the royals themselves: for there was an unspoken but widely accepted hierarchy of the royals who 'did' independence days (and the Queen and the Queen Mother, he adds, did not). When a high-ranking royal was welcomed by nationalist leaders, argues Murphy, this was clearly regarded by London as a tacit acceptance of the 'old order'; so, too, was disappointment at a low-ranking royal.

Chandrika Kaul's contribution to this book looks at the role of the British media at Indian independence and at Mountbatten's careful management of official publicity. British newspapers, she argues, were critically important in creating the first draft of the history of British decolonization and the images associated today with Indian independence. She examines the ways in which decolonization was viewed as an orderly and planned 'transfer of power', which involved the minimum disruption and which served as the fulfilment of long-cherished 19th-century ideals that purportedly underlay the very establishment of the empire.

Within a few days of independence, sections of the British press (as well as some US newspapers) began to reassess and question the capacity for self-governance of the Indians. The consequences of independence were increasingly seen as bearing out the warnings of those who, like Churchill, had seen the empire as necessary for good governance and stability within India—the so-called *Pax Britannica*. In this way, both the act of independence and its aftermath—though for very different reasons—were seen to justify imperial rule. As a result, two dominant accounts of Indian independence emerged: a pro-empire version, apparently co-existing with a celebration of decolonization.

Beginnings—Expectations and Reality

In "The Ending of an Empire: From Imagined Communities to Nation States in India and Pakistan", Yasmin Khan explores a recurrent theme in this book the contrast between expectations and reality, especially for the 'ordinary' populations of the nascent state. At the independence of Pakistan on 14 August 1947 and of India on the following day, there was immense confusion at many levels of society about the changes taking place. Euphoric understandings of freedom and heightened expectations accompanying the moment of independence, shows Khan, did not sit happily with the realities of nation-state formation and a bloody Partition, which displaced at least 12 million people and led to the deaths of up to a million.

Despite the pageantry of the Independence Days in August 1947, transitions from imperialism to postcolonialism in South Asia were protracted over several years. They cannot, asserts Khan, be defined by one brief moment. This was especially so in the case of the border regions of Punjab and Bengal, where there was a lack of clarity about what becoming 'Indian' or 'Pakistani' citizens meant—how these states would differ from each other and how citizens of the two new nations would relate to each other in the future.

Ten years after the independence of India and Pakistan, on 6 March 1957, Ghana achieved self-rule. The whole show, observes Richard Rathbone in his contribution to this book, was "a combination of two wonderful sets of invented regal traditions":

> Ghanaian fancy dress, sumptuous woven cloth, seriously heavyweight gold bling and ornamented sandals met its British equivalents, tiaras, anachronistic feathered hats and appliquéd braid. Rams' horns vied with trumpet fanfares, libations to the ancestors matched loyal toasts.

At the time, Kwame Nkrumah was undoubtedly the most famous African in history. He and his political party have "deservedly", comments Rathbone, been given credit by history for the attainment of independence. Nkrumah did his best to fuel this credit and collaborated with his publisher to ensure that *Ghana*, his autobiography, would be published on Independence Day itself.

But behind "the pomp and the partying", there were some messy politics: Independence Day was a troubled transition, which "was a triumph for Nkrumah and a disaster for his opponents". The internal struggle over power has been largely ignored outside Ghana, argues Rathbone, because "interest focussed and still focuses upon the political struggle for independence from British rule". In fact, the losers in 1957 were to be the major beneficiaries of the *coup d'état* which toppled Nkrumah's regime nine years after independence.

The British bore in mind their preparations for Ghana's independence day as Malaya's *Merdeka* (independence) approached nearly six months later. Ceremonies derived from

Malay coronation rites accompanied rituals which the British devised to cover their retreat from empire. Both sides shows A. J. Stockwell in his chapter in this book, worked for a cordial handover in order to confound common enemies and convince the world that the process was natural, legitimate and effective. The transition appeared almost too smooth to some, suggesting that Malayan independence itself was being compromised. In fact, as Stockwell argues, Malaya advanced to independence much faster than the British had intended: that notwithstanding their anxieties about Malaya's prospects, they had no practical alternative to falling in with a timetable set by the Tunku Abdul Rahman.

In "Whose Freedom at Midnight? Machinations towards Guyana's Independence", Clem Seecharan looks at the background to Guyana's independence on 26 May 1966. He explains that for nearly 20 years, Cheddi Jagan, of Indian extraction—"buoyed up by the independence of India"—had championed Guyana's struggle for freedom from British rule. It was not Jagan's political party, however, but that of Forbes Burnham, the African leader, which won the 'prize' at independence. This was largely the result of interventions by President Kennedy and the British government, who feared that Jagan—an honest politician, but "naïvely addicted to Marxist rhetoric and dazzled by Castro"—would bring about a Cuban-type revolution, on the mainland of South America. As a result of Anglo-American collusion, shows Seecharan, Burnham took Guyana to independence and Jagan was a "virtual spectator" at the celebrations. Like Nkrumah in Ghana, Jagan published his autobiography at independence; but unlike Nkrumah, he wrote in a spirit of angry defeat—*The West on Trial: My Fight for Guyana's Freedom*.

Racism and racial conflict were inherent problems in the lead-up to independence. African Guyanese, argues Seecharan, "would have opted for remaining colonials indefinitely rather than support independence under a party led by an Indian". Even today, her African and Indian peoples define themselves primarily through their ethnicity. Guyana, suggests Seecharan, has failed to develop a cohesive national identity.

In Rhodesia on 11 November 1965, an aberrant and illegal independence was proclaimed, which was no freedom at all for the majority population. Unwilling to accept the British government's commitment to NIBMAR (No Independence Before Majority Rule), Ian Smith and his white minority government made the Unilateral Declaration of Independence (UDI) of Rhodesia. This meant that 220 000 white Rhodesians took power for themselves, at the expense of four million blacks. Bizarrely, the proclamation document drew heavily on the 1776 United States Declaration of Independence. Smith declared that there would be no majority rule in his own or his children's lifetimes—"I don't believe in majority rule ever for Rhodesia, not in a thousand years".

Smith was 985 years out: the colony became free 15 years later, on 11 April 1980, when the nation's first non-racial, democratically elected government took the reins of power. All over the world (except in apartheid South Africa), the independence of Zimbabwe was welcomed as the overthrow of racial segregation and inequality. This moment of freedom, shows Sue Onslow in her contribution to this book, seemed then to represent a triumph of hope and the human spirit, exemplified in Robert Mugabe's rhetoric of reconciliation.

Onslow examines the way in which Zimbabwe appeared at that time to have made an extraordinary transition to democracy—against all the odds, and against a background of violence, brutalization and a profoundly traumatized society. None of the world's press, which had flocked to Salisbury (now Harare), anticipated the subsequent violence in the *Gukuruhundi* campaign, when the Zimbabwean Fifth Brigade in 1982 killed an estimated 10 000 people in Matabeleland. Nor did they predict the way in which a single narrative (the victor's history, as supplied by Mugabe's political party, ZANU-PF) would come to dominate the political and educational discourse. Was this national liberation from oppression, asks Onslow, or the imposed will of the majority?

Other 'Freedoms at Midnight'

The final contribution to this book, by Martin Shipway, draws comparisons with French decolonization. It explores the absence of a concept of 'transfer of power' in French decolonization—whether in constitutional and philosophical terms, or simply because the most important transfers of French power occurred in traumatic circumstances at the end of the wars in Indochina and Algeria. The French empire, he shows, was rooted in a constitutional myth of permanence quite different from the corresponding British guiding principle of evolution towards self-government. The equivalent moments of celebration, notably de Gaulle's two grandiose '*discours de Brazzaville*', in 1944 and 1958, were therefore ostensibly intended to mark the continuity of empire, rather than its end.

Shipway develops his argument by examining cases where French policy makers nonetheless found themselves grappling with concepts of independence, whether in Vietnam during the implementation of the so-called 'Bao Dai' solution, or in sub-Saharan Africa after de Gaulle's return to power in 1958. Perhaps surprisingly, and notwithstanding Republican French distaste for British-style 'ornamentalism', French independence ceremonies, however low-key, tended to follow some aspects of the pattern established by the British, not least in echoing the rhetoric and timing of Nehru's 'freedom at midnight'.

On one Independence Day, British and French traditions came together uneasily—when the New Hebrides became Vanuatu on 30 July 1980. For this was an Anglo-French condominium. The last British Resident Commissioner, Andrew Stuart, was well-acquainted with British convention, having witnessed Uganda's independence. But in Vanuatu, he now had to accept a hybrid mix of conventions. In the first place, he later recalled,

> there was not one single colonial authority to hand over its power, but two. The Queen's Representative (in our case the entirely admirable Duke of Gloucester) had to share the stage with a political minister from republican France ... Whether symptomatic or not of a French belief that decolonization from France is an act of self-destruction, not of rebirth, Paris had decreed that there must be no lowering of the French flag in public. Instead it was to be secreted away in the middle of the night, 24 hours before independence ... I was determined that come what may, the Union Jack would come down with dignity.

The affair was run on a shoestring. The French were dignified but determinedly non-celebratory, observed Stuart. But, he added, "In the middle of all their worries about their divided nation and their concerns for the future, the Nivanuatu were having themselves a ball."[8]

These examples highlight an important area for future research: comparative studies looking at the independence of territories that were colonized by other European nations, as well as Britain—France, Belgium, Portugal, the Netherlands, and Italy. What were the similarities and dissimilarities and what were the reasons for them? Another area for future research is the significance of informal celebrations, especially in regard to the experience of the peoples of the newly independent nations. For example, *Indépendance cha cha cha*, one of the great jazz songs of the liberation movement in the Belgian Congo (now Democratic Republic of Congo), became part of non-official independence celebrations in several African countries.

The enactment of independence in the Belgian Congo reflected the expectations not only of the Congolese, but of the outgoing colonizing state. At the celebrations on 30 June 1960, King Baudouin of Belgium gave a speech that was grudging and paternalistic. He began by praising early Belgian colonizers, particularly King Léopold II, and claiming that Belgium had made many sacrifices for the Congo. Then he declared that it was now the job of the Congolese to show Belgium that it had been right to trust them with independence. Outside Parliament, where thousands of Congolese listened over loudspeakers, there was outrage. Patrice Lumumba, the democratically elected Prime Minister, stood up to challenge the King in an impromptu speech. "No Congolese worthy of the name", he replied, "will ever be able to forget that this independence has been won through a struggle, an urgent and idealistic struggle from day to day in which we did not spare our energy or our blood. We have experienced contempt, insults and blows endured morning and night; we knew law was never the same for the whites and blacks." Who could forget, he asked, "the hangings and shootings in which perished so many?"[9]

But Baudouin's words had not been simply a matter of bad taste. They also reflected the sham of the independence ceremonies: for Belgium had already made plans to maintain control. Within a week of Independence Day, the Belgian government had intervened militarily in its former colony.

In the case of the Portuguese colonies, independence followed suddenly—and hard upon—the Carnation Revolution in Lisbon on 25 April 1974, when a left-wing military coup in Portugal overthrew Marcelo Caetano, the right-wing Salazarist dictator. The haste to independence recalls the rush to freedom in India; but in the case of the Portuguese territories, there was no Mountbatten to choreograph a dignified imperial departure. Angola was born in the midst of conflict and confusion, as different liberation movements and foreign governments competed for power. On 10 November 1975, the day before independence, the Portuguese armed forces withdrew from Angola. On the same day, in the capital Luanda, a truck drove around the city and removed the statues of the Portuguese conquerors from their plinths (whereas in the former British colonies, as Cannadine notes, the statues of British monarchs and proconsuls were toppled later on).

Angola followed the model of freedom at midnight. In the afternoon, an airplane flew in to Luanda, carrying foreign delegations – but only a few, because of rumours that a squadron from Zaire (Democratic Republic of Congo) was planning to bomb the airport that day. As the midnight hour grew nearer, thousands of people gathered at night in one of the squares. The Polish journalist Ryszard Kapuscinski reported the scene:

> The cathedral clock struck twelve.
> November the eleventh, 1975.
>   Quiet reigned on the square. From the speakers' platform, Agostinho Neto [the leader of the MPLA, the dominant liberation movement] read a text proclaiming the People's Republic of Angola. His voice broke and he had to pause several times. When he finished, there was applause from the invisible crowd, and the people cheered. There were no more speeches. After a moment the lights on the platform went out and everyone departed rather hastily, lost in the darkness...
>   On the northern front, the artillery was silent. But suddenly the soldiers in town began shooting wildly in the air in celebration. There was a chaotic uproar and the night came alive.
>   Meanwhile, the FNLA and Unita [the competing liberation movements] formed their own government with a capital in Huambo.[10]

Anniversaries

Independence Days have been followed by Independence Anniversaries, when 'freedom at midnight' is recalled in midnight ceremonies. By the time of Ghana's 50th anniversary in 2007, notes Richard Rathbone in this book, most of what Ghanaians knew about the colonial period had been derived from school text books and the memories of older members of their families or villages—for the majority of the population were born after 1957. At the celebrations of this anniversary, called *Ghana@50*, it was inconceivable to exclude the image of Nkrumah, who was widely regarded as the father of the nation. So although he and his party had been responsible for oppressing the current government's antecedents, ways were found to link them: one poster, much in evidence in Accra, showed the juxtaposed heads of John Kufuor, the Prime Minister, and Nkrumah. "Searching for comparisons," comments Rathbone, "combinations of Lafayette and Robespierre or Charles I and Protector Cromwell seemed to fit."

In his memoir of growing up in Malawi, *The Jive Talker*, the conceptual artist Samson Kambalu recalls Malawi's 20th anniversary of Independence Day on 6 July 1984. As well as watching a celebration football match (Malawi v Kenya), the nine-year Kambalu attended a youth rally, where he participated in an iconographic celebration of the rule of Dr Hastings Kamuzu Banda, the President for Life, and Banda's political party. It was the task of schoolchildren like Kambalu to sit in one of the open stands and to carry

> a set of cards that formed part of the giant stand-sized images of the rising sun on the Malawian flag, the MCP slogan—'Unity Loyalty Obedience and Discipline'—Banda's portrait, and the black rooster with the word *kwacha* (dawn) under his feet.

"Sitting there," he remembers, "you had to be attentive so you could put the right colour in the jigsaw when called."[11]

xviii *Preface*

At the 40th anniversary of Botswana's independence on 30 September 2006, hundreds of schoolchildren also lifted and changed cards, at the independence stadium in Gaborone. But although the choreography was similar, the iconography was different. One image showed the ballot box, to emphasise the importance of democratic rights; another spelt out the words, *Pula! Pula! Pula!* ('Rain!'), to signify happiness and hope. The final image showed the words 'Vision 2016', referring to the list of social and economic goals towards which Botswana is working for its 50th anniversary of independence in 2016. The memory of 1966 was still strong at Botswana's 40th anniversary. But there was a powerful sense of looking to the future—not to the past. This was emphasized by the theme of the 40th anniversary celebrations: 'Economic Diversification: The Key to Sustainable Development.'[12]

The Final Transition

Imperial closure has had different meanings, depending on a range of factors. In particular, it has depended on whether it was seen as a beginning, or an ending. One of the British guests at Botswana's independence, John Stonehouse, the Colonial Under-Secretary of State, complained that the celebrations were "Spartan"[13]; but from the point of view of Botswana, this was appropriate for a nation leaving colonial rule as one of the poorest nations of the world. For the royal minders at many independence events, the threat—or worse, the reality—of rain, was a continual headache; on Kenya's day of independence on 12 December 1963, a torrent of rain prevented the British Secretary of State from getting to the ceremony at all. But for many nascent states, especially in Africa, rain was received as a promise of hope. In Luanda, the falling of rain on Independence Day was gratefully welcomed—"warm like a blessing, in the best tradition of African culture".[14]

Insofar as there is a model for the celebration of independence from Britain, this has been the Indian model of freedom at midnight. This was enacted for the very last time at the final transition—the handover of Hong Kong to China on 30 June 1997. The pomp and ceremony of these first and last transitions were probably the most carefully planned and most spectacular of all the transfers that took place in the half-century after 1947. In Hong Kong, the links between these two transitions were highlighted: when Chris Patten, the Governor, referred in his departure speech to Hong Kong's "unshakeable destiny",[15] this echo of Nehru's "tryst with destiny" speech was surely deliberate. The significance of the "stroke of midnight" was amplified and emphasised by the countdown clock, where large red digits ticked down to zero. Even nature offered a repeat performance: both Independence Days were flooded by rain.

But there was little confidence that on the following day, to use Nehru's words, Hong Kong would "awake to life and freedom". At all the transfers of power from Britain since 1947, a new national flag had replaced the Union Jack. In the arena in Hong Kong in 1997, it was otherwise: just after midnight, the new flags raised were the Chinese flag and a flag representing the territory's new status as a special administrative region (SAR) of the People's Republic of China.

"History is not just a matter of dates", observed Chris Patten at the handover of Hong Kong. "What makes history," he went on, "is what comes before and what comes after the dates that we all remember."[16] Of course this is right. Even so, the transitions and their ceremonies merit careful research and analysis. For they had various simultaneous meanings: they were about the birth of the individual independent states; they were about the winding-up of the British empire; and they were intrinsic to the reshaping of the world order in the second half of the 20th century. The 'midnight hour' was experienced, in its own way, by each member of the growing community of Commonwealth nations—a milestone in a shared history.

Notes

1. We are indebted to Gervase Hood for his valuable comments on earlier drafts of this Preface.
2. Quoted in Gopal, S. ([1989]2004) *Jawaharlal Nehru. A Biography* (New Delhi: Oxford University Press), p. 178.
3. Brown, J. (2003) *Nehru. A Political Life* (New Haven and London: Yale University Press), p. 175.
4. Rushdie, S. (1981) *Midnight's Children* (London: Jonathan Cape), p. 1.
5. Sir Henry Storks to Duke of Newcastle (Col. Secretary) 15 March 1864, The UK National Archives (TNA): CO 136/184.
6. C. M. James to M. Brown, 8 September 1966, TNA: FO 371/188143.
7. Williams, S. (2006) *Colour Bar. The Triumph of Seretse Khama and His Nation* (London: Penguin), p. 317.
8. Stuart, A. (2001) *Of Cargoes, Colonies and Kings: Diplomatic and Administrative Service from Africa to the Pacific* (London: Radcliffe Press), pp. 224–232.
9. *The Times*, 1 July 1960.
10. Kapuscinski, R. ([1976] 2001) *Another Day of Life*, trans. W. R. Brand (London: Penguin), pp. 120–123.
11. Kambalu, S. (2008) *The Jive Talker* (London: Jonathan Cape), p. 36.
12. Personal reminiscence, Susan Williams.
13. Stonehouse, J. (1975) *Death of an Idealist* (London: W. H. Allen), p. 63.
14. Fernando, E. (2005) *O Último Adeus Português* (Lisboa: Oficina do Livro), p. 17.
15. Quoted in Moss, P. (1997) *Hong Kong Handover* (Hong Kong: FormAsia Books).
16. *Ibid*.

Introduction: Independence Day Ceremonials in Historical Perspective[1]

DAVID CANNADINE
Institute of Historical Research, University of London

> Colony by colony, the [British] Empire was dismantled ... The procedure became almost standard, like an investiture ... Down came the flag, out rang the last bugle .... Out from England had come some scion of royalty; and there was an Independence Day ball, at which the new Prime Minister danced enthusiastically with Her Royal Highness; and there were sundry ceremonies of goodwill and fraternity ... Just for a moment they all meant it, and it seemed hardly more than a passing of tradition from one hand to another, or a coming-of-age.[2]

When I was growing up in Birmingham during the 1960s, there were two unforgettable images that repeatedly appeared on the evening news bulletins on our recently-acquired television. They were from distant places, to none of which I had yet travelled, but they intruded themselves so regularly and so insistently into our living room that they were formative influences on my youth, as I suspect they were for many members of the immediate post-war generation to which I belong. From one perspective, these pictures were as different in their frequency as they were dissimilar in the stories they made so vividly visible. Night after night, or so it seemed, there were horrifying images of B52 bombers dropping napalm on the cities and rice fields and peoples of Vietnam, in a violent, brutal and ultimately vain projection of American military might and global reach to a far-off land of which most of us knew nothing. Less often, but at least once, and sometimes twice or three or even four times a year, there was a very different item on the television news, reporting that the Union Jack had been pulled down at midnight, in a former British colony, in the presence of a member of the royal family, and in a newly built stadium located in the capital city.[3] Thus was power transferred from the old empire to a new nation, and from a pro-consular elite to a popularly elected government, in the orderly and dignified manner described by James Morris, and on what would thereafter become known in the newly begotten country, following the American precedent of the fourth of July, as its Independence Day.[4]

At the time, these different and discrepant images seemed to be depicting two distinct and disparate worlds and, as such, they were particularly reassuring to those in Britain who believed (as many did then, and some still do now) that *we* were much better at dealing with non-western parts of the globe than were the Americans. The British understood empire, so this argument ran, which meant we were able to end our own dominion over palm and pine relatively amicably and successfully, with the result that many former colonies, on achieving their independence, immediately joined the Commonwealth; the Americans, by contrast, never comprehended or appreciated empire, and so it was scarcely surprising that they botched their neo-imperialistic intervention in the former colonies of French Indo-China.[5] Yet for all these contrasts and dissimilarities, the traumas of Vietnam (and of neighbouring Laos and Cambodia), and the ceremonial obsequies of the British Empire, were parallel and simultaneous manifestations of the same contemporary trend: for they were both part of that process whereby relations between 'the west' and those large areas of the rest of the world which had previously been European colonies, were being re-negotiated and re-configured.[6] And the decade in which those relations were most significantly altered and fundamentally adjusted was the 1960s: at the beginning of it, as Harold Macmillan made plain in his 'winds of change' speech, delivered to the South African parliament in Cape Town in February 1960, the British Empire had become unsustainable; by the end of it, the American intrusion into Indo-China was doomed to failure.[7]

Such were the mood and the mores of that decade, so it was scarcely surprising that, when Bernard Levin produced his coruscating contemporary history of Britain during the 1960s, which was published in London as *The Pendulum Years*, it was re-packaged in the United States, more resonantly and more imaginatively, as *Run Down the Flagpole*.[8] It was a good alternative title, for while it took the British half a century to wind up their global imperium, from the independence (and partition) of India and Pakistan in 1947 to the Hong Kong handover precisely 50 years later, it was during the 1960s that that process of imperial withdrawal was at its most intense, and there were more independence celebrations across that decade than during the 1950s (when the momentum of African decolonization was only beginning to gather), or the 1970s (by which time most of the British Empire was truly one with Nineveh and Tyre). Indeed, so frequent were these imperial departures and goodbyes between the years 1960 to 1970 that a retired British army officer, named Colonel

Eric Hefford, embarked on a new (but essentially time-limited) career as a sort of late-imperial, trans-oceanic, globe-trotting Earl Marshal, organizing the events that declared and proclaimed 'freedom at midnight': in one guise he was the undertaker of the British Empire, orchestrating valedictory colonial observances, in the other he was the impresario of freedom, planning the independence day celebrations by which new nations came to birth.[9]

Taking a longer view across the half century from 1947 to 1997, there were more than 50 such occasions in as many years, and they form an extraordinary and unique sequence of hybrid spectaculars—collectively for the British Empire whose end they signified and symbolized, and individually for the post-imperial, successor states whose beginning they marked and memorialized. To those who regard such state-sponsored flummery as nothing more (or better) than insubstantial pageants and tinsel ephemera, such happenings are of no scholarly interest or historical significance; but since the British Empire had (among other things) existed and endured as a pageant, it was at least consistent with that element of caparisoned theatricality that it ended and expired in a succession of valedictory rituals, which were not so much, as Colonel Hefford claimed, "plucked from the book of ancient British traditions", but were deliberately made up and self-consciously invented.[10] It is more than ten years after the Hong Kong handover, it is nearly 40 years since the peak decade of independence ceremonials by which I was so struck when I was growing up, and it is over 60 years since the initial celebrations took place in New Delhi and (less enthusiastically) in Karachi; and this means there is now sufficient distance on these episodes and events to see and study them in a historical perspective which, as so often in imperial and post-imperial matters, is simultaneously global and general, yet also place-bound and particular.

I

The independence ceremonials that took place in Britain's former colonies between 1947 and 1997 form, in all conscience, a large enough topic, encompassing substantial parts of the globe across half a century; but like many aspects of the history of empire and of decolonization, they also need to be de-parochialized, and set in a longer historical time-frame and a broader geographical perspective.[11] Before 1776, the very notion of a former colony becoming 'independent' of its conquering coloniser was scarcely conceivable, and in the early modern period (and in certain instances thereafter) the great European powers regarded their overseas territories as possessions, which might be won or lost or (occasionally) exchanged, but which never gained or were granted something called 'freedom'. The Mediterranean island of Menorca, for instance, was traded back and forth across the 18th century between Britain, Spain and France, and was eventually ceded by Britain to Spain in 1802.[12] In the same way, the Ionian Islands were given to Greece in 1864, Heligoland was returned to Germany in 1890, and Wei Hai Wei went back to China in 1930. Indeed, it is in this venerable category of territorial transfer and exchange between great powers, rather than that of colonial liberation from a European empire, that the handover of Hong Kong to the Chinese government ought to be set. For no one seriously believed that Britain's last great colony was becoming a free and independent nation state in 1997.[13]

There were also three instances of colonial separation from the British Empire, well before 1947, and none of them were marked by the sort of celebrations and fireworks and transient expressions of mutual admiration that subsequently became so familiar. The first 'British experience of decolonization' was the rejection of imperial authority by the 13 colonies from the mid 1770s: royal statues and coats of arms were torn down by rebellious Americans; the Declaration of Independence denounced George III as an evil and wicked tyrant; and after the British defeat at Yorktown in 1782, there was nothing for it but for the King's troops to cut and run and scuttle.[14] The second was the creation of the Irish Free State in the aftermath of the Anglo-Irish Treaty of 1921. Unlike the 13 former colonies, this new nation did not initially repudiate the British connection, but instead became a dominion within the Empire. Yet once again, there were no independence celebrations: the last British Lord Lieutenant, Viscount Fitzalan, departed from Dublin Castle in 1922 in a private car; the low-key successor post of governor general was abolished in 1937; and Eire eventually became a fully independent republic outside the British Commonwealth on Easter Monday 1949, the anniversary of the 1916 Rising.[15] The third was the ostensible 'independence' of Egypt, which the British proclaimed in March 1922, when they formally relinquished their protectorate. But unlike the United States and the Irish Free State, Egyptian independence was more nominal than real, the ensuing ceremonials were concerned with the establishment of an Egyptian monarchy rather than with the celebration of Egyptian freedom, and there were widespread protests by the nationalists against the continuing de facto British presence.[16]

This was not the way in which colonial ties would later be severed across the half century after 1947, in those 'ceremonies of goodwill and fraternity' which reached their climax in the 1960s.[17] Yet even during the era of 'freedoms at midnight', there was another non-ceremonial path to independence taken by the 'old' imperial dominions of Canada, Australia, New Zealand and South Africa, which was less complete than in the case of the United States or the Irish Republic, but was more so than had been true of inter-war Egypt. In 1914, Britain had declared war on behalf of the whole Empire, but after 1918, and increasingly after 1945, the four dominions gradually moved towards an autonomy which did not mean the complete rejection and belligerent repudiation of the British imperial connection. In all four instances, the process that has infelicitously but accurately been described as 'de-dominionization' involved some or all of the following: the acceptance of the Statute of Westminster, the appointment of home-grown governors general, the replacement of the Union Jack by a new national flag, the repudiation of the imperial honours system, the composing of a new national anthem, and the end of constitutional subordination to London (South Africa went the furthest of the four, declaring itself a republic in 1961, although it rejoined the Commonwealth in 1990). As a result of this long, gradual yet incremental sequence, there was no single date on which dominion 'independence' from the British Empire could be publicly proclaimed and ceremonially recognized in the presence of a member of the royal family.[18]

Equally non-ceremonial, albeit for very different reasons, were Britain's departures from their territories in the Middle East, which took place at much the same time as this process of 'de-dominionization'. In May 1948, less than a year after the celebrations in Delhi and Karachi, the British withdrew from Palestine, where they had failed to broker a peace deal between Jews and Arabs, and the last High Commissioner, General Sir Alan Cunningham, retreated to the docks at Haifa in a bullet-proof car that had been built to protect King George VI from German bombs in wartime London.[19] In Egypt, real independence came suddenly and acrimoniously in the mid-1950s: the monarchy was overthrown and a republic established; British troops withdrew from their bases; the Suez Canal was nationalized; and Nasser was the hero of the hour. Meanwhile, to the south, in what had previously been the Anglo-Egyptian condominium of the Sudan, a new radical government proclaimed itself independent in January 1956, and no member of the British royal family was invited to be present.[20] Further east, Iraq and Jordan had ostensibly become independent in 1932 and 1946 respectively, when the League of Nations mandates expired; but in the aftermath of Suez, the pro-British monarchy in Iraq was brutally overthrown in 1958, and King Hussein only survived in Jordan by publicly repudiating the British connection, dismissing General Sir John Glubb from his command of the Arab Legion in March 1956.[21] But the greatest humiliation was in Aden in November 1967: as in Palestine, the British failed to broker a deal between local notables, and they took flight in their helicopters. "We left without glory but without disaster", the last Governor, Sir Humphrey Trevelyan later recalled; yet others described the episode more brutally as "the worst shambles of the end of Empire".[22]

No-where, in these once-wide dominions of the British Middle East, were there the sort of ceremonial farewells, signifying the 'orderly transfer of power', that were taking place at the same time elsewhere in the Empire; and this was also the case in those rare instances where the British departed on relatively good terms, leaving the traditional rulers intact, as in Libya (which the British ruled briefly after the Second World War), and the Gulf sheikhdoms of Kuwait, Qatar and Bahrain (which they had protected for much longer).[23] Moreover, none of these successor states, having repudiated the British and having rejected the staging of 'ceremonies of goodwill and fraternity', subsequently joined the Commonwealth: the separation, when it finally (and often brutally) came, was absolute and complete. There are many reasons for this. With the exception of Egypt and the Sudan, British dominion across the Middle East was 'shallowly rooted' and of relatively short duration, in some cases lasting scarcely a generation. Many of the mandates, protectorates and bases were never colonies in a formal sense, which meant that even when the separation was amicable, ceremonials of independence were scarcely appropriate. But often there was a deeper failure, deriving from a lack of mutual sympathy or regard: in part because many Arabs loathed the British as unwelcome invaders and unwanted (and pro-Jewish) infidels; and in part because, and unlike in (most of) Africa and South Asia, the British made no serious attempt to accommodate the forces and leaders of Arab nationalism (Anthony Eden famously likened Nasser to Mussolini, and wanted him 'destroyed'). From the unhappy and disordered perspective of the Middle East, and also from the gradualist viewpoint of the 'old' dominions, the independence celebrations taking place elsewhere in the British Empire in the half century from 1947 were the exception rather than the norm.[24]

II

To be sure, they were the most significant sequence and symbols of the 'end of empire'; but even in the case of the 'freedom at midnight' ceremonials, there were more variations to the pattern than has generally been recognized or recollected. The spectacles and fiestas were well planned and carefully choreographed, and according to Sir Colin Allan, who was the last Governor of the Seychelles (1973–76) and of the Solomon Islands (1976–78), and who thus had good cause to know, there was "a check-list of about eighty points under two main headings. They are ticked off in a bureaucratic way one by one—relevant or not—it is as simple as that". But although from the British perspective, these events formed a recognizable and inter-connected series, they were very much one-off happenings in each colony, which meant that no two independence observances were ever wholly alike.[25] Depending on the size, population and wealth of the new nation to be, the cost and scale of the ceremonials varied markedly: in Colonel Hefford's experience, they ranged from £180 000 in Malta to £2 250 000 in Nigeria, with most of them averaging between £300 000 and £400 000. The joyous crowds did not always behave as they were expected to: in New Delhi, Lord Mountbatten had planned a solemn moment when he and his staff would salute the new Indian flag, but large crowds "surged into the specially prepared arena and threw the display into turmoil".[26] Individual participants could not always be relied upon to perform as required: at the inauguration of Malaysia in September 1963, the new governor of Sarawak collapsed under the strain. The weather was not always co-operative: on Kenya's day of independence in December 1963, heavy rain caused such chaos on the route to the stadium in Nairobi that the British Secretary of State missed the entire ceremony; and at the Hong Kong handover, there was a torrential downpour, while the last British Governor, Chris Patten, not only refused to wear the customary proconsular uniform and plumed hat, but visibly shed a tear when receiving the British flag after it had been hauled down for the last time.[27]

Despite these local variations, it is often supposed that all of these independence celebrations were graced by a member of the British royal family; but on a quarter of these occasions, no member of the House of Windsor was present. As with Palestine and Aden, the British were sometimes unable to manage decolonization in the orderly, dignified and consensual manner which was deemed the essential precondition for the presence of a royal representative. In the case of Burma, the country had been occupied by the Japanese during the Second World War, the return of the British administration in late 1945 was a provocation to the Burmese nationalists, and General Aung San, to whom they hoped to transfer power, was murdered. Accordingly, it was the last Governor, Sir Hubert Rance, who acted as the sovereign's representative in January 1948, when Burma became an independent republic and, unlike India, Pakistan and (subsequently) Ceylon, it did not join the Commonwealth.[28] A decade later, independence was only slightly better handled on the island of Cyprus, where thousands of British troops were tied down in the mid-1950s dealing with the 'state of emergency', where British officials were unable to hold the balance between Greek and Turkish Cypriots, and where they seriously misjudged and underestimated the politician-prelate Archbishop Makarios. In August 1960, the Governor, Sir Hugh Foot, left the island after saying goodbye to the (by then) President Makarios and making a final troop inspection, but there were no speeches, no sentimental songs, and there was no royal presence (although Cyprus, unlike Burma, did elect to join the Commonwealth).[29]

Members of the British royal family were also not called upon when former British colonies, on being granted their freedom, were immediately merged with other countries, or reconfigured into new nations. In the cases of British Somaliland (July 1960) and the South Cameroons (October 1961), these two newly independent countries were immediately merged with their larger neighbours (respectively Somalia and Cameroun), they became republics outside the Commonwealth, and no member of the House of Windsor attended. Across the Indian Ocean, Singapore, North Borneo and Sarawak all became independent on 16–17 September 1963, and they were merged into a federation, which also included Malaya (which had become independent in 1957, when the Duke of Gloucester had represented the Queen). This new federation, named Malaysia, came into being immediately, and once again, no member of the British royal family was present, since the merger was deemed more important than the independence.[30] Instead, the British government was represented by Duncan Sandys and Lord Lansdowne. There was a further reason why these celebrations were relatively low key (i.e. non-royal): Malaysia's giant neighbour, Indonesia, refused to recognize what it regarded as a neo-colonial confection, and on 18 September, a mob stormed the British embassy in Djakarta, and set it on fire. (But there were no absolutely hard and fast rules about these matters: in the case of Zanzibar, Prince Philip *did* attend the island's independence celebrations in December 1963, even though it subsequently merged with Tanganyika to become Tanzania.)

Elsewhere in the dissolving Empire, members of the royal family were sometimes scheduled to appear at independence celebrations, but for reasons ranging from the political to the personal, their visits were cancelled at the last minute. Although the circumstances were rarely as fraught as in Palestine or Aden or Burma or Cyprus, there were occasions when a sudden and unexpected deterioration in public order meant that the planned royal visit was aborted. In Mauritius, the ceremonials had been arranged along customary lines in March 1968, and Princess Alexandra had agreed to represent the sovereign; but the security situation subsequently worsened, her visit was cancelled, and her place was taken instead by Lord Greenwood. Likewise, when Grenada was scheduled to become independent, early in 1974, Prince Richard of Gloucester was deputed to attend, but violent clashes between the government and the opposition meant that the visit was aborted. There were also family and health reasons for occasional royal non-shows. In September 1968, the Duke of Kent had to withdraw from attending the independence celebrations of Swaziland, because of the sudden death of his mother, Princess Marina, and his place was taken by George Thomson, the last British Secretary of State for Commonwealth Relations.[31] In the case of the Ellice Islands in the Pacific, Princess Margaret was scheduled to be present in October 1978, but in the event she was unable to do so, as she was stricken with pneumonia, and she was represented by her private secretary, Lord Napier and Errick.[32]

These were the most commonplace variations on the standard 'freedom at midnight' ceremonial, as the British Empire decolonized, but there were also others.

One very unusual case was that of Southern Rhodesia, which had unilaterally (and illegally) declared its independence in 1965; but this was from the British government rather than from the British crown, and the colony only became officially free in April 1980, when Prince Charles attended the celebrations.[33] There were also former League of Nations mandates which had been assigned to the imperial dominions after the First World War, and which in their turn became independent: Western Samoa from New Zealand; Papua New Guinea and Nauru from Australia; and Namibia from South Africa. But only in the case of Papua New Guinea was the British crown represented, and once again by the Prince of Wales. Finally, there were nations which became independent twice, once from the British Empire, and again as members of the Commonwealth. East Pakistan had participated in the freedom celebrations of August 1947, but it subsequently declared its independence of West Pakistan, and became Bangladesh, in December 1971. Two years after the creation of the federation of Malaysia in 1963, Singapore seceded from it, and declared itself a sovereign republic within the Commonwealth. And what had once been the colony of British Somaliland and the mandate of the British Cameroons both subsequently seceded from the greater Somalia and greater Cameroun which they had initially joined on independence. But these were very much post-imperial developments, and neither the British government nor the British monarchy was in any way involved in them.

III

Set in this broader perspective and longer time-frame, the ceremonials of independence turn out to have been much less central to the wider processes of British decolonization and 'de-dominionization' than it is commonplace to suppose; and even when the 'freedom at midnight' rituals did occur, there were more local variations than is often appreciated. But these end-of-empire observances also shared common characteristics, and it is well worth trying to tease out some general themes. Many of them emerge from a brief examination of the first such occasions, in India and Pakistan; although it is only in retrospect that they may be seen as initiating a trend, for in 1947, few people (and even fewer policymakers) believed that most of the British Empire would be gone in the next 20 years.[34] As the central figure in both independence pageants, the last Viceroy, Lord Mountbatten was determined to ensure that the transfer of power was well stage-managed: he wanted the new nations of India and Pakistan to begin with peace and order and with feelings of goodwill towards the former imperial power; he wanted the British to leave with dignity and prestige and with as much residual influence as they could retain; he sought to present independence as the triumphant realization, in his hands, of Britain's long-cherished wish to make India free; and he insisted that the accelerated timetable to independence had concentrated minds, and resulted in many fewer deaths than would otherwise have been the case. The joyous crowds, the glittering processions, the new national flags and the memorable and moving speeches certainly went some way to conveying this impression; and although in neither India nor in Pakistan was the British flag actually hauled down at midnight, these observances would provide the model and the inspiration for all subsequent independence celebrations as the Empire ended.[35]

Yet despite the impression of order and amity which these ceremonials gave, there was much that was at variance with what was in many ways a carefully crafted and deliberately contrived image. The partition of the sub-continent was regarded by many, including Field Marshall Sir Claude Auchinleck, who was the head of the Indian Army, not so much as a triumph, but as the negation and betrayal of Britain's imperial mission. Mountbatten himself had hoped to limit the effects of partition by acting as Governor-General of both new nations, and by chairing a common defence council, but in this ambition he was defeated. The rulers of the princely states, who had looked upon the King-Emperor and the Viceroy as their guardian and guarantor, felt a deep sense of betrayal when the British government abandoned its treaty obligations, and when Mountbatten gave them no choice but to throw in their lot with the two new successor nations. Many critics felt that the move to independence was too rushed, which meant that, *pace* Mountbatten, the violence was intensified rather than contained, and that, far from being the fulfilment of Britain's imperial designs, the result was (in Churchill's words) a policy of "general surrender and scuttle". (The Viceroy was also accused of delaying the detailed announcements of partition until after independence, so that he would not be held responsible for the bloodshed that subsequently ensued.)[36] Although the three nations had parted on amicable terms, subsequent relations between Britain and India, and Britain and Pakistan, were nothing like as cordial as had been hoped, and the residual influence of the former imperial power soon dwindled.[37] Moreover, later relations between India and Pakistan were often very tense, Pakistan soon abandoned democracy for martial rule, the eastern and western parts of the nation broke apart, and from the killing of Mahatma Gandhi to that of Benazir Bhutto, assassination became a frequent occurrence in the politics of the sub-continent.

No historian (or anthropologist or sociologist) of state-sponsored rituals would be surprised at such contradictions, ambiguities and paradoxes: from the triumphs of Roman emperors and commanders, via the rituals of Renaissance Venice, to the imperial and local spectacles associated with the British monarchy and Communist Russia, real and deep conflicts have often been concealed beneath a ceremonial consensus that was simultaneously both manufactured yet also spontaneous.[38] Thus it was for what became, in retrospect, the prototypical independence observances that took place in south Asia, and so it was for those which were subsequently played out in other parts of the British Empire, albeit with their own marked and particular local variations, and also with fewer people involved. As in India and Pakistan, the aim of the 'freedom at midnight' ceremonials was to give the impression that independence had always been the intention of the British imperial mission; that power was being transferred voluntarily, with dignity and with mutual expressions of esteem and good will; that a member of the British royal family would appear to set a regal seal of approval on the proceedings; that Britain and its former colony would remain on good terms thereafter, with the former still wielding some benevolent influence over the latter; and that the new nation, happy and secure in the annual observance of its independence day, would go on to enjoy freedom, democracy, prosperity, unity and consensus. From the Gold Coast to Kenya to Southern Rhodesia, this was the public rhetoric of independence, and the expression of high hopes for the future, that was articulated by such enemies-turned-friends of Britain and its Empire as Kwame Nkrumah, Jomo Kenyatta and Robert Mugabe.

But as had been the case with the independence celebrations in India and Pakistan, the reality was at best more complex, and at worst very different. However much delight there was in the prospect of 'freedom at midnight' from British imperial rule, the consensus that characterized such independence celebrations was often little more than superficial, temporarily papering over significant disagreements and deep-rooted tensions and briefly erasing unhappy memories and bitter resentments. In Malaya, freedom came after a tumultuous decade and a half which still left many scars: the Japanese invasion, the British surrender and return, the Communist insurgency, racial strife between Malays and Chinese, and the still-continuing state of emergency: all of which invested the independence celebrations of August 1957 with varied and contradictory meanings. In Kenya, freedom followed the decade-long Mau Mau emergency, the detention of thousands of Africans, the imprisonment and release of Jomo Kenyatta, and the constant complaints of British settlers that they were being betrayed: at independence, Kenyatta was determined to 'forget' Mau Mau, though many of his fellow countrymen were not.[39] In the Gold Coast, the politics of independence meant the traditional tribal chiefs of the north had been out-manoeuvred by the urban-based, middle-class nationalists of the south, led by Kwame Nkrumah, to whom the British transferred power: like the ruling princes in India, ten years before, they found little at which to rejoice in their nation's freedom.[40] And in Southern Rhodesia, the official independence from Britain took place after more than a decade of international sanctions, civil war, settler bitterness and economic deterioration, which cast its shadow over the 'freedom at midnight' observances. Margaret Thatcher conspicuously refused to attend, many white Rhodesians felt betrayed, and so did Joshua Nkomo, who had expected to be the new leader of the new nation, but who had been defeated by Robert Mugabe.

Thus regarded, the independence celebrations of these colonies-becoming-countries afforded only a brief, temporary respite in the nationalist struggle against Britain, and they also intensified the internal battle between parties and tribes and personalities for the control of the post-colonial state. Despite their fulsome expressions of gratitude and friendship, and (in most cases) their decision to join the Commonwealth, the new leaders of new nations soon distanced themselves from Britain, and they re-branded their countries in further repudiation of their imperial past: the Gold Coast became Ghana, Nyasaland became Malawi, Basutoland became Lesotho, British Honduras became Belize, and so on. In capital cities across Asia and Africa, statues of British monarchs and proconsuls were toppled and banished, and streets and roads with royal or imperial appellations were re-named. Most former colonies soon became republics, and instituted their own systems of indigenous honours, thereby rejecting the monarchical and hierarchical aspects of the British Empire that had last been asserted in the royal presence at the independence day celebrations.[41] As for the parliamentary democracy which the British were so eager to bequeath to the successor states of Empire: this was the first and greatest casualty of the post-independence struggles for power, which often resulted in one party rule, military dictatorship, tribal conflict, civil war, the abuse of human rights and economic ruin (as is all too apparent today in Zimbabwe). This in turn means that the subsequent annual observance of independence day in many former colonies has become a celebration of indigenous culture, of an adored (and feared) charismatic leader, and of a long and glorious history, into which the British

Empire often seems little more than a relatively brief and now un-lamented intrusion.

In retrospect, the midnight celebrations in India and Pakistan in August 1947 had portended this de-imperializing half-century of ceremonial contradictions and ambiguities, of high hopes and false dawns; and the Hong Kong handover on 30 June 1997 completed the cycle in a no less paradoxical and multi-layered way. Since the colony was being returned to China, rather than given its independence, the sinologists in the Foreign Office believed that the most important priority for Chris Patten, the last British governor, appointed by John Major in 1992, was to keep on good terms with the Chinese authorities, for the sake of the future of Sino-British relations. But Patten regretted that Hong Kong had not become a more democratic colony while it had been under British rule; he was determined to make significant advances in that direction, however hostile the government might be in Beijing; and he was equally determined to seek guarantees from the Chinese that they would respect such reforms as he was able to implement once Hong Kong reverted to them. These very significant differences of policy were fought out in public, and in London and Beijing as well as in Hong Kong itself, and to this day, Patten's record remains controversial, just as Hong Kong's future remains unclear.[42] But although the Chinese government was itching to move in and reclaim it, they did allow the British a dignified exit from their last great colony. The Prince of Wales represented the queen, John Major and Tony Blair were both present, and after the ceremonials, the British dignitaries departed in the royal yacht *Britannia*, which was subsequently laid up in Scotland, on the Firth of Forth at Leith, and not replaced. And so Britain's seaborne empire, and Britain's maritime monarchy both came to an end in 1997—the year which was also, by agreeable coincidence, the 100th anniversary of the Diamond Jubilee of Queen Victoria, which may not have witnessed the climax of the British Empire in terms of its territorial extent, but which certainly did so in terms of imperial consciousness on the streets of London.

IV

So much for independence celebrations in the British Empire, the pomp and the partying and the paradoxes of imperial closure: yet what, meanwhile, of the imperial metropolis itself? For as John Darwin has rightly written, the United Kingdom was no less "a successor state of the old imperial system" than India or Pakistan, or the Sudan or Malaya, or Nigeria or Ghana, or Barbados or Antigua. In other European nations that were the epicentres of empires, post-war decolonization was marked, not so much by celebration or by ceremonial, but rather by bitter, divisive and sometimes extreme domestic politics: witness France over Algeria in the 1950s and 1960s, and Portugal over Mozambique and Angola in the 1970s.[43] This was not true in Britain: partly because Clement Attlee and Harold Macmillan handled the crucial phases of south Asian and African decolonization with considerable political skill; partly because the far-right section of the Conservative party, which opposed such policies of 'scuttle', never gained serious traction in parliament or in the country; partly because, as with the case of the old dominions, Britain de-imperialized incrementally rather than instantaneously; and partly because the peak years of decolonization were also the time when applying to join what was then called 'Europe' seemed to offer an attractive and appealing alternative, whereby Britain might continue to exert influence in what was rapidly becoming a post-imperial world, but through a neighbouring continent rather than a distant empire.[44]

Appropriately enough, then, such observances of decolonization as did take place in London were more concerned with the colonies than with the metropolis, and they tended to be rather low-key ceremonial affairs. On the same day that independence was being declared and celebrated, and provided that the former colony had embraced the Christian religion, a service of thanksgiving and dedication was held, usually in Westminster Abbey. It was attended by another member of the British royal family, by the High Commissioner and his entourage from the new nation, by members of the Christian bodies who had been at work there, and by representatives of the growing number of free and autonomous Commonwealth countries. Like the independence ceremonials themselves, these religious services followed what had become, by the mid- 1960s, a recognizable pattern. The new flag of the new country, "the sign of its nationhood and the promise of its unity", was borne in procession in the Abbey, and placed upon the high altar. The (British) national anthem was sung, along with some rousing 19th-century hymns, such as "Now Thank We All Our God", or "Hills of the North, Rejoice". During the prayers, God's blessing was sought for the new country: "that it may be an instrument for good in His hands who is the lord of all nations"; "that it may be strengthened against those forces that would divide or weaken it from without or from within"; and "that it may never lack the men and women of wisdom, honour and righteousness to guide its destinies". And the service ended with a fanfare and with the singing of the new country's new national anthem (in the English version).

Such was the sequence of de-colonization observances that took place in London, reaching its climax during the 1960s, and which attracted significantly less attention than the more extended and elaborate ceremonials that took place overseas. (I have no recollection of any such events being televised, either live or as reported on the news.) But there were also much grander, one-off ceremonials in the former imperial capital, and they carried with them an unmistakable sense of recessional and retreat. There was the long-delayed dedication of the Chapel of the Order of the British Empire in the crypt of St Paul's Cathedral in 1960, ironically in the very same year that Macmillan's 'wind of change' speech portended that Empire's end.[45] There were Winston Churchill's magnificent obsequies on a grey January day in 1965: not only the last rites of the great man himself, but also, as it seemed to many, the requiem for Britain as a great imperial power.[46] There was Lord Mountbatten's ceremonial funeral in August 1980: mourning the passing of the last of the great captains and the last Viceroy of India. There was the service held in Westminster Abbey in June 1998, in the presence of the Queen, to mark the formal end, after the Hong Kong handover, of what had once been known as the Colonial Service. And there was Queen Mother's state funeral in March 2000: the last British queen consort who had also been Empress of India.[47] But that metropolitan sequence of imperial valedictions is not yet over, for when the reign of Queen Elizabeth II ends, it will surely be recalled that on her 21st birthday, which she celebrated in South Africa in April 1947, she had pledged herself "to the service of our great imperial family to which we all belong".[48] In the course of her reign, that great imperial family has dissolved, the imperial children have grown up and left home, and it was the 'freedom at midnight' ceremonials which set many of them on their way.

Notes

1. For help and assistance in preparing this essay for publication, I am deeply grateful to Terry Barringer, Lizzie Edwards, Rob Holland, Helen McCarthy and Tony Stockwell.
2. Morris, J. (1978) *Farewell the Trumpets: An Imperial Retreat* (London: Faber), pp. 518–519.
3. The peak years for the granting of independence within the British Empire, when four former colonies were freed, were 1961, 1962, 1963 and 1966; only in 1969 were there no such celebrations: see below, appendix; for my own recollections of these events, see Cannadine, D. (2001) *Ornamentalism: How the British Saw Their Empire* (London: Allen Lane), p. 188. Memoirs of colonial governors and colonial administrators are a rich source of accounts of preparations for independence and Independence Day celebrations. Examples are to be found in Johnson, J. (Ed.) (2002) *Colony to Nation: British Administrators in Kenya 1940–1963* (Banham: Erskine Press) pp. 21–273 and Stuart, A. (2001) *Of Cargoes, Colonies and Kings: Diplomatic and Administrative Service from Africa to the Pacific* (London: Radcliffe Press), pp. 58–67 (Uganda) and pp. 224–232 (New Hebrides). For a guide to this burgeoning memoir literature see Barringer, T. (2004) *Administering Empire: An Annotated Checklist of Personal Memoirs and Related Studies* (London: University of London Institute of Commonwealth Studies).
4. Karter Appelbaum, D. (1989) *The Glorious Fourth: An American Holiday, An American History* (New York: Facts on File); Travers, L. (2007) *Celebrating the Fourth: Independence Day and the Rites of Nationalism in the Early Republic* (Amherst: University of Massachusetts Press); Heintze, J. R. (2008) *The Fourth of July Encyclopedia* (Jefferson, NC: McFarland). Independence days were also established in the Latin American republics when they became free of Spanish dominion in the early 19th century. For Mexico, see: Costeloe, M. (1997) The Junta patriotica and the celebration of independence in Mexico City, 1825–1855, *Mexican Studies/Estudios Mexicanas*, 23, pp. 21–53; Duncan, R.H. (1998) Embracing a suitable past: independence celebrations under Mexico's Second Empire, 1864–6, *Journal of Latin American Studies*, 30, pp. 249–277.
5. For the belief that the British ended their Empire relatively well, see: Annan, N. (1990) *Our Age: Portrait of a Generation* (London: Weidenfeld & Nicolson), p. 357; Jenkins, R. (2002) *Twelve Cities: A Memoir* (London: Macmillan), p. 6. See also Sandbrook, D. (2005) *Never Had It So Good: A History of Britain from Suez to the Beatles* (London: Little Brown), pp. 287–289; Nasson, B. (2004) *Britannia's Empire: Making a British World* (Stroud: Tempus), pp. 190–194.
6. For a recent survey of European decolonization, see Judt, T. (2005) *Postwar: A History of Europe since 1945* (London: Heinemann), pp. 278–299.
7. Horne, A. (1989) *Harold Macmillan*, Vol. 2, *1957–1986* (London: Viking), pp. 193–198; Louis, W.R. (2002) The dissolution of the British Empire in the era of Vietnam, *American Historical Review*, 107, pp. 1–25; Hyam, R. (2006) *Britain's Declining Empire: The Road to Decolonisation, 1918–1968* (Cambridge: Cambridge University Press), pp. 250–262.
8. Levin, B. (1970) *The Pendulum Years: Britain and the Sixties* (London: Jonathan Cape); idem (1971) *Run Down the Flagpole: Britain in the Sixties* (New York: Atheneum). In both editions, chapter 8 was entitled 'Run down the flagpole', and the end of the British Empire is discussed on pp. 121–174.
9. Faulkner, A. (1979) The man who makes a show of independence, *Sunday Telegraph Magazine*, February 11, pp. 39–40; Morrissey, P. (1980) The man who makes a show of independence, *Journal of the Orders and Medals Research Society*, 29, pp. 164–165.
10. Cannadine, *Ornamentalism*, p. 161; Faulkner, The man who makes a show of independence, p. 39.
11. Cannadine, D. (2008) *Making History Now and Then: Discoveries, Controversies and Explorations* (London: Palgrave), pp. 214, 233–234; Maier, C.S. (2006) *Among Empires: American Ascendancy and its Predecessors* (Cambridge, MA: Harvard University Press); Darwin, J. (2007) *After Tamerlane: The Global History of Empire* (London: Allen Lane).
12. Colley, L. (2007) *The Ordeal of Elizabeth Marsh: A Woman in World History* (London: Harper Press), pp. 42, 48, 108, 259.
13. Hyam, *Britain's Declining Empire*, p. 412.

14. Boyce, D. G. (1999) *Decolonisation and the British Empire, 1775–1997* (Basingstoke: Macmillan), pp. 12, 27; Armitage, D. (2006) *The Declaration of Independence: A Global History* (Cambridge, MA: Harvard University Press), pp. 52–57, 166–169; McConville, B. (2006) *The King's Three Faces: The Rise and Fall of Royal America, 1688–1776* (Chapel Hill: University of North Carolina Press), pp. 280–316. So loathed was George III by the 1770s by many in the 13 colonies that it is difficult to agree with the view of the Prince of Wales, namely that if it had been possible for the king to visit the eastern seaboard of America, the colonists would have realized what a splendid and agreeable person he was, and would have remained loyal rather than become rebellious. ('Foreword' in Brooke, J. (1972) *King George III* (London: Constable), pp. 10–11).
15. Cannadine, *Ornamentalism*, pp. 154–156; Dean, D. W. (1992) Final exit? Britain, Eire, the Commonwealth, and the repeal of the External Relations Act, 1945–49, *Journal of Imperial and Commonwealth History*, 20, pp. 391–418; McEvoy, F. J. (1985) Canada, Ireland and the Commonwealth: the Declaration of the Irish Republic, *Irish Historical Studies*, 24, pp. 506–517.
16. Darwin, *After Tamerlane*, pp. 383–384; Beinin, J. and Lockman, Z.,1919: Labour Upsurge and National Revolution, in: A. P. Hourani, P. S. Khoury and M. C. Wilson (Eds) (1993) *The Modern Middle East* (London: I. B. Tauris), pp. 395–428.
17. Morris, *Farewell the Trumpets*, p. 519.
18. Tsokhas, K. (1994) Dedominionization: the Anglo-Australian experience, 1939–1945, *Historical Journal*, 37, pp. 861–883; McIntyre, W. D. (1999) The strange death of dominion status, *Journal of Imperial and Commonwealth History*, 27, pp. 193–212; Buckner, P. (2008) Canada and the end of Empire, 1939–1982, in: P. Buckner (Ed.) *Canada and the British Empire* (Oxford: Oxford University Press), pp. 107–126; Schreuder, D. M. and Ward, S. (2008) Epilogue: after empire, in: D. M. Schreuder and S. Ward (Eds) *Australia's Empire* (Oxford: Oxford University Press), pp. 389–402. A. G. Hopkins (2008) 'Rethinking decolonization', *Past and Present*, 200, pp. 211–247.
19. Louis, W.R. (1988) Sir Alan Cunningham and the End of British Rule in Palestine in: A. N. Porter and R. Holland (Eds) *Theory and Practice in the History of European Expansion Overseas: Essays in Honour of R. E. Robinson* (London: Cass), p. 143; Shepherd, N. (1999) *Ploughing Sand: British Rule in Palestine, 1917–1948* (London: John Murray), pp. 242–243; Fieldhouse, D. K. (2006) *Western Imperialism in the Middle East, 1914–1958* (Oxford: Oxford University Press), pp. 194–219; Lapping, B. (1985) *End of Empire* (London: Granada), p. 142.
20. Hyam, *Britain's Declining Empire*, pp. 221–240; Louis, W. R. (1991) The coming of independence in the Sudan, *Journal of Imperial and Commonwealth History*, 29, pp. 137–158.
21. Fieldhouse, *Western Imperialism in the Middle East*, pp. 69–116, 220–244.
22. Lapping, *End of Empire*, pp. 309–310. Trevelyan's predecessor in Aden, Sir Richard Turnbull, told Denis Healey "that when the British Empire finally sank beneath the waves of history, it would leave behind only two monuments: one was the game of Association Football, the other was the expression 'Fuck off'". Healey, D. (1989) *The Time of My Life* (London: Politico's), pp. 283–284.
23. Louis, W. R. (2003) The British withdrawal from the Gulf, 1961–1971, *Journal of Imperial and Commonwealth History*, 31, pp. 83–108; Smith, S. C. (2004) *Britain's Revival and Fall in the Gulf: Kuwait, Bahrain, Qatar, and the Trucial States, 1950–1971* (London: RoutledgeCurzon); Boyce, *Decolonisation and the British Empire*, pp. 180, 205. Libya became independent, under the newly-proclaimed King Idris, in December 1951: see Louis, W. R. (1988) Libyan independence, 1951: the creation of a client state, in: P. Gifford and W. R. Louis (Eds) *Decolonisation and African Independence: The Transfer of Power, 1960–1980* (New Haven and London: Yale University Press), pp. 159–184.
24. Darwin, *After Tamerlane*, p. 387; Fieldhouse, *Western Imperialism in the Middle East*, pp. 340–348; Boyce, *Decolonisation and the British Empire*, pp. 150–176.
25. Allan, C. (1980) Bureaucratic organisation for development in small island states, in: R. T. Shand (Ed.) *The Island States of the Pacific and Indian Oceans: The Autonomy of Development* (Development Studies Centre Monograph no. 23, Canberra), p. 403.
26. Faulkner, The man who makes a show of independence, p. 39; Bayly, C. and Harpur, T. (2007) *Forgotten Wars: The End of Britain's Asian Empire* (Allen Lane), p. 292.
27. Devonshire, A. (2004) *Accidents of Fortune* (Norwich: Michael Russell), p. 78; Sanger, C. (1995) *Malcolm MacDonald: Bringing an End to Empire* (Liverpool: Liverpool University Press), p. 3; Hyam, *Britain's Declining Empire*, p. 400.
28. Hyam, *Britain's Declining Empire*, pp. 116–119.

29. Hyam, *Britain's Declining Empire*, pp. 269–272, 399; Holland, R. F. (1998) *Britain and the Revolt in Cyprus, 1954–1959* (Oxford: Clarendon Press), pp. 329, 336.
30. Jones, M. (2000) Creating Malaysia: Singapore security, the North Borneo Territories, and the contours of British policy, 1961–3, *Journal of Imperial and Commonwealth History*, 28, pp. 85–109.
31. Hyam, Britain's *Declining Empire*, pp. 400–401.
32. Warwick, C. (1983) *Princess Margaret* (London: Weidenfeld and Nicolson), pp. 156–159.
33. The full text is printed in Armitage, *Declaration of Independence*, pp. 243–245.
34. The two pioneering studies are Masselos, J. (1990) 'The magic touch of being free': the rituals of independence on August 15, in J. Masselos (Ed.) *India: Creating a Modern Nation* (New Delhi: Sterling), pp. 37–53; Owen, N. (1992) 'More than a transfer of power': Independence Day ceremonies in India, 15 August 1947, *Contemporary Record*, 6, pp. 415–451.
35. Owen, 'More than a transfer of power', pp. 443–444.
36. Boyce, *Decolonisation and the British Empire*, p. 157; Gilbert, M. (1988) *Winston S. Churchill*, Vol. viii, *'Never Despair', 1945–1965* (London: Heinemann) pp. 299–300; Zamindar, V.-Y (2007) *The Long Partition and the Making of Modern South Asia: Refugees, Boundaries, Histories* (New York: Columbia University Press); Khan, Y. (2007) *The Great Partition: The Making of India and Pakistan* (New Haven and London: Yale University Press).
37. Ashton, S. R. (2005) Mountbatten, the Royal family and British influence in post-independence India and Burma, *Journal of Imperial and Commonwealth History*, 33, pp. 51–72.
38. Lukes, S. (1977) *Essays in Social Theory* (London: Macmillan), p. 52–73; Cannadine, D. and Price, S. (1987) (Eds), *Rituals of Royalty: Power and Ceremonial in Traditional Societies* (Cambridge: Cambridge University Press); Beard, M. (2007) *The Roman Triumph* (Cambridge, MA: Harvard University Press); Muir, E. (1981) *Civic Ritual in Renaissance Venice* (Princeton: Princeton University Press); Wilentz, S. (1985) (Ed.), *Rites of Power: Symbolism, Ritual and Politics Since the Middle Ages* (Philadelphia: University of Pennsylvania Press); Cannadine, D. and Hammerton, E. (1981) Conflict and consensus on a ceremonial occasion: the Diamond Jubilee in Cambridge in 1897, *Historical Journal*, 24, pp. 111–146; Lane, C. (1981) *The Rites of Rulers: Ritual in Industrial Society – the Soviet Case* (Cambridge: Cambridge University Press).
39. Anderson, D. (2005) *Histories of the Hanged: Britain's Dirty War in Kenya and the End of Empire* (London: Weidenfeld & Nicolson), pp. 335–337.
40. Rathbone, R. (2000) *Nkrumah and Chiefs: The Politics of Chieftancy in Ghana, 1951–60* (Oxford: James Currey).
41. Cannadine, *Ornamentalism*, pp. 166–173.
42. Luce, R. (2007) *Ringing the Changes: A Memoir* (Norwich: Michael Russell), pp. 100–103; Welsh, F. (1996) *A Borrowed Place: The History of Hong Kong* (New York: Kodansha International), pp. 502–536; Dimbleby, J. (1997) *The Last Governor: Chris Patten and the Handover of Hong Kong* (London: Little Brown); Patten, C. (1998) *East and West* (London: Macmillan); Fenby, J. (2008) *The Penguin History of Modern China: The Fall and Rise of a Great Power, 1850–2008* (London: Allen Lane), pp. 659–661.
43. Nasson, *Britannia's Empire*, pp. 189–190; Darwin, J. (1988) *Britain and Decolonization: The Retreat from Empire in the Post-War World* (London; Macmillan), pp. 324, 327–328.
44. Darwin, J. (1986) The fear of falling: British politics and imperial decline since 1900, *Transactions of the Royal Historical Society*, 5th series, 36, pp. 27–43.
45. Sandbrook, *Never Had It So Good*, pp. 265–266; Hood, F. (1967) *The Chapel of the Most Excellent Order of the British Empire* (Oxford: Oxford University Press), pp. 14–17; Burman, P. (2004) Decoration, furnishings and art since 1900, in: D. Keene, A. Burns and A. Saint (Eds) *St Paul's: The Cathedral Church of London, 604–2004* (New Haven and London: Yale University Press), pp. 14–17.
46. Morris, *Farewell the Trumpets*, pp. 545–557; Dimbleby, J. (1977) *Richard Dimbleby* (London: Hodder & Stoughton), pp. 370–375; Levin, *Pendulum Years*, pp. 399–411; Gilbert, '*Never Despair*', pp. 1360–1364.
47. Kirk-Greene, A. (1999) *On Crown Service: A History of HM Colonial and Overseas Civil Services, 1837–1997* (Londo: I. B. Tauris), pp. 90–91; Luce, *Ringing the Changes*, pp. 54, 182–185; Nasson, *Britannia's Empire*, p. 7.
48. Bradford, S. (1996) *Elizabeth: A Biography of Her Majesty the Queen* (London: Heinemann), p. 120; Pimlott, B. (1996) *The Queen: A Biography of Elizabeth II* (London: Harper Collins), pp. 117–119.

16 D. Cannadine

Appendix. Independence dates and royal participation, 1947–97

Dependency	Date	Royal participant
1. The British Empire		
India	August 1947	Lord Mountbatten
Pakistan	August 1947	Lord Mountbatten
Burma	January 1948	None
Ceylon	February 1948	Duke of Gloucester
Palestine	May 1948	None
Libya	December 1951	None
Sudan	January 1956	None
Gold Coast	March 1957	Princess Marina
Malaya	August 1957	Duke of Gloucester
British Somaliland	July 1960	None
Cyprus	August 1960	None
Nigeria	October 1960	Princess Alexandra
Sierra Leone	April 1961	Duke of Kent
Kuwait	June 1961	None
Southern Cameroons	October 1961	None
Tanganyika	December 1961	Prince Philip
Trinidad	August 1962	Princess Royal
Jamaica	August 1962	Princess Margaret
Uganda	December 1962	Duke of Kent
Sarawak	September 1963	None
Singapore	September 1963	None
British North Borneo	September 1963	None
Kenya	December 1963	Prince Philip
Zanzibar	December 1963	Prince Philip
Nyasaland	July 1964	Prince Philip
Malta	September 1964	Prince Philip
Northern Rhodesia	October 1964	Princess Royal
The Gambia	February 1965	Duke of Kent
Maldive Islands	July 1965	None
British Guiana	May 1966	Duke of Kent
Bechuanaland	September 1966	Princess Marina
Basutoland	October 1966	Princess Marina
Barbados	November 1966	Duke of Kent
Aden	November 1967	None
Mauritius	March 1968	None
Swaziland	September 1968	None
Tonga	June 1970	Prince William of Gloucester
Fiji	October 1970	Prince Charles
Bahrain	August 1971	None
Qatar	September 1971	None
Bahamas	July 1973	Prince Charles
Grenada	February 1974	None
Seychelles	June 1976	Prince Richard of Gloucester
Solomon Islands	July 1978	Prince Richard of Gloucester
Ellice Island	October 1978	None
Dominica	November 1978	Princess Margaret
St Lucia	February 1979	Princess Alexandra
Gilbert Islands	July 1979	Princess Anne
St Vincent and the Grenadines	October 1979	Prince Richard of Gloucester

(*continued*)

Appendix. (*Continued*)

Dependency	Date	Royal participant
Southern Rhodesia	April 1980	Prince Charles
New Hebrides	July 1980	Prince Richard of Gloucester
British Honduras	September 1981	Prince Michael of Kent
Antigua and Barbuda	November 1981	Princess Margaret
St Kitts-Nevis	September 1983	Princess Margaret
Brunei	January 1984	Prince Charles
Hong Kong	June 1997	Prince Charles
2. Dominions		
Western Samoa (New Zealand)	January 1962	None
Nauru (Australia)	February 1968	None
Papua New Guinea (Australia)	September 1975	Prince Charles
Namibia (South Africa)	March 1990	None

Sources: Lapping, B. (1985) *End of Empire* (London: Granada), rear endpaper; Kirk-Greene, A. (1999) *On Crown Service: A History of HM Colonial and Overseas Civil Services, 1837–1997* (London: I. B. Tauris), p. 81; Hyam, R. (2006) *Britain's Declining Empire: The Road to Decolonisation, 1918–1968* (Cambridge: Cambridge University Press), pp. 411–412.

Independence Day and the Crown

PHILIP MURPHY
Department of History, University of Reading, UK

The phenomenon of royal tours of the Empire/Commonwealth has attracted a considerable amount of scholarly attention in recent years.[1] Yet the role of royal family at independence ceremonies remains a neglected subject. Compared with the complex practical issues that had to be settled in negotiations leading to independence, the choice of the British monarch's representative at the ceremony marking the transfer of power might well seem a relatively trivial detail. Yet a great deal of energy and anxiety was devoted to it by Whitehall, by the Palace and to a lesser extent, by independence leaders themselves. Indeed, on at least one occasion an independence day was actually re-scheduled to enable a particularly prestigious royal to be present. A clue as to why the British government took such a close interest in this aspect of the arrangements is provided by David Cannadine's suggestion that the end of empire could be seen as "embodying, portending and meaning the end of hierarchy".[2] The dispatch of royal representatives to independence ceremonies was an important symbolic assertion by Britain that the hierarchical structures on which Empire rested had not been entirely dissolved by the loosening of imperial ties.

A largely unspoken but widely accepted hierarchy governed the choice of potential royal representatives. At its pinnacle were the 'unattainable' royals. The first category shrank by a factor of 50% between 1957 and 1961. When the question of royal representation at Ghanaian independence in 1957 was considered, it was decided by the Colonial and Commonwealth Relations offices that neither "the Queen herself nor Prince Philip nor the Queen Mother nor Princess Margaret should be asked to undertake this sort of ceremony". The reason given was that the task "would be a recurring one—though not in quick succession".[3] Hence, when Malaya's Prime Minister, Tunku Abdul Rahman, asked if Princess Margaret could represent the Queen at Malaya's independence ceremony which followed a few months after Ghana's, he was told this would not be possible. While the prohibitions on Princess Margaret and Prince Philip were lifted relatively quickly, by May 1966 the permanent under-secretary at the Colonial Office, Sir Hilton Poynton, could describe as "a well established Palace rule" the convention that neither the Queen nor the Queen Mother presided over independence celebrations.[4] Queens—and even former Queens—did not give things away.[5]

The first entrant into the category of 'elite' royals, whose presence at independence ceremonies was expected to be particularly prized, was Princess Margaret. She was scheduled to attend the Nigerian independence celebrations in 1960, but she withdrew a few months beforehand in favour of Princess Alexandra of Kent. This, it was explained by the Palace, was to allow her some months of privacy following her marriage to Anthony Armstrong-Jones in May.[6] Indeed, having settled down to marriage and having given birth to her first child, it seems to have proved a little difficult to coax the Princess back onto the official circuit. In February 1962, after discussing with the Queen the possibility of Margaret representing her at Jamaican independence, Harold Macmillan pointedly recorded his own support for the proposal, claiming that "she should do Jamaica for the sake of the island (where she is popular) and for her own sake".

It took a little longer for the Colonial Office to reconcile itself with the idea of Prince Philip attending independence celebrations. This was very much a recognition of the Prince's special status. Officials feared that his presence might create 'jealousies' in other newly independent countries.[7] Yet Colonial Secretary Iain Macleod, for reasons that are considered below, overruled the objections of his officials, and Prince Philip represented the Queen at Tanganyika's independence celebrations in December 1961. Thereafter, he became the prize catch for any independence day. In July 1966, the Colonial Office told the Palace of the preferred 'batting order' of Barbados ministers for their country's independence day: "first Prince Philip; second, the Prince of Wales; third the Duke of Kent, with Princess Alexandra in reserve if she was able to undertake public engagements again".[8] At that time, however, the Palace felt that Charles was too young to undertake such engagements, and it was not until 1970 that he attended his first independence celebration, that of Fiji.

In a third category came George VI's sister Mary, the Princess Royal, who presided over the independence days of Trinidad and Tobago in 1962, and Zambia in 1964. More prolifically, there were those great stalwarts of independence ceremonies, the Gloucesters and the Kents. These royals were very much the 'default position' of independence celebrations—acceptably senior, but hardly a mark of special favour. The Duke of Gloucester, a younger brother of George VI, presided over the independence days of Ceylon in 1948 and Malaya in 1957. His elder son, Prince William of Gloucester, represented the Queen at Tonga's independence celebrations in 1970, and his younger son, Richard, the current Duke of Gloucester, did so in the Seychelles, the Solomon Islands, St Vincent and the Grenadines, and Vanuatu. Princess Marina, the widow of another of George VI's brothers, George, Duke of Kent, represented the Queen at Ghana's independence in 1957. Her daughter, Princess Alexandra, did so in Nigeria three years later, and her younger son, Prince Michael of Kent, represented the Queen at the independence day of Belize in 1981.

The member of the family who notched up the most independence day celebrations was Marina's elder son, Edward Duke of Kent. He acted as the Queen's representative in Sierra Leone, Uganda, the Gambia and British Guiana.[9] At times, the Kents seemed to accept these engagements in the way that other families select package holidays. In January 1966, Hilton Poynton noted, "I understand that it has been virtually decided that the Duke of Kent should do British Guiana and that Princess Marina should do Basutoland and Bechuanaland. We had originally thought the other way round; but Princess Marina has apparently said that she is particularly keen to do the African ones and the Duke of Kent, who has never been to the Western hemisphere, would like to do British Guiana."[10]

In the fourth category came the more distant royal relations whose potential deployment raised official anxieties about slighting the territory in question. In January 1966, the Colonial Office told the Palace that the Governor of British Guiana had proved unenthusiastic about the proposal that Lord Mountbatten should represent the Queen at the territory's independence celebrations. He claimed that there would be real disappointment if a 'Royal proper' could not do it. One official at the Colonial Office sympathized with this view. He suggested that "it would not help British Guiana to feel any less slighted than they already showed signs of being, if they were to get Lord Mountbatten instead of a Royal".[11]

While this unspoken hierarchy was broadly accepted, some territories had special requirements, which cut across these categories. In 1973, for example, the Governor of the Bahamas specifically requested an *unaccompanied male royal*. This, it was explained, was because Government House was in such a run-down condition, that it could not easily accommodate a female royal, who was expected to have a somewhat larger retinue than a male one.[12] This left one four possible candidates: Prince Charles, the Duke of Edinburgh, the Duke of Kent and Prince Richard of Gloucester. The latter two were thought to be too uxorious to want to leave their wives at home, and the Duke of Edinburgh's engagement diary was already full. This left Prince Charles, who was currently serving as a naval officer on HMS *Minerva*, stationed conveniently in the West Indies.

It is only by appreciating the nature of this unspoken hierarchy, that we can understand the dual significance of dispatching members of the royal family to independence day ceremonies. The first aspect related to the perceived expectations of the newly independent states themselves. It was regarded as natural in London they would want a 'proper royal', and if possible a senior one. The provision of such a royal was therefore a gesture of goodwill by the former imperial power—one that would be welcomed by the newly independent nation and would have the effect of cementing its relations with Britain. In at least one case, that of Tanganyika, London's willingness to accede to the request for an 'elite' royal, in the interests of promoting good relations with the territory had a direct impact on the date of independence. Independence had originally been set for 28 December 1961, but Julius Nyerere objected that a date so close to Christmas might make it difficult for foreign dignitaries to travel to the country. It was therefore proposed to bring it forward to 20 December. Before an announcement of the change was made, however, Nyerere and his Cabinet requested that the Queen be represented at the celebrations by the Duke of Edinburgh. The Colonial Office learned from the Queen's Private Secretary, Sir Michael Adeane, that this might be possible.

Since the Duke was due to end a tour of West Africa on 6 December, however, the date of independence would have to be brought forward still further to fit into his programme.[13] Officials at the Colonial Office were, as we have already seen, reluctant to allow the Duke to be used in this way.[14] Macleod, however, overruled them. His enthusiasm for the Duke's visit was due at least in part to the fact that the Tanganyikan government had been contemplating adopting a republican constitution. He hoped that "to meet their request for the presence of the Duke of Edinburgh at their independence celebrations might avert this".[15] Macleod also felt that the earlier date would be easier to defend at the UN as it would appear that it had been chosen so as to allow Tanganyika's admission to the General Assembly before it went into recess. Hence, on 4 July 1961, Macleod announced that Tanganyika's independence was to be brought forward to 9 December, although he neglected to explain that the new date had been chosen to fit into the royal schedule.

Thereafter, the particular prestige of having the Duke of Edinburgh present on independence day was a bargaining counter the British government was prepared to use in its negotiations with nationalist leaders. At a meeting of the Cabinet Committee on Royal Visits[16] in May 1966, it was suggested that if, as appeared likely, the granting of independence to Mauritius was delayed from March to June 1967, it would be possible for the Duke of Edinburgh to attend the celebrations on his way back from a visit to Australia.[17] The Colonial Office hoped to be able to use the prospect of the Duke attending the independence celebrations of Mauritius in person as a means of reconciling the country's chief minister, Sir Seewoosagur Ramgoolam to a slightly longer transfer of power than had originally been contemplated. Indeed, one official suggested that it "might well prevent the Premier from pressing for earlier independence and thus avoid his raising with us the question of going back on the six month period of internal self-government".[18]

If nationalist leaders were thought to be sensitive to the level of seniority of their independence day royal, they were also thought to expect a suitable level of formality and pomp to be attached to their visit. In advance of her visit to Jamaica in 1962 for the country's independence celebrations, Princess Margaret—clearly stung by press-criticism of her lifestyle, and anxious in the words one Downing Street official "not to expose herself to any charge of extravagance"—asked the Prime Minister to decide whether she should travel to the West Indies on a specially chartered flight, or whether she should take the considerably cheaper option of a scheduled flight.[19] The Palace itself, however, had its own firm views on the matter. Michael Adeane told Downing Street that:

> he was a little worried about the possible local reaction if Princess Margaret did not go in a special aircraft but came out of an ordinary scheduled one. He said that he was not concerned with Princess Margaret's comfort or convenience but with the fact that she would be The Queen's representative on this occasion and that the Jamaicans might make unfavourable comparisons between what was done for them and what had been done for other Commonwealth countries.[20]

We now come to the second important characteristic of the royal presence on independence days: it was a powerful symbolic assertion that the transfer of power was a voluntary and calculated decision by a country whose power, dignity and sense of hierarchy were undiminished by the act of granting independence. The corollary of this personification of national prestige and the established order was that the British government was highly sensitive about any possibility that the significance of the royal visitor would not be properly acknowledged, or that they might be exposed to embarrassment, indignity or even danger.

Anxieties of this kind meant that, in the cases of Ghana and Malaya in 1957, serious questions were raised about whether the royal visitor should actually be present at the transfer of power. In the case of Ghana, it was initially suggested by the Colonial and Commonwealth Relations secretaries that Princess Marina of Kent, who was due to open the first session of the territory's new legislature, should not be present on Independence Day. They feared "there would be a real risk that the significance of her presence would be overlooked in the excitement of the celebrations".[21] The acting governor of the Gold Coast, however, insisted that it was important that the Princess should be present on independence day itself, and insisted that her 'significance' would not be overlooked. With the messy aftermath of the Suez Crisis dominating the agenda in Whitehall, Nkrumah was prevailed upon to provide a 'categorical assurance' that neither Nasser nor any other official representative of Egypt would be invited to the celebrations. On the basis of these assurances, the government overturned its earlier decision and approached the Queen with the suggestion that the Duchess open the Ghanaian parliament on 6 March—Independence Day itself. British anxieties, however, continued to focus on the way in which the Princess would be perceived, and the prospect of her opening the Ghanaian parliament led one official to complain that "such politically unsophisticated people as the Gold Coasters would all too easily identify the royal representative with one political party, and this would be most undesirable at a time when we are striving to promote unity".[22]

In the case of Malaya, the problem, in the eyes of the Colonial Office, arose from the fact that the Queen would not be the head of state on independence. Instead, one of the Malay Sultans would be installed as Yang di-Pertuan Besar, the representative of the collective sovereignty of the rulers. The Colonial Office worried that ceremonies involving the new Malayan head of state might raise "awkward questions" regarding "the precedence of the member of the Royal Family representing the Queen, in relation to the Yang di-Pertuan Besar", particularly given the probable desire of the Malays "to surround their own head of state with the maximum pomp and circumstance".[23] The Colonial Office suggested to the British High Commissioner in Malaya that it might be better if the Queen were represented not by a member of the British royal family but by "one of the high officers of state" such as the Lord Chamberlain or Lord Steward. Tunku Abdul Rahman, however, was extremely keen that a member of the royal family should attend, and the authorities in Malaya assured London that "the ceremonies could and would, be so arranged that all possible courtesies would be paid and that no embarrassment to the royal personage could possibly result".[24] Like Nkrumah, the Tunku was also obliged to undertake that no official representative of the Egyptian government would be invited. On the basis of these undertakings, the government recommended that the Queen choose the Duke of Gloucester as her representative.[25]

Rather bizarrely, on his previous such engagement, attending the independence celebrations of Ceylon in 1948, there had been fears that the Duke of Gloucester and his wife might be upstaged by an empty chair—or more precisely, by an empty throne. This was the throne of the last King of Kandy, which had been returned to the country by Britain as part of the Duke's visit. It was proposed that the throne be placed in the Ceylonese parliament, which the Duke was due to open, and it was argued "that as the King is not opening Parliament in person, it would be in accordance with United Kingdom practice to leave [the] Kandyan throne empty and for [the] Duke and Duchess to occupy special seats just below".[26] The governor of Ceylon worried, however, that "the ordinary spectator ... may regard the empty throne as something superior to the Duke as King's Representative".

These concerns did not entirely disappear as independence days became more regular events. In July 1963, when it was decided that the Duke of Edinburgh should represent the Queen at Kenya's independence celebrations in December, the question arose over whether he should also stay on to attend the inauguration of the East African Federation, which was expected to occur a few days later. The Colonial Secretary, Duncan Sandys, had his doubts about this—and again the Egyptians were a factor. As one of Sandys' officials explained, "At the Kenya Celebrations, the Duke of Edinburgh would naturally take pride of place. There is, however, some possibility that at the East African Federal Celebrations he might be simply 'lumped in' with various dignitaries. It may even be that the occasion will be used for Pan-African gestures, e.g., by President Nasser, though this seems unlikely."[27]

Questions of gender certainly featured in and exacerbated these sorts of anxieties. Male royals were considered to be more robust than their female counterparts and hence less susceptible to embarrassment and less likely to sustain injuries to national prestige. Having warned London in October 1972 of "the real possibility that the [Bahamas' independence] celebrations will be so ill-organised that it could prove prudent not to expose the Royal Visitor to the resultant shambles", the governor of the territory was relieved to learn that Prince Charles would be representing the Queen. He suggested that "now that the Prince of Wales has been selected and there is no Royal Lady involved, there will be slightly greater license for confusion".[28]

This syndrome unmistakably played a role in the arrangements for the independence celebrations of Mauritius in 1968, a rare case in which a royal visit was cancelled altogether because of security concerns. Again, however, the anxieties of those responsible for organizing the visit related not merely to the possibility that physical harm might come to the royal representative, but that their dignity might in some way be undermined. In this respect, it was significant that the intended royal visitor was a woman—Princess Alexandra. In March 1968, with a state of emergency in place aimed at containing communal violence, Lord Shepherd, the governor of Mauritius, advised that the visit should be cancelled. While admitting that the likelihood of any direct personal attack was remote, Shepherd noted that "a degree of risk of embarrassment, marginal though it might be in the eyes of the security experts does exist".[29] It was clearly assumed that a man would be less susceptible to embarrassment and less of a concern for the security experts, and both the Cabinet of Mauritius and officials in London were keen to explore the possibilities of sending a male member of the royal family in Princess Alexandra's place. In the end, however, the security situation was judged to be such that no royal should be sent.

An instructive parallel can be drawn with the situation in Sierra Leone in 1961. In this case, the prospective royal representative at the independence celebrations was a man—the Duke of Kent. With Independence Day approaching, the governor proposed declaring a state of emergency, principally aimed at opposition from Siaka Stevens's All People's Congress. He told London that once some of the instigators of unrest were detained "everything should be perfectly quiet for HRH's visit".[30] The Queen was consulted about the matter, and she appears to have agreed with the Colonial Secretary's view that unless the situation deteriorated, the royal visit should go ahead.[31] In the case of Sierra Leone, the threat of violence seems to have been considerably less than it was in Mauritius seven years later. Yet the discourse of 'embarrassment' which attached itself so firmly to discussions about the safety of a female member of the royal family was noticeably absent from the correspondence relating to the Duke of Kent's visit in 1961. Indeed, it was even suggested that the Duke should send a personal letter to the governor of Sierra Leone, expressing his regret at the unrest but saying that he was still looking forward to his visit.[32]

In November 2005, the British press published extracts from a private diary kept by Prince Charles during his visit to Hong Kong for the territory's hand-over ceremony eight years before. They attracted attention for the Prince's highly critical remarks about the Chinese regime, describing its officials as "appalling old waxworks" and bemoaning the "awful Soviet-style display" which attended the transfer of power. Yet one of the Prince's most striking comments related not to the former colony's new rulers, but to his own treatment on the flight from Britain to Hong Kong. He recorded that he and his staff were seated "on the top deck in what is normally club class. It took me some time to realise that this was not first class although it puzzled me as to why the seat seemed so uncomfortable". He then discovered that a party of other British dignitaries, including the former Prime Minister, Edward Heath, *had* been placed in first class. "Such is the end of Empire", the Prince sighed to himself.[33]

The Prince's remarks nicely reinforce David Cannadine's 'Ornamentalist' view of the British Empire as having had at its heart an obsession with social rank and status. For all their Gilbertian overtones, the arrangements for the attendance of members of the royal family at independence day ceremonies in the 1950s and 1960s deserve more serious attention than they have hitherto received, not least because they suggest a rearguard action to uphold the notion of hierarchy even at the moment of the transfer of power. The negotiations over which member of the royal family should represent the British monarch were themselves a tacit acknowledgement by independence leaders of the glamour and dignity of Britain's ruling house. During the actual celebrations, every effort was made by the British authorities to ensure that this sense of dignity was preserved and projected. With the transfer of power in Hong Kong in 1997, only a few tens of thousands of inhabitants remained within the British dependent territories. The main contrast with those earlier transfers of power, however, was not so much the vastly diminished size of the 'Imperial' population, as the steady erosion within Britain itself of the clearly-defined and broadly accepted structures of hierarchy and authority upon which Empire had rested. This indeed was the end of Empire.

Notes

1. See, for example, Potter, S. J. (2006) The BBC, the CBC, and the 1939 royal tour of Canada, *Cultural and Social History*, 3(4), pp. 424–444; Buckner, P. (2005) The last great royal tour: Queen Elizabeth's 1959 tour to Canada, in: P. Buckner (Ed.) *Canada and the End of Empire* (Vancouver: UBC Press), pp. 66–93; Buckner, P. (2003) Casting daylight upon magic: deconstructing the royal tour of 1901 to Canada, *Journal of Imperial and Commonwealth History*, 31(2), pp.158–189; Kaul, C. (2003) *Reporting the Raj: The British Press and India, c.1880–1922* (Manchester and New York: Manchester University Press); Connors, J. (1993) The 1954 royal tour of Australia, *Australian Historical Studies*, 25(100), pp. 371–382.
2. Cannadine, D. (2001) *Ornamentalism: How the British Saw Their Empire* (London: Allan Lane), p. 152.
3. Lennox-Boyd to Home, 12 February 1957, DO 35/9747.
4. Minute by Poynton, 18 May 1966, CO 1032/496.
5. This did not, however, prevent colonial governments from inviting the Queen to their ceremonies. In August 1963, for example, the governor of Kenya, Malcolm MacDonald, told the Colonial Secretary, Duncan Sandys, that "the Kenyan Cabinet have unanimously decided that Her Majesty the Queen should be invited to preside at the Independence Day Celebrations in Kenya on December 12th" (MacDonald to Sandys, 3 August 1963, CO 822/3238). MacDonald commended this proposal to London on the grounds that the Queen had been in Kenya when she received news of her father's death and had not returned since. She had been presented with Sagana Lodge as a wedding present by the Kenya government, but had never used it. Michael Adeane had told MacDonald that the Queen was considering giving the Lodge to the government and people of Kenya as an independence present, and MacDonald suggested that a visit by the Queen would provide an opportunity to visit the Lodge and make this gesture in person. MacDonald's logic proved far too fanciful for Sandys, who minuted: "There can be no question of advising the Queen to go to the Independence celebrations" (Minute by Milton, 12 August 1963, CO 822/3238). Instead, he confirmed what had already effectively been decided within the government—that the Duke of Edinburgh should represent the Queen.
6. *The Times*, 1 April 1960.
7. Pearson to Macleod, 4 July 1961, CAB 21/4962.
8. Minute by Williams, 7 July 1966, CO 1031/5179.
9. Following her marriage to the Duke in June 1961, Duchess of Kent, played a major part in these celebrations. She proved a great success at Uganda's independence ceremony in 1962. When shortly before their marriage, however, the Duke had suggested taking his then fiancée with him to Sierra Leone's celebrations, the country's prime minister had expressed doubts to the governor about "whether Creole Church people of Freetown would think it proper. It might not be acceptable in England either." (Dorman to Poynton, 15 March 1961, CO 554/2529).
10. Minute by Poynton, 24 January 1966, CO 1031/5179.
11. Minute by Fairlie, 12 January 1966, CO 1031/5179.
12. Goodison to Muirhead, 2 April 1973, FCO 63/1205.
13. Pearson to Macleod, 4 July 1961, CAB 21/4962.
14. *Ibid.*
15. *Ibid.*
16. A Cabinet committee on 'Royal Visits Overseas and Visits by Foreign Heads of State', which met for the first time in July 1959, included representatives from the Foreign Office, the Colonial Office, the Commonwealth Relations Office, the Treasury and the Palace.
17. Cabinet Committee on Royal visits, RV (66), first meeting, 17 May 1966, CO 1032/496.
18. Minute by Galsworthy, 17 May 1966, CO 1032/496.
19. Zulueta to Macmillan, 22 June 1962, PREM 11/3851.
20. Zulueta to Macmillan, 25 June 1962, PREM 11/3851.
21. Home and Lennox-Boyd to Eden, 9 November 1956, PREM 11/1859.
22. Minute by Terry, 10 February 1957, CO 554/1390.
23. Draft letter from Sir John Macpherson to Sir Donald MacGillivray, forwarded Macpherson to Laithwaite, 11 December 1956, DO 35/9747.
24. Lennox-Boyd to Home, 12 February 1957, DO 35/9747.
25. Salisbury to Adeane, 8 March 1957, DO 35/9747.

26. Moore to Creech Jones, 13 December 1947, CO 537/2214, in: K. M. De Silva and S. R. Ashton (Eds) (1997) *British Documents on the End of Empire: Sri Lanka* (London: Stationery Office), Pt 2, p. 441.
27. Minute by Gilmore, 8 July 1963, CO 822/3238.
28. Paul to Roberts, 15 March 1973, FCO 63/1205, recalling his earlier letter in October 1972.
29. Shepherd to Secretary of State, 6 March 1968, FCO 32/337.
30. Macleod to Macmillan, 17 April 1961, CO 554/2529.
31. Adeane to Poynton, 18 April 1961; Adeane to Poynton, 19 April 1961, CO 554/2529.
32. Colonial Office to Bligh, 18 April 1961, CO 554/2529.
33. *Daily Telegraph*, 23 February 2006.

"At the Stroke of the Midnight Hour": Lord Mountbatten and the British Media at Indian Independence

CHANDRIKA KAUL
School of History, University of St Andrews, St Andrews, UK

The first major decolonization of the 20th century took place over 48 hours during mid-August 1947, in the Indian sub-continent. This article seeks to analyse how this defining event was interpreted at the metropolitan heart of empire by examining its portrayal in the British media, focussing primarily on the national press.[1] The organization of official publicity under the last Viceroy, Lord Louis Mountbatten, forms a key aspect of this analysis for the light it throws on the transformed imperial context within which the public mediation of these events transpired.

Newspapers were critical in creating the first draft of the history of British decolonization, and in significant ways impacted on future remembrances of the occasion. Over the 20th century, the press became inextricably linked with Britain's imperial enterprise and its pro-empire thrust was widely acknowledged. At Independence, and in some significant ways till today, a widespread British perception of decolonization was to view it as an orderly and planned *transfer of power* that involved the minimum disruption and served as the fulfilment of long cherished 19th-century Macaulayite ideals that underlay the very establishment of the empire. What role, if any, did the press play in furthering the official line on decolonization? James Epstein has recently argued that to understand the "constitutive impact" of empire on Britain requires moving beyond generalizations to "analysing specific contexts".[2] It is hoped that this investigation will contribute in some small measure towards a more empirically sensitive history of just such a specific context in the process of India's impact on Britain and help tease out some of the ways in which the end of empire was explained to a popular audience.

Fleet Street in Delhi

If you had walked into the Imperial Hotel in Delhi during the summer of 1947, you might be forgiven for thinking that you had inadvertently entered a Fleet Street pub, so thick was the air with media talk. The majority of the foreign press had been encamped in the Imperial for months and included news agencies like Reuters, the Associated Press of America, Agence France Presse, Tass, and the Central News agency, China. Amongst the non-British papers represented were the *New York Post, New York Times, Life, Time, Chicago Daily News, Chicago Tribune* and the *Sydney Morning Herald*. Apart from Doon Campbell of Reuters and Bob Stimson and Gordon Mosley from the BBC, there were over 15 special correspondents from the British national press, with both quality dailies like *The Times* and *Daily Telegraph and Morning Post*, and more popular papers like the *Daily Express* and *Daily Mail*, electing to have two or more journalists reporting from the field. Fleet Street also had long-established links with English-language newspapers in the main provincial capitals like the *Statesman* in Calcutta, the *Times of India* in Bombay, and the *Civil and Military Gazette* in Lahore, and was able to report with an immediacy from these cities.[3] In addition to their traditional reliance on Reuters, papers also teamed up to establish a news-share syndicate like *The Times and Manchester Guardian* service. Even so the quality and range of coverage was far from uniform across India. Thus the north-west was historically a problematic area for recruiting reliable local correspondents, as witnessed by the travails of, for example, *The Times*. Large centres like Peshawar remained unrepresented and others like Karachi were covered by *The Times* Bombay representative, Sir Francis Low, who was also editor of the *Times of India*, on the basis that the time lag between Karachi and Bombay was less than between Karachi and New Delhi, and that Sindh was insufficiently important to warrant a permanent correspondent.[4]

Freedom at Midnight

How, then, did the British national press interpret decolonization in the subcontinent? Fleet Street accorded the story pride of place on the front page with no lead being spared in making the headlines bolder and larger than before. Coverage extended into editorials and featured reports and by-lines from special correspondents strewn throughout their pages. In terms of column inches *The Times* and the *Manchester Guardian* more than made up for their relatively sedate presentation, with the conservative *Daily Telegraph*, the liberal *News Chronicle* and the Labour *Daily Herald* providing more moderate coverage, with the picture-led *Daily Mirror* making up the rear, devoting only 14 lines or 66 words on its front page to the story. The *Illustrated London News* had an impressive set of photographs in features over the summer and in depth coverage in its Independence issue (23 Aug.). Prospective maps of the new nations were produced in the *Daily Mail* and *The Times* (which had its own cartographic department), while awaiting the recommendations of the

Boundary Commission. The following headlines, from both quality and popular papers, capture some of the spirit of the coverage:

"Power is transferred at Midnight" (*Daily Telegraph*)
"Power is handed over in India", "Lord Mountbatten on a friendly parting", "The End of an Era" (*The Times*)
"India is pledged to peace" "Midnight guns greet two new dominions"
"An Accidental Empire ends" "Freedom day" (*Daily Herald*)
"The New Beginning" (*News Chronicle*)
"India: 11 words mark end of an empire" (*Daily Mail*)
"India greets dawn of Independence" (*Daily Worker*)
"Farewell and Hail" (*Manchester Guardian*)
"India: the end of an epoch" (*Spectator*)
"Indians Link Arms – Greet Freedom" (*Daily Mirror*)

For the majority of Fleet Street, however, the symbolic image of change was the new flags and most did a creditable job of explaining the symbolism of the icons used. In this context one photograph took centre stage. There had been some official concern at public reactions to the lowering of the Union Jack from the ramparts of the ruined British Residency in Lucknow, "from which", the *Telegraph* informed its readers, "it had never been lowered since recapture of the town after the siege of 1857". The *Illustrated London News* devoted the entire front page to this image and how the flag was replaced at midnight, "secretly and without ceremony" (*Mail*), by the Indian tricolour. The *Contemporary Review* had a detailed feature on the subject of "A Flag Hauled Down" where A. F. Fremantle quoted Wordsworth's lament over the fall of a great city: "And what if she had seen those glories fade, Those titles vanish, and that strength decay; Yet shall some tribute of regret be paid." Fremantle offered his "tribute of regret" in the form of an account of the fall of the Residency and what it meant "and means still, to those who have known it and something of its history".[5] For their readers this served as an emotive symbol of the heroic sacrifice of empire and its inclusion as part of the Independence celebrations is not without significance.

The flag symbolism was also carried through in features recording the hoisting of the tricolour from the India Office and the Pakistani flag from Lancaster House. Thus, the popular evening daily *Star* noted how the western avenue of Aldwych "sparkled with all the colour of an Indian scene". In the socialist weekly *New Statesman and Nation*—which, under the editorship of Kingsley Martin, had been a relentless champion of the nationalist cause—Martin writing under the pseudonym "Critic" in the "London Diary", could not contain his joy: "To see the Indian flag hoisted at Aldwych was a wonderful cure for cynicism. Few aspirations for the good have succeeded in our time, and we are so accustomed to worthy defeat and barren victories that a victory that fulfils a worthy aspiration deserves all the emphasis we can give it."[6] The *Telegraph* and the "democratic" *Reynolds* newspaper were the only ones to profile the new Indian High Commissioner with a photograph of Krishna Menon. However, the former contended that the appointment "may be received with mixed feelings" since Menon, as long-serving secretary of the India League and a Socialist member of the St Pancras Borough council, was not "*persona gratissima*" in

Whitehall. By contrast, Peter Yorke in the *Reynolds* ("This man saw his dream come true"), extolled the sacrifice and achievements of Menon.

While Fleet Street across the political spectrum was unanimous in extending the "universal goodwill" of Britain (*Spectator*) and promises of "unstinting" support (*Telegraph, Chronicle*), one predictable, overarching theme to emerge was the self-congratulatory tone of most papers. Witnesses to history in the making, journalists of both quality and popular papers portrayed the "transfer of power" as peaceful and as the "fulfilment of the British mission".[7] Victor Thompson writing in the *Herald* appeared to encapsulate press sentiment when he noted that "The empire which began as an accident has ended on purpose."[8] Macaulay's 1833 dictum on Britain's "proudest day" was widely quoted,[9] giving the lie, argued the conservative *Mail*, "to those on the other side of the Atlantic and elsewhere who proclaimed us oppressors". The *Guardian* emphasized how "freedom by a voluntary transfer of power was unique in history".[10] Indians, its editorial noted, were able to "rejoice at achieving their independence without the prelude of country-wide civil war to which some months ago many had resigned themselves".[11] Similarly, Norman Cliff, the *News Chronicle*'s special correspondent, contended: "Never has a great Imperial Power surrendered its proud domain or freedom been acquired by subject millions by so peaceful and friendly a transition."[12]

The *Times*, *Guardian*, and *Herald* also featured a potted history of the Raj. The *Guardian* stressed how Britain went to India "not to conquer but to trade. Events not intention created the British Raj". Indeed, it was the Raj that by enabling "contact with the outer world" facilitated the "recovery of a vitality and self confidence" by the Indians. "As soon as this happened, the political changes now being completed could only be a matter of time, for Great Britain had neither the desire nor the ability to rule a people which had recovered the will to rule itself."[13] Having acquired the empire, the civilizing agency of the Raj was to the fore, the fruits of which were now the abiding legacy for Indians. The *Observer* was convinced of the "moral and material benefits" that the Raj had brought to India, which for *The Times* leader writer, H. M. Stannard, included "the strength and adaptability of the British tradition of political freedom", "political ideas and constitutional methods for reconciling liberty with order" and "a new conception of public service".[14] Institutions like the Indian Army and the Indian Civil Service (ICS) were universally commended. Thus Sir George Schuster in the *Guardian* wrote of the ICS as displaying "such integrity, such single hearted devotion, such thoroughness and accuracy", that it would be "a priceless heritage".[15] While Sir Malcolm Darling recorded a touching tribute of his service since 1904, "An ICS farewell to India", giving due regard to the struggle of the Congress party.[16] The *New Statesman* admitted that at the moment of departure, nostalgia would "tug at the hearts", but despite these "last-minute looks over the shoulder", Indians and Europeans were beginning to enjoy a friendship between equals.[17] It was also the case that in Pakistan Britons continued to occupy key posts: six out of nine government departments were under their supervision at Independence.

In true media tradition, there was the inevitable personalization of politics. Taking the lead from Attlee, Wavell was all but forgotten, the press hailing Mountbatten as Britain and India's saviour: the *Guardian* noted how less than a century after

Victoria, her great-grandson stood as the freely chosen constitutional head of a free state.[18] Mountbatten's charismatic personality, good looks and royal connections no doubt played a large part in feeding this press adulation. In the words of the *Mail*: "By his own remarkable powers of personality he brought the Indian leaders together and achieved in less than five months what others for more than a decade had sought in vain to do." Attlee, too, came in for a fair share of the praise "for the firmness of his Indian policy" (*Mail*), with the *Guardian* reminding readers that his statecraft "was the culmination of years of devotion to India", beginning with his membership of the Simon Commission in 1927.[19] Erstwhile critics like the *Spectator* also acknowledged the "courage" displayed by the Prime Minister "in committing himself to a great act of faith".[20]

Indian protagonists did not, however, fare as well. While Nehru's "tryst with destiny" speech was quoted by several papers and he was the recipient of a few positive though passing references, what many like the conservative *Express*, *Mail* and *Telegraph* as well as the labour *Herald* chose to emphasise was the gratitude expressed towards Britain by Indian leaders, selecting excerpts from their speeches in the Constituent Assembly directed to this end. For instance, Sarvapalli Radhakrishnan was quoted as saying: "When we see what the Dutch are doing in Indonesia and the French in Indo-China, we cannot but admire the sagacity and genius of the British people. ... As from midnight tonight we can no longer blame the Britisher."[21] Similarly, Rajendra Prasad, the Assembly's President, was cited as maintaining that Indian freedom was "the consummation and fulfilment of the historic traditions and economic ideals of the British race".[22] The imagery of the grateful imperial subject/student and the wise and benevolent colonial master/teacher was a recurrent underlying motif in many newspaper accounts.

Notable also by its absence was any detailed discussion of Indian nationalism or the freedom struggle. The few references that were made came predictably in the liberal and labour papers. Thus the *Guardian* alluded to the key personalities of the Congress and Martin stressed that Britain "has been induced to keep that promise [of independence] at least in part by the work of many devoted individuals, both in England and India. We should not forget that this is a victory for the idealists, for Gandhi and Nehru and countless others who suffered for their persistence with long periods in stifling gaols".[23] Victor Thompson in the *Herald* made a passing reference to the Indian struggle and the consequent "bitterness and violence".[24] However, even he attributed the rise of the nationalist movement to the seeds sown chiefly by British liberals who "continually questioned British rule, insisted that self government must always be the eventual goal, [and] forced the authorities to proceed with the Indianization of administration and services".[25] When Gandhi is mentioned, he is invariably portrayed as aloof from the celebrations: "His creed rejected, his dream of a united India shattered, the architect of India's freedom is a sad, lonely figure on this day of official rejoicing."[26] Gandhi "cannot reconcile himself to violence and division, although he believes that Pakistan has come to stay".[27]

Partition that enabled the creation of Pakistan, was widely regarded as a misfortune, responsibility for which was laid squarely at the door of the Indians. Sir Stanley Reed, Conservative MP and erstwhile editor of the *Times of India*, referred to it as "a tragedy" (*Spectator*). The "fissures", claimed Reed, between Hindus and

Muslims "have continuously developed with the transfer of power which began with the advent of the Liberal Government in 1906". This veiled reference to the constitutional separatism enshrined in the separate electorates awarded in the subsequent 1909 Constitutional Act, is striking in its singularity. Reed reiterated the oblique references contained in many papers when he referred to the "astute leadership" of Jinnah in consolidating a feeling of inferiority and cultural difference of the Muslims.[28] The veteran *Times* correspondent Ian Morrison, writing from Delhi, stressed how the unavoidable balkanization of the sub-continent, "has come in a way that has been a disappointment to many Indians who have devoted their lives to the struggle for independence. The vision which they have always had of a strong united India has proved impossible of attainment. Partition has brought sadness to many, and joy in the ceremonies ... is not unalloyed".[29] Cliff claimed that the Hindus were "more likely to deplore the partition of their country than to rejoice at its liberation".

While Jinnah was not universally championed, there was a prominent pro-Muslim and anti-Sikh and anti-Congress position in the two quality conservative weeklies, the *Observer* and the *Spectator*. Writing in the latter, Sir Evelyn Wrench—who claimed authority on the basis of personal association with Jinnah until 1944—noted that, "Englishmen can remember with gratitude the fact that he refused to embarrass" the government in 1942, when Congress launched the Quit India movement.[30] Amongst detractors of Jinnah was the radical H. N. Brailsford, who found a congenial home in the *New Statesman* but also wrote for periodicals such as the *Contemporary Review*, where he argued that Jinnah had worked "at every turn to widen the breach" and "fought only for his own community, in the feud which he has steadily embittered, without a thought for the good of India".[31] While the *Chronicle* contended that Partition was "largely the creation of one man, and all indications are that at the outset it will be mainly under his personal rule". The British were more or less absolved of blame. As "Sagittarius" wrote in the *New Statesman* (in a homage to the Kipling classic "White Man's Burden"):

> They would not be united
> According to your plan –
> You frowned upon partition
> But yielded Pakistan.

Likewise the *Observer*'s editorial position stated that while the new Dominions "should have been born without the pangs of war is good; it is for the two Indias to sustain the peace".[32] Even the *Guardian*, long the stalwart of Indian nationalism, maintained: "We have handed over India to the Indians: they have chosen what ... seems a second best—a divided India. But it is their choice; if they come together well and good, but their destiny is in their own hands."[33]

There also appeared to be a consensus in Fleet Street not to dwell on the communal troubles on the day of Independence. However, there were prominent exceptions where reports of celebrations were juxtaposed with those of massacres under graphic headlines. "High Death Roll in Punjab", "Fierce Communal Battles" ran *The Times'* story. "Lahore Ablaze" reported Ralph Izzard, the *Mail*'s special correspondent and the *Star*'s headlines read: "India Celebrates As Thousands Riot", while the *Herald*'s header declared: "120 Killed as India riots and feasts."[34] The triangular communal situation in the Punjab, where Sikh sentiments were embroiled in the general Hindu–Muslim clashes, was discussed in the weeks leading up to Independence in *The Times*, the *Guardian,* the *Telegraph* and the *Observer*. Several papers also singled out what the *Guardian* claimed was the "Curious Apathy" in Karachi on 14 August, a lethargy that was in sharp contrast to the next day when India appeared to erupt with festivities.[35] Special mention was accorded to the fraternization on the streets of Calcutta where "Hindus and Moslems linked arms" (*Mirror*) and "drove round the city roaring their joint welcome to independence" (*Daily Worker*). While in Pakistan, the *Chronicle* noted how the Muslims "show more delight at release from Hindu than from British domination". For *The Times* correspondent possible explanations included the "lethargic temperament of the ordinary Sindhi", the fact that the majority of Karachi's population were Hindus, and a general realization of the "tremendous problems" overshadowing the birth of Pakistan. Only the *Herald's* Andrew Mellor and the newsreel footage from Paramount and Gaumont, seemed to contradict this somewhat subdued impression. Mellor referred to Karachi as "The City of Flags", where "Cars hooted and bumped each other, people climbed lamp posts and stood on roofs or got jammed in the dense masses in the roads."

However, most papers were unanimous in highlighting as a dereliction of British duty the fate of the princely states that comprised two-fifths of the sub-continent. Long the bulwarks of conservative imperialism in the face of rising nationalist agitation, the special relationship between the Raj and princely India, came to an abrupt end with Independence. "That Britain should have had to default in its obligations to the Princes is deeply to be regretted", argued the *Spectator*. "Nothing could be more repugnant to public opinion in Great Britain than any enforced severance from the Commonwealth of rulers who have, in many cases, given loyal support to it in war and in almost all cases value their British connection highly."[36] The *Contemporary Review* featured a detailed survey of the new constitutional status of the States by V. S. Swaminathan,[37] while the *Express* correspondent Sydney Smith chose to give prominence to the largest of these, Hyderabad, where there were no celebrations on 15 August. With a photo of the Nizam who "insists on maintaining independent relations" with Britain, Smith informed his readers that its ruler had a yearly income of £3 000 000, yet spent barely £5 a month on himself and "prefers to live on a verandah with a pet goat as companion". It is not clear how far this picture of an eccentric rich potentate was meant to endear him to a British audience or help consolidate his claim for an independent status within the Commonwealth.

Finally, most of Fleet Street echoed the sentiments expressed in the ever optimistic *New Statesman* that the Indians were "not a bitter, or an unforgiving race ... they will not allow memories of the past to vitiate the potentialities of the future".[38] Yet, there was an overwhelming acknowledgment that a new balance of power needed to be created in the East and that British foreign policy would have to be reassessed. "The substitution of such a balkanised system for the unity which existed before can hardly fail to increase international tension", was how the *Guardian* put it.[39] Other underlying anxieties were exposed by the caricaturists' pen. *Punch* in its inimitable style depicted Mountbatten as the cameraman attempting to orchestrate a picture of an unstable triumvirate with a smiling British Lion flanked by two ferocious tigers on either side representing the two new dominions, with the caption: "Tria Juncta in Uno", while a cartoon in the *News of the World* depicted a conversation between a fruit seller and a flower girl beneath a statute of Disraeli as Lord Beaconsfield, who had done so much to make India a jewel in Britain's crown, with the caption: "Egypt gone, and India. Blimey 'e wouldn't 'arf 'ave used some unparliamentary language!"[40]

The role of the Commonwealth was in this context considered critical. There was some doubt about whether both the new Dominions would join the Commonwealth and some sentiment that suggested (incorrectly as it turned out) that Pakistan could be relied on to do so more than India, there was no hesitancy in emphasising its unique role. Thus the *Spectator* was convinced that: "By severance from the Commonwealth they can gain no freedom which is not theirs already; by association with it they will ensure a co-operation that must inure in every way to their advantage."[41] There was also a sense that India and Pakistan, with their ancient civilization and traditions, were uniquely placed to act as mediators between the East and West in ways which the *Mail* argued "may profoundly affect the future of the world. Their statesmen now have the power, if they use it right, to bridge the gap between East and West; to make us both, in a true sense, one world".[42] In addition, the significance of the creation of Pakistan as "the leading State of the Muslim world", meant, according to *The Times*, that Karachi had emerged as "a new centre of Muslim cohesion and rallying point for Muslim thought and aspirations".[43] A prescient sentiment, indeed, given the context of world politics today.

Figure 1. Tria Juncta in Uno, *Punch*, 23 July 1947. © *Punch*

The Mountbatten Factor

In analysis of imperial coverage the bounded context is pre-eminently important for, though Fleet Street prided itself on its independent stance, in reality the constraints of coercive rule and imperial subjugation that underlay the Raj always threatened to impinge in significant ways upon the extent and nature of its coverage. With combined circulations of the daily national press reaching 15.5 million, officials were not in a position to underestimate its potential to influence the voting and consuming public. In 1947, there was the added factor in the shape of the new Viceroy and his publicity team.

Lord Wavell, Mountbatten's predecessor, had been warmly endorsed by the British press upon his appointment, undoubtedly influenced by his war record, but while aware of the role of public opinion, Wavell did not feel the necessity to cultivate the media on a systematic footing. I. M. Stephens, editor of the *Statesman*, felt that the Viceroy came across as "reticent, enigmatic" with "no particular liking for social events and wholly lack[ing] interest in or capacity for self-display".[44] Wavell did, however, reserve special regard for *The Times*, whose special correspondents Alexander Inglis and James Holburn, "understood how Governments work. ... and could be relied upon to give a balanced view. They were also most discreet and did not misuse inside information."[45] "Delhi has become an acute problem", noted Ralph Deakin, *The Times* foreign editor, when conveying both Wavell and the Secretary of State Leo Amery's urgent request to have Holburn reinstated in 1945: "There is some compensation in the keen desire that high authority has displayed to have you back."[46]

The contrast could not have been more striking with Mountbatten who was "extrovert and sociable" and functioned "in a blaze of publicity".[47] His capacity for self publicity is legendary: while being filmed for an ITV series in the 1970s, he insisted on directing the lighting and camera angles as "it was important for him to be shot from 6 inches above his eye line".[48] He was excited by the communication revolution of his times, an interest stimulated early in his naval career as a wireless officer, and, throughout his life he invested in innovation; for instance, in 1959 he backed Cockerell, the inventor of the Hovercraft.[49] Mountbatten transformed the traditional approach to the office of the Viceroy by appreciating the extraordinary demands of the situation—as one commentator remarked: "India in March 1947 was a ship on fire in mid-ocean with ammunition in the hold."[50] Against precedence, he handpicked a new public relations team to accompany him, in which a key player was Alan Campbell-Johnson who became the first (and only) press attaché appointed to the Viceroy's staff, heading a team that successfully orchestrated the stage management of the Mountbatten handover of power and helped create the mythic dimensions of his personal role in this process. Campbell-Johnson, with a background in the Royal Air Force, had worked closely with Mountbatten at the Combined Operations Headquarters in South East Asia and was in a unique position to witness Mountbatten as a 'communicator'. Mountbatten, he claimed, "wanted always to simplify, to popularise, and in particular to photograph. He was a believer in developing and using an image" and was "at his very best in public".[51]

Such synergy is apparent in the negotiations prior to the departure of the Viceregal party for India. It was felt important to develop a strategy *vis-à-vis* the press.

38 C. Kaul

THE ROPE TRICK

Figure 2. The Rope Trick, *Punch*, 28 May 1947. © *Punch*

Campbell-Johnson liaised extensively with the India Office Information department and with Sudhir Ghosh, the Press Officer at the Indian High Commission in London. The consensus was weighted against any regular question-and-answer sessions with the Indian press since the danger of misrepresentation was felt to outweigh any potential benefits. Instead, it was planned to have "an editorial tea-party" soon after Mountbatten's arrival, to be followed by off-the-record meetings with them individually.[52] Mountbatten set the ball of his diplomatic charm offensive rolling almost immediately by going against protocol to make a speech at his inauguration where he stressed that it was "not a normal Viceroyalty" on which he was embarking: "I shall need the greatest goodwill of the greatest possible number, and I am asking India today for that goodwill."[53] And for the first time "film cameras whirred and flash bulbs went off" in the Durbar Hall to capture the swearing-in ceremony on celluloid.[54] By the tone of not just the Anglo-Indian but also the Indian-run press, Mountbatten appeared to have got off to a good start with papers commenting upon his engaging frankness and charm of manner (*Hindustan Times*), his readiness to take quick decisions in an emergency (*Pioneer*), his embodying "that combination of natural authority and progressive spirit which characterizes the British Royal House" (*Statesman*).[55] The *Tribune* argued that Mountbatten would need to do his utmost to "enable transfer of power to keep India united" in which case India would remain Britain's friend, while the *Sind Observer* warned that the need of the hour was a firm hand and not vague generalities, and *Dawn* was convinced that Mountbatten had "great and unprecedented responsibilities" but would "doubtless be wooed and fawned upon, cajoled and alternately threatened, a time honoured Congress way".[56]

Once in office, the minutes of every staff meeting demonstrate how systematically press comment was scrutinized and how keen an interest Mountbatten took in cultivating journalists both Indian and foreign: proffering advice, correcting misstatements and being available to lunch as occasion demanded. The favoured few like Eric Britter of *The Times*, were also invited to join the Mountbattens at their hill station retreat at Mashobra. One high point of this interaction came at the Viceroy's press conference in Delhi when he expounded the Plan of 3 June with respect of Independence with Partition. Campbell-Johnson enthused how the event had been "a tremendous success, and has done much to clarify and stabilize the situation and control the whole tone of press comment." The reactions of nearly 300 correspondents present "were quite the most enthusiastic I have ever experienced".[57] Mountbatten, speaking without notes, demonstrated a command over the subject that moved Stephens to recall years later: "For sheer intellectual range and vigour, for assured grasp of minutiae, yet brilliant marshalling of the main lines of a long, difficult argument, it was an extraordinary performance."[58] Mellor of the *Herald* claimed to be "stunned" by the performance, while Britter called it a "*tour de force*".[59] Only two major Indian papers—the *Hindustan Times* and the *Indian News Chronicle*—were critical of the balkanization of the sub-continent as envisaged in the plan, but significantly not about the Viceroy's performance. All India Radio (AIR) covered it in special bulletins, provincial governors had it translated for distribution in regional languages, and British representatives in London, Washington, Canberra, Toronto, Singapore, Rangoon and Shanghai received copies in time for a near simultaneous release.[60] Fleet Street and the BBC were seminal to Mountbatten as he attached "the greatest importance to clear transmission in England and America".[61] He was also keen to have "the widest broadcast publicity" for speeches by Nehru, Jinnah and Baldev Singh,[62] for to be seen to be endorsed by the Congress, League and Sikh political interest groups was deemed critical to achieve a positive public response. In the event, the BBC's coverage of the 3 June announcement was considered to have been "magnificent" and as Campbell-Johnson noted: "it is good to see that they have at last woken up to the full importance of India".[63]

Campbell-Johnson thus operated in an imperial context that put enormous store by image and presentation. His own attention to detail, frequent press conferences, informal press briefings and overall attempts to personalize the government–press interface bore handsome dividends. In his words: "By dint of giving up some of the hours of the day and sacrificing some of the paper work, I have managed to achieve fairly good relations with most of the correspondents here. I am sure it pays to be available even if one has not a lot to say, and the Indians undoubtedly react favourably to minor courtesies which the European correspondents might take for granted."[64] Throughout these tense months, and particularly during the partition civil strife following Independence, Campbell-Johnson was able to maintain harmonious working relations with both the foreign and the Indian press. He was, for instance, instrumental in having Mountbatten dissuade Nehru from imposing censorship on the foreign media, which he had threatened to do during a press conference on 28 August. He collaborated with his counterpart A. H. Joyce, the

Adviser on Publicity Questions at the India Office, to help advise Fleet Street editors and the London representatives of Indian newspapers. By 1947, the latter were a substantial presence in the capital and it was arranged for them to have separate weekly press conferences from May to August in recognition of the fact that they had a special interest to serve, and their quota in the Parliamentary press gallery was supplemented whenever possible. Joyce had a wealth of direct Indian experience as he had been seconded from the India Office to work for the Bureau of Public Information in Delhi during 1935 and again in 1936–37, helping reorganize government publicity. And he reassured Campbell-Johnson that despite the fact that the adverse newsprint situation meant that Indian and international news "suffers to an appalling extent": "You can always rely ... on our giving the fullest possible prominence" to Mountbatten's statements, and to his "efforts to bring HMG's [His Majesty's Government] policy to a successful issue".[65] The smooth operation of the official co-operation between London and New Delhi, what Campbell-Johnson referred to as "a good piece of teamwork from 7 000 miles range", owed a great deal to the personal commitment and shared vision of these two administrators and lay at the heart of the successful government publicity arrangements during these months.

BBC and Newsreels

Despite their hectic schedules during trips back to London before August, Mountbatten and Campbell-Johnson prioritized meetings with the British media including the BBC and newsreel companies. The audio-visual was felt to be a pivotal aspect of official publicity and the BBC and AIR broadcasts (in the latter case working closely with Sardar Patel, the head of communications in the Interim government) were utilized on an unprecedented scale with AIR being especially influential for its rural programmes, which reached listeners who might not be able to read newspapers. Meeting with Sir William Haley, the Director General of the BBC, Mountbatten was able to secure the Corporation's "very full attention to the period of the transfer of power". Haley informed the Viceroy that the BBC were sending a team of three news observers—Wynford Vaughan Thomas, Edward Ward, and Richard Sharp, two feature writers—Francis Dillon and Louis MacNeice, and three mobile recording units, with the objective "to report fully in this country and all over the world the progress of transfer from August onwards and further most importantly to provide material for programmes describing the British record of achievement in India".[66]

While there was approval of measures to cover the events just before and after 15 August, there was concern, as articulated by the Secretary of State Lord Listowel, that should there be continued communal violence after the transfer of power, then the BBC's aim of emphasizing British achievement might give offence unintentionally as "we should appear to be trying to emphasise awful consequences of abandonment of power".[67] Mountbatten concurred: "It would be far better to let the new Dominions find their own feet within the Commonwealth, rather than overstress the whole business at the start."[68] Campbell-Johnson was "in very close touch" with the BBC's chief in India, Bob Stimson, and Mountbatten was confident that "in the end we shall be able to get the right stand on things".[69] He was also "anxious that all important phases of the ceremonies, should be covered by newsreel men",[70] but was "appalled at the indifference" of the major companies who, apart from the American-financed Paramount and Movietone, had no outlay on covering the celebrations.[71] Thus with only four weeks to go, John Turner of Gaumont News was hastily appointed as the official representative of the Newsreel Association working on a rota agreement. Mountbatten was assiduous in ensuring official support, with the government paying for his travel within India though he was not attached to Mountbatten's staff since it was emphasized that Turner was "to publicise India and not the Viceroy".[72]

Concluding Remarks

This article has had two prime foci: one, the influential British press and the diverse arguments put forth into contemporary popular debate about the end of empire, and second, the powerful government propaganda machinery in New Delhi and the India Office, and its evolving relationship with the media, especially under the direction of the publicity conscious Louis Mountbatten, who played a seminal role in mediating the public image of decolonization.

Overall, Campbell-Johnson felt that the independence celebrations "went off very well from the publicity viewpoint", and the reception accorded to the Mountbattens in both Delhi and Bombay was "quite extraordinary".[73] Despite last-minute preparations, the film rota agreement had worked successfully resulting in both Gaumont and Paramount producing "excellent newsreels".[74] In fact, as Turner's own reminiscences reveal, and, as historians like Wood have argued, the overwhelming emphasis in the newsreels took the shape of eulogistic accounts of the official ceremonies revolving around the Mountbattens, with key Indian and Pakistani protagonists and events often sidelined or ignored completely.[75] Fleet Street was in a strong position—its journalists enjoyed unprecedented access to the locus of imperial power and to sources of information and comment. Special correspondents were deployed in large numbers and its leader writers in London were men of ability and longstanding experience of the East, like Professor Rushbrook Williams, who wrote the majority of the leaders in *The Times*. Williams had been successively Professor of History at Allahabad University, chief propaganda officer to the Government of India during the Great War, and adviser at the Ministry of Information during the Second World War. Colin Reid, the *Telegraph*'s special correspondent, was a considerable expert on Middle Eastern affairs and on the Muslim culture of Egypt and the Levant.[76]

Although the majority of the national press broadly supported the imperial project, they appeared to reach, with only a few murmurings of regret, a remarkably consensual verdict on the loss of the proverbial jewel in the Imperial Crown. As the *Herald*'s special correspondent concluded, India was "willingly relinquished" by the imperial nation as "a shining act of faith and justice".[77] Distinctions between papers of different political persuasions, so marked in domestic politics and indeed in the lead up to independence, appeared to dissolve in the moment of its realization. The extent to which this reflected a pragmatic response to what was perceived as an inevitable change given the general political consensus at Westminster or was influenced by new international pressures operating in a post-war world and specifically from the self-proclaimed leader of the free world, the USA, needs further investigation. There is less doubt, however, that sophisticated systems of information management and political propaganda were deployed by a government anxiously looking towards the world's stage for approval and keen to maintain productive ties with the new nations of the East. British enterprise and capital investment "dominated India's private foreign sector in 1947". Britain still had a powerful stake in India economically and strategically, and official priority was to protect this scenario. By the end of the 1950s British private capital in India "was well above the 1948 level".[78]

To deny that official media management and what *The Times* referred to as Mountbatten's "high powered diplomacy of discussion", and, Pamela Mountbatten as her father's "Operation seduction",[79] had an impact in fashioning the story conveyed to the British reading public would be absurd, though it is problematic to gauge the extent and nature of this influence across the press. What is also of import is the impact of Fleet Street coverage within the sub-continent, where it was taken to reflect a wider British popular opinion. What is open to much less debate, however, is that this honeymoon period in press reportage of the sub-continent was over almost as soon as it began. And herein lies the seminal paradox. The narrative as structured on Independence Day was one of the fulfilment of Britain's imperial destiny in India: Macaulay's dream in the 1830s. The press were able to portray Independence as a British achievement—as something arising almost organically out of her long-term policy and vindicating British rule. However, within a few days, sections of the British, particularly conservative press (as well as some US newspapers) began to reassess and question the capacity for self governance of the Indians. The consequences of Independence were increasingly seen as bearing out the warnings of those like Churchill, who had seen the empire as necessary for good governance and stability within India—the so-called *Pax Britannica*. Therefore, both the act of Independence and its aftermath—though for very different reasons—were seen as justifying imperial rule. Thus the *Observer*'s editorial argued on 31 August that "the Punjab massacres are a sad commentary on India's attainment of independence, barely a fortnight old".[80] The fact that the mass of the foreign correspondents were based in Delhi, and the few that tried to report from West Pakistan experienced severe logistical difficulties, further directed the critical spotlight on the Indian government and imposed in effect a news blackout from Pakistan. The attribution of blame for the communal troubles was laid almost unequivocally at India's door, a sentiment apparently reinforced when Delhi was engulfed in the crisis during September.

For the *New Statesman* this "deliberate press campaign designed to convince the British public that the end of British rule in India has thrown the entire country into a state of anarchy is as wicked as it is misleading. Every incident in the Punjab tragedy indicative of local breakdown in administration is exaggerated and distorted to give the impression of nation-wide collapse". In the *Express*, it contended, "No effort is spared to hold up the Governments of two Member states of the British Commonwealth to contempt and ridicule and to label them after three weeks as unfit to rule". While acknowledging that the suffering and killings were immense, the *New Statesman* maintained that even this provided "no justification for the silly suggestion in some newspapers that the Indian settlement was a mistake". And while these massacres were "a ghastly by-product of painful re-birth" in India, they were "much less serious" than for example the 1943 famine which was "barely reported in England when one and a half million died".[81]

Thus, there emerged two main accounts of Indian independence: a pro-empire version apparently co-existing with a celebration of decolonization. In other words, press comment vindicated British rule for achieving a peaceful transfer of power and at the same time British rule was also vindicated by the subsequent violence that engulfed the new nation states. How do we explain this apparent dichotomy? Perhaps one could suggest that both approaches contained essential truths about the British imperial experience. The British had always been divided as to the meaning of its Indian Raj—a paternalist despotism in the name of superior Christian civilization or a progressive programme of improvements leading to eventual self-rule? Of the two, the former had deeper roots in the mainstream British press and helps to explain the reversion to this kind of coverage in the post-independence period. What requires explanation, therefore, is why the more optimistic view prevailed in the lead up to and during August. To some extent this can be attributed to the Mountbatten-India Office media operation. Both Mountbatten and the decisive plan he enunciated inspired confidence. He provided a narrative for Independence that seemed to render it a progressive British achievement. The positive newspaper reportage was not entirely unexpected, and, in following the official position on empire in 1947, it was consistent with its coverage of the 1930s when the bulk of the press backed a policy of appeasing Indian nationalists through the devolution of self-government. In a sense, therefore, Mountbatten reaffirmed this position with his skill in imperial choreography, his role being to dramatize a script that was already largely written and in so doing to provide the imagery that would fix how the world saw 15 August then and how we see it now.

Yet, while this was true for the lead up to and Independence day itself, it could hardly be sustained against the facts of the communal bloodbaths and civil war that accompanied Partition and the mass migration in its aftermath during the autumn of 1947. This helped to create deep fault-lines both within Fleet Street as well as between the foreign and the Indian press and political opinion, fracturing trust in western perceptions of the new post-colonial realities and feeding into demands for the setting up of a Third World Information Order.

Notes

1. **Dailies:** *Daily Telegraph, The Times, Manchester Guardian, News Chronicle, Daily Mail, Daily Express, Daily Herald, Daily Mirror, Daily Worker, Star*; **Weeklies & Periodicals:** *Spectator, Observer, New Statesman and Nation (NS&N), News of the World, Illustrated London News, Radio Times, Reynolds Newspaper, Contemporary Review, Quarterly Review, Nineteenth Century and After, Punch.*
2. Epstein, J. (2006) Taking class notes on empire, in: C. Hall and S. Rose (Eds) *At Home with the Empire* (Cambridge: Cambridge University Press), p. 274.
3. For development of Fleet Street links with the Indian press, see Kaul, C. (2003) *Reporting the Raj, the British Press and India* (Manchester: Manchester University Press).
4. Eric Britter to Ralph Deakin, 31 Dec 1946, Foreign Editors file, TNL archives, London.
5. *Cont. Review*, Jan. 1948, Vol CLXXIII, pp. 14–15.
6. *NS&N*, 23 Aug, *Star*, 15 Aug.
7. *Guardian*, 11 July.
8. *Herald*, 15 Aug.
9. See *Times, Guardian, Chronicle, Herald,* and *Mail*, 15 Aug.

10. *Guardian*, 11 July.
11. *Guardian*, 15 Aug.
12. *Herald,* Freedom day, 15 Aug.
13. *Guardian*, 15 Aug.
14. *Observer*, 10 Aug, *Guardian* 15 Aug.
15. Cited in *Guardian*, 15 Aug.
16. *Guardian,* 16 Aug.
17. Comment, *NS&N*, 16 Aug.
18. *Guardian*, 16 Aug.
19. *Ibid.*
20. *Spectator*, 18 July; Comments, *NS&N*, 14 June.
21. *Mail, Express, Telegraph*, 15 Aug.
22. Quoted in *Herald*, 16 Aug.
23. *NS&N*, 23 Aug.
24. *Herald*, 15 Aug.
25. *Ibid.*
26. *Herald*, 15 Aug.
27. *Chronicle,* 15 Aug.
28. *Spectator*, 15 Aug.
29. *Times,* 15 Aug.
30. *Spectator*, 22 Aug.
31. *Cont. Review*, June, vol. CLXXI, p. 21.
32. *Observer*, 17 Aug.
33. *Guardian*, 15 Aug.
34. *Herald, Star*, 14 Aug.
35. *Ibid*, p. 5.
36. *Spectator*, 18 July.
37. *Cont. Review*, Aug., pp. 82–87.
38. *NS&N*, Comments, 23 Aug.
39. *Guardian*, 9 Aug.
40. *News of the World*, 24 Aug.
41. *Spectator*, 15 Aug.
42. *Mail*, 15 Aug; also *Guardian*, 15 Aug.
43. *Times*, 15 Aug.
44. Stephens, I. M. (1964) *Pakistan* (London: Penguin), p. 148.
45. Lord Wavell to Leo Amery, 20 Dec 1944, L/I/1/267, IOLR, London.
46. Deakin to Holburn, 11 Jan. 1945, Foreign Editors file, TNL.
47. Stephens, *Pakistan*, p. 148.
48. Cited in Hoey, B. (1994) *Mountbatten: The Private Story* (London: Sidgwick and Jackson), p. 4.
49. Terraine, J. (1980) *The Life and Times of Lord Mountbatten* (London: Arrow Books), p. 179.
50. Lord Ismay cited in Campbell-Johnson, A. (1951) *Mission with Mountbatten* (London: Robert Hale), p. 221.
51. Campbell-Johnson, A. (1997) *Mountbatten in Retrospect* (South Godstone: Spantech & Lancer), pp. 49–50.
52. Campbell-Johnson to Mountbatten, 14 Mar. 1947, Mss Eur F 200/114, IOLR.
53. L/I/1/1467, fol 162.
54. Campbell-Johnson, *Mission*, p. 42.
55. *Hindustan Times*, 23 Mar., *Pioneer*, 24 Mar, *Statesman*, 23 Mar.
56. *Sind Observer*, 21 Mar., *Dawn*, 23 Mar.
57. Johnson to Joyce 5 June 1947, F 200/114.
58. Stephens, *Pakistan*, p. 148.
59. Cited in Campbell-Johnson, *Mission*, p. 110.
60. Memo by Johnson, 27 May 1947, F 200/114.
61. Johnson to Joyce, 1 June 1947, F 200/163.
62. Johnson to Joyce, 3 June 1947, F 200/163.
63. Johnson to Joyce, 25 June 1947, L/I/1/1456.

64. *Ibid.*
65. Joyce to Johnson, 31 Mar 1947, L/I/1/1467.
66. Haley to Mountbatten, 14 June 1947, F200/114.
67. Listowel to Viceroy, 13 July 1947, F 200/114.
68. Viceroy to Listowel, 15 July 1947, F 200/114.
69. Viceroy to Listowel, 1 Aug 1947, F200/163.
70. Viceroy to Listowel, 14 July 1947, F 200/114.
71. Turner, J. (2001) *Filming History* (London: BUFVC), p. 114.
72. Viceroy to Listowel, 16 July 1947, F200/114.
73. Johnson to Joyce, 24 Sept 1947, L/I/1/515, IOLR.
74. *Ibid.*
75. Wood, P., in: C. Kaul (Ed.) (2006) *Media and the British Empire* (Basingstoke and New York: Palgrave Macmillan), pp. 145–159.
76. Campbell-Johnson, *Mission*, p. 68.
77. *Herald*, 15 Aug.
78. Lipton, M. and Firn, J. (1975) *The Erosion of a Relationship* (London: OUP), p. 86.
79. Mountbatten, P. and Hicks, I. (2007) *India Remembered* (London: Anova Books), p. 66.
80. *Observer*, 31 Aug.
81. *NS&N,* The Punjab's price for freedom, 6 Sept.

Reference

N.B. Unless stated otherwise, all press references are to the year 1947. The author would like to thank the Punch Library and its archivist for permission to reproduce the two cartoons.

The Ending of an Empire: From Imagined Communities to Nation States in India and Pakistan

YASMIN KHAN
Department of Politics, Royal Holloway College, University of London, UK

The story of Independence Day in South Asia is a schizoid one; on the one hand there are the familiar tropes and clichés of well-orchestrated rituals and speeches in New Delhi and Karachi on 14 and 15 August 1947; the Mountbattens in full courtly regalia, the packed streets and All India Radio commentaries. This is a story of jubilation, of the passing of sovereignty and the celebration of a long-fought for independence as the British Union Flag was replaced by the Indian and Pakistani colours. This is the moment still heralded each year by the Indian prime minister's speech from the ramparts of the Red Fort in Delhi and marked by sweets, songs and national holidays. On the other hand there stand the accompanying stories of devastation, ruination and misery caused by the catastrophic upheaval of an unforeseen partition and mass migration which uprooted more than 12 million people from their homes in Punjab, Bengal and North India and led to the violent deaths of perhaps a million men, women and children. At times these two stories coincided, at other times they diverged widely: how are they to be reconciled?

The high moments of state ritual and the passing of official sovereignty were celebrated in Pakistan and India on 14 and 15 August respectively. In many ways the very orderliness and elaborate design, planning and execution of these rituals was a self-conscious manifestation of state sovereignty intended to inscribe state power at a time of acute crisis in the legal, policing and governmental strategies of the state. "At the stroke of the midnight hour, when the world sleeps, India will awake to life and freedom." Jawarhalal Nehru's haunting words filled the night air of the midnight assembly session of the Constituent Assembly in New Delhi's Council House. The remarkable speech was broadcast throughout the country and reproduced in special newspaper editions. Huge jostling crowds thronged Lutyens' commanding sandstone buildings in New Delhi to take part in the tryst with destiny. Many carried small flags and distributed sweets. Impromptu firework displays occurred all over the country.

In Karachi just 24 hours previously, in parallel, Jinnah had inaugurated the Pakistani Constituent Assembly meeting and spoken to the people over the airwaves of a "supreme moment" and of "the fulfilment of the destiny of the Muslim nation". The celebrations were "carried off with very scanty means and not in as perfect a manner as at Delhi" recalled one member of the audience, "but that never struck one as incongruous ... it was improvised, Pakistan itself was being improvised".[1] Euphoria, an unprecedented collective feeling, marks many of the recollections of those who stood in the vast crowds, dazzled by the fireworks and illuminated buildings, not only in Delhi, but in the major cities throughout South Asia. "We have to celebrate 15 August in such a way that people's psychology is metamorphosed into that befitting the citizens of an independent nation,"[2] instructed a Congress secretary, and every effort was made to make it a memorable occasion. There was a profound sense of catharsis; a feeling of order upended and old constraints removed.

However, despite a coherent, strongly unified 'language of legitimacy' spoken by the Congress leadership, especially by Nehru, which drew on liberal, democratic nationalist principles (and was later reflected in the constitution of 1950) millions of Indian Congress supporters had quite different and heightened expectations of Independence.[3] In places these expectations overlapped with the official party-line but in other places were completely at variance with the national leadership. Notions such as *swaraj* (literally meaning 'self-rule' and invoked by Gandhi to convey freedom from imperialism) and 'Pakistan' were understood by people in 1947 in a varied and diverse set of ways which may seem obtuse or puzzling to us now; among the Leaguers some associated Pakistan with utopia, complete freedom or a radical new form of social justice. The League's membership reached one million, and millenarian expectations of a coming Islamic kingdom had been nurtured alongside utopian ideals of radical social justice in a fictive Pakistan. Among Congress followers, similarly, the conditions were ripe for raised expectations of freedom, localized and community interpretations of its meaning and even wildly improbable millenarian dreams. Many of these visions and expectations had very little overlap with the legalistic exchange of sovereignty being engineered between the British and their nationalist heirs in the imperial capitals.

The meanings of *swaraj* among Indian Congress supporters had particular manifestations and localized interpretations which looked forward to moral renewal, spiritual leadership, the promotion of community or linguistic rights or a reordering of social hierarchies. This will to power often took priority over policy designed and promulgated from Delhi. All these deeply complex movements were subsumed within Congress nationalism and, as Independence Day dawned, the Congress leadership was faced with the complicated task of meeting these expectations, sitting astride a social powder-keg of social unrest, strikes and violence, while at the same time pushing forward its own social democratic agenda. These popular, euphoric expressions of independence have been missing from traditional histories of independence, which have tended to be overshadowed by partition and the hiving-off of a South Asian Muslim state. One example of the ways in which popular expectations outstripped political policy is the opening up of jails and the widespread early release of prisoners at the moment of independence: releasing prisoners was a popular act—it was cheap and easy to implement at the stroke of a pen. Jail populations had increased significantly during the Second World War, especially during the backlash against Gandhi's Quit India movement of 1942. By the end of 1942, 18 000 people had been detained by the British for political activities under the Defence of India rules. British arrests on political charges had been widespread and unforgiving during the war, and although political prisoners punitively locked up by the imperial state had been freed in a series of releases during 1945 and 1946, prison populations were still swollen at the date of independence. Blurred terminology and lack of clarity about the nature of the crimes of prisoners meant that it was not always easy to comb out specifically political detainees from the others in jail. For this reason popular amnesties were proclaimed at the moment of independence. Some states went even further though: in Bombay the provincial government decided to fling open the prison doors. On Independence Day all prisoners who had been behind bars for ten years or more were allowed to walk free, alongside those who had served two-thirds of their sentences. Death sentences were commuted to prison terms. Some of the recently arrested prisoners charged with communal violence in the riots of the preceding months were also promised early release. "In all, more than 3,000 prisoners, which is roughly 40 per cent of the jail population [of Bombay city], will be released on the evening of August 14", reported *The Times of India*. This practice was mimicked all over the subcontinent. Remarkably, some 13 000 prisoners were released on 15 August in the Central Provinces.[4]

There was a darker side to freedom, though. The particular irony of independence, and its interlocking with partition, was the way in which it forced a new moment of national identification. From myriad, localized groups, patriotic allegiance to either India or Pakistan was now mandatory. No Muslim was immune now from the charge of disloyalty and many had to bend over backwards to try and prove themselves. "Half of my life I had to suffer such humiliation as a Congressman at the hands of the British Government in India", protested the Muslim Congressman from Bihar, Syed Mahmud. "Now it seems for the remaining period of my life I have to suffer all these indignities and insults at the hand of the Congress Government. Am I wrong in this conclusion?"[5] Questions of national identity even several years after partition were problematic. The 'gravitational pull' of Pakistan was strong for some Muslims, who weighed up the decision to migrate to Pakistan, whether for economic, familial or security reasons. The only definition that the state allowed, though, was the sharp distinction between national loyalty to India and national loyalty to Pakistan. This was difficult to prove, as most people were not motivated by these ideologies: had those Muslims who had gone to Pakistan and then returned to India really displayed their loyalty to the state? In addition, the minorities of both states were now involved in strategic calculations.

Employees in intelligence branches intercepted letters to Pakistan and prosecuted anti-national behaviour—the familiar actions of governments which start to suspect the fidelity of their own citizens during a time of terror. Some Muslims, especially those with families living across the border in Pakistan, wavered and did not express their allegiance to either India or Pakistan, as they continued to reside in a grey netherworld in which these new borders remained porous. Others used subterfuge in order to explore the possibilities of making a new life elsewhere. One police sub-inspector in the northern industrial city of Kanpur, Mohammad Rizvi, caught corresponding with relations in Pakistan under a fictitious name while attempting to secure a permanent settlement permit in Pakistan, was arrested on discovery of the correspondence and dismissed. Considerations about whether to depart for Pakistan, often driven by more mundane economic motives, were always interpreted by the government in the paradigm of loyalty or disloyalty to the nation state.[6] This was a complex emotional and political process for all those people living in the former Raj, but particularly difficult for millions of people who felt themselves to be in the 'wrong' country, were financially or physically ruined by partition or had other, deeply felt, sub-nationalist identities. Was it right to celebrate in the middle of violence? Who was an Indian or Pakistani citizen now? Should you celebrate the creation of one state, both states or none? How could people's 'psychology' be 'metamorphosed' so that they became loyal citizens? Furthermore, as the first states to gain independence from British colonial rule, these meanings of statehood and independence were being thrashed out for the first time—there were no precedents and no other Asian or African postcolonial states to look to as a point of comparison.

Celebrating Independence Day became an important signifier of national loyalty and, conversely, in the future, neglecting Independence Day could be used to unearth 'disloyalty' to the state. Dismissals and suspensions for suspected disloyalty became common in the police force during the first three years of independence. Government returns highlight the tenuous reasons given for these dismissals and the importance of proving loyalty to the new regime. One sub-inspector was suspended for nearly a year for arriving late at the local Independence Day celebrations in August 1948. Another, Abdul Majid Khan, a sub inspector in Deoria, was overheard discussing the case of Muslims in Hyderabad in the Urdu library and was suspended. Although he was ultimately acquitted, he avoided returning to work on medical grounds.[7]

Given the contingencies and trauma of the ongoing violence, there was also ambivalence about whether independence should be a day of jubilation at all. Veer Sarvarkar, the Hindu nationalist supreme, and others in the Hindu Mahasabha and Rashtriya Swayam Sevak Sangh (RSS) who staunchly opposed Partition, completely boycotted the celebrations. Gandhi was also conspicuously absent, praying and fasting in Calcutta and promoting peace. "This much I certainly believe that coming August 15 should be no day for rejoicing whilst the minorities contemplate the day with a heavy heart". He urged a day of fasting, praying and spinning instead: "It must be a day for prayer and deep heart-searching."[8] Gandhi's refusal to endorse the festivities was sensitive to the perversity of holding firework displays, dances and feasting as massacres continued elsewhere, but also placed another question mark over the legitimacy of Pakistan and the new Partition settlement.

In public places, the line between religious rituals, holy institutions and the national cause was blurred. Both India and Pakistan included a significant, religious component in their official state rituals of celebration. Listeners to Pakistan Radio at one minute past midnight on 14 August heard the announcement of Pakistan's birth followed by readings from the Quran. In New Delhi, at a private residence, Nehru

From Imagined Communities to Nation States in India and Pakistan 51

and his ministerial colleagues sat cross-legged around a holy fire as Hindu priests from Tanjore chanted hymns and sprinkled holy water on them. N. A. Sherwani, a Congress minister and a Muslim, unfurled the striped gold, green and white national flag over the Bharat Mata, or Mother India temple in the sacred city of Varanasi.[9] Elsewhere, diverse and impulsive ceremonies centred on historic sites associated with the heroes who had fought the British in the uprising of 1857, or the Quit India movement of 1942. Others organised ecumenical, multi-faith ceremonies with readings and prayers from all religions. In the Punjabi cities where massacres were still taking place, there were far fewer signs of celebration. When Penderel Moon arrived in the imperial centre of Lahore on 15 August he recalled a deathly stillness:

> The Lawrence Gardens were full of troops; the Mall empty, every shop shut and as silent as the grave. I made for the railway station to find out about trains to Simla. As I passed down Empress Road a fire station was coping with a burning house, and to the left, from the city proper, numerous dense columns of smoke were rising from the air.[10]

At the 'festivities', later that day, only one Hindu and no Sikhs attended the Governor's inauguration for which only one-fifth of invitations could be delivered. For many who had not yet escaped the risk of violence, the memories of Independence Day were overshadowed by fear and this fuelled the resentment of refugees who felt abandoned by their compatriots. A refugee from Lahore recalled:

> The evening was drawing to a close. I turned the radio to Delhi. The babble of tongues, the excitement of the vast assembled crowd near the Red Fort could be clearly heard. The announcer was giving a running commentary on the whole show; the Independence of India was being inaugurated ... Just then a bullet was fired in the Sanda Road Chowk, hardly fifty yards from my kothi .... Of course the Delhiwalas must have had a gala night, stuffing themselves with fruit, sweets and drinks, soft or strong, they must have gone to sleep dreaming of pleasant dreams .... Of course, a few of them had seen but many of them had only heard that there was 'some trouble' in the Punjab. But what was Punjab's trouble as compared to the Azadi [freedom] of the other parts of the country? A.N. Bali, *Now it can be told* (Jullundur: Akash Vani Prakashan, 1949), p. 39.

Meanwhile, in private homes some people fused the secular and the profane, improvising their own ceremonies, distributing coloured sweets or hoisting flags. Families and individuals found their own way to negotiate rocky questions about national loyalty and allegiance to one state or the other. "On Independence day, when the announcement came on the radio," remembered the Punjabi journalist Amjad Husain, who was in Lahore in 1947, "father took the Holy Quran in hand and made all family members take an oath of loyalty to Pakistan. I still remember that every family member took an oath."[11] In much the same way, in Bombay, people were busy designing and improvising their own ceremonies to mark the occasion of Independence. A Sikh, Saroj Pachauri, a child at the time, remembered painting Pakistani flags and watching her father participate on the dais in the

Punjabi town of Rawalpindi during the Independence Day celebrations, only weeks before the whole family fled to safety in India.[12] Many people celebrated Independence Day in the 'wrong' country, as they later moved as refugees from India to Pakistan or vice versa. Some even celebrated it twice, once in each state. For some, participating itself was a kind of insurance against violence and 'proof' of loyalty to the new nation, and for the terrified, newly converted Muslims, seen along the roadside near a hamlet in Bahawalpur, it must have been a strange kind of 'freedom'. They were jigging desperately around "a miserable bit of green cloth" which was "a stick with a little green flag tied to the end" and protesting "this is our flag. We now have Pakistan and Muslim Raj."[13] In fact, the group had been forcibly made to convert to Islam and had gathered under the flag for safety, to try and prove their 'Pakistani-ness'.

As the 3 June plan, which decreed the Partition, had been so rushed and inadequately thought out, there had been little meditation on who was a rightful Indian and who was a rightful Pakistani. At the heart of these uncertainties and dilemmas was the undefined question of citizenship. Did this just depend on religious identity? As each new government tried to earmark its own citizens, a diplomatic quarrel erupted about *who* should be celebrating independence, and which country they should be endorsing. The Congressman, Acharya Kripalani, suffered his own family's displacement from Sindh. He was personally badly shaken by Partition's events. Now he issued a directive to provincial Congressmen living in areas that were soon to become Pakistan, "The hearts of all Congressmen and Congress sympathisers in Sind, East Bengal, West Punjab and the North-West Frontier Province are lacerated at the division of the country," he wrote; "they are, therefore, in no mood to rejoice with the rest of India. Under these circumstances there is no need of celebrating August 15, in these areas which have been separated from India."[14] A bad-tempered row broke out immediately with Pakistani politicians who saw things in a different light; weren't these Hindu and Sikhs now Pakistani citizens and, if so, why should they not take pride in Pakistan's green and white crescent moon flag?

Flags had become powerful, sometimes lethal symbols. The Pakistani flag had unmissable Islamic connotations. This provoked anger and confusion among Hindus and Sikhs in Pakistan, as they contemplated staying in the country. The Pakistani prime minister tried to fudge this issue, rebuffing a complainant with the claim that it is "not a religious flag" and arguing that the "Moon and stars are as common to my Honourable friend and they are as much his property as mine." Such disingenuous claims hardly washed with a community already shattered by violence and frightened about the protection of its religious freedoms.[15] Similarly in India, Krishna Sobti recollected the fuzzy sense of belonging among different people, depending on their status, religion and outlook:

> Our entire family was gathered around the radio. Our servants, many of whom were Muslims, were also present. When Nehru spoke our reaction was very different from theirs. After tea, sweets were passed round (green and orange ones known as ashrafian). None of the Muslim servants touched them. But when the national anthem was sung and we stood up, they did too. They realized that they too, had paid a price for freedom.[16]

We do not know what was going through the minds of these particular servants. But as loyalty to the Congress *party* and allegiance to an Indian *state* got rolled up together, this could cause confusion and panic.

Emphasis on loyalty to Congress symbols, such as *khadi*, the Gandhi cap, and the spinning wheel, alienated many people who had been political opponents of the Congress but now felt pressure to submit to the emblems of the *party* as well as to those of the *nation state* in order to gain acceptance as loyal and law-abiding citizens. The Congress Chief Minister of Uttar Pradesh made all the police in his province wear a Congress armband on Independence Day in August 1947. As the departing British governor noted, "Pant would have his pound of flesh out of the police in the UP."[17] The Congress flag and the national flag—which were very similar in any case—were used interchangeably on Independence Day. People who had been involved in the intense electoral campaign in 1946 in opposition to the Congress or policemen and officials who had worked in the service of the colonial state strongly associated these symbols with an old adversary. In the past, they had rallied against this flags and ripped them down. This sea-change could be hard to swallow, and the insistence upon these old symbols could be regarded as a show of Congress triumphalism.[18]

Now formally labelled as 'minorities' in the official mindset, groups of Hindus and Sikhs in Pakistan and Muslims in India, felt thoroughly compromised. "You are free; you are free to go to your temples, you are free to go to your mosques or to any other place of worship in this state of Pakistan", Jinnah told Hindus and Sikhs in Pakistan in an acclaimed speech at the time of independence, even as arson attacks on these religious buildings and the murder of their worshippers continued unabated.[19] Jinnah's commitment to a plural state was both a principled and economically pragmatic, given Pakistan's position on an economic precipice. As the chief minister of the North West Frontier Province put it bluntly six months later: "We had more than one reason for wishing the Hindus and Sikhs to stay on. They controlled all the banking, trade and industry in this Province and their sudden departure has hit us very hard."[20] Some Pakistani leaders realized that the state had much to gain from stemming the flow of migration.

It was also possible for non Muslims to be, at least in the early days of the state, enthusiastic Pakistanis. J. N. Mandal, an untouchable from Bengal, was elected chairman of the Pakistani constituent assembly. The other members cheered as he signed the roll book in Karachi on Independence Day and he called on other Pakistani 'minorities' to be "responsible, loyal and faithful to the state". Soon afterwards he was promoted to a coveted ministerial position. Mandal's experience was hardly typical, though. Everywhere minorities were feeling deeply insecure about their own physical safety and their own citizenship rights. It was these fears which drove people from their homes and started one of the greatest mass migrations in history.

As well as marking the end of a nationalist struggle against colonialism, 15 August also underscored a moment at which a new project began. People felt compelled to decide upon unalloyed national attachments, clearly demarcate their patriotism and express unwavering belief in the power of one nation state or another. This was all vastly different from the melange of communities and national beliefs which had been in co-existence at the end of the Second World War in India.

'Independence Day' was, then, in South Asia a loaded term which, after 1947, continued to have complex and difficult meanings for those who had lived through it. Independence Day was used by political groups to heighten attention to their cause; the Hindu Mahasabha became interested in several disputed sites of worship simultaneously in late 1949 and passed a resolution for the restoration of the Ayodhya temple on the day before Independence Day. It was also a time of increased anxiety around security and a moment during which violence broke out in the stormy years following Independence as sporadic Hindu–Muslim rioting continued to occur; in Agra, in 1948, there was a conflict between refugees and Muslims on Independence Day, which led to an exchange of fire between the refugees and the police. For Bangladeshis, of course, there were other layers of complexity: the original August 1947 dates later being replaced by the anniversary of liberation during the civil war of 1970–71. Right up until the present day, Independence Day celebrations in India are sometimes a state-sponsored initiative designed to test and promote uncertain loyalties to the state; the empty streets and squares of Kashmir's chief city, Srinigar, on annual Independence Days are a recurrent reminder of the state's efforts to establish its sovereignty and the symbolic use of boycott and *hartal*, or public strike, by those who want to protest this claim made by the Indian state.

Above all, the moment of independence in South Asia came at a catastrophic price. One of the most critical but least understood aspects of the moment of Independence, on 14 and 15 August—for India and Pakistan respectively—was the lack of awareness—in fact, complete ignorance—about what was being delivered, what kind of states were coming into existence and what their ideological orientation would mean for the inhabitants of those states. The reasons for the confusion were complex and multiple; some historians have argued, in particular, Ayesha Jalal, that the lack of conceptual clarity and high-stakes game-playing by Jinnah meant that there were multiple versions of what Pakistan might constitute on the table well into the early months of 1947. This highly plausible and convincing theory means that, in essence, many of those who had supported the Muslim League for their own localized reasons had very little sense of how India and Pakistan were actually going to take shape on a map; in real terms the comprehension of nation-statehood was limited and unexplored and nations, in the compulsions of nationalist discourse, had become far more about *nationalism* than *nation state-hood*; the fabric of state construction had been reduced down to something simplistic and one-dimensional: flags, maps, anthems; the actual reality of communities and peoples permanently separated had barely been contemplated. As Vazira Zamindar has carefully and persuasively traced, this meant a complicated disentanglement of nationality, citizenship and the meanings of community belonging over many years as the state tried to sever communities which transcended these neat imagined lines of citizenship.[21]

Independence Day was not without real legal meaning in South Asia. Sovereign power was transferred to the hands of Indian and Pakistani politicians. Nevertheless, this transition must be viewed with some scepticism and with an eye upon the multiple complications of establishing new forms of sovereignty in the wake of empire. There is a general consensus that colonial India's law and order apparatus was not simply dismantled at independence. Continuities in the civil service, army and police force outweighed discontinuities, at least during the years of Nehru's premiership. Histories of the transition to independence in South Asia tend to vacillate on the question of colonial continuities in the everyday operation of the state.[22] How far was independence explicitly relevant and meaningful for ordinary Indians? Or was it, instead, a legalistic, symbolic exchange of power with great import for political players at the apex of the historical pyramid but with little real significance to the actual lives of Indians, beyond its figurative manifestations? The suggestion made here is that 14–15 August 1947 marked an important ritualistic moment but that, simultaneously, it posited complex new questions of nationality and citizenship that have taken much longer to settle. This is not intended to belittle the meanings of a longed-for independence but to suggest the need for complicating moments of 'independence' from colonial empire as times of painful transition during which new nationalisms and sovereign forms emerge, unfortunately, often with bloody and desperate consequences.

Notes

1. Whitehead, A. (1997, 2000) *Oral Archive: India: a People Partitioned* (London: School of Oriental and African Studies); Sahabzada Yaqub Khan, interviewed in Delhi, 15 March 1997.
2. Mangla Prasad, United Provinces Provincial Congress Secretary, Lucknow, to all district and town Congress committees, 30 July 1947. Quoted in T. Y. Tan and G. Kudaisya (2000) *The Aftermath of Partition in South Asia* (London: Routledge), p. 37.
3. The phrase language of legitimacy is drawn from the work of Zachariah, B. (2005) *Developing India: An Intellectual and Social History* (New Delhi: Oxford University Press).
4. *Times of India*, 13 August 1947 and 18 August 1947.
5. Datta, V. N., and Cleghorn, B. E. (Eds) (1974) *A Nationalist Muslim and Indian Politics: Selected Letters of Syed Mahmud* (Delhi: Macmillan).
6. UPSA (United Provinces State Archives, India), Home Department Police (A), Box 22, 63/1948.
7. UPSA, Home Department Police (A), Box 22, 63/1948.
8. *Hindustan Times*, 22 July 1947. Cited in Tan and Kudaisya, *The Aftermath of Partition in South Asia*, p. 42. For a very detailed account of Independence Day ceremonies and celebrations, from which my account draws, see Tan and Kudaisya, idem, pp. 29–77.
9. Tan and Kudaisya, *The Aftermath of Partition*, pp. 29–7.
10. Moon, P. (1998) *Divide and Quit: An Eyewitness Account of the Partition of India* (Delhi: Oxford University Press), p. 115.
11. Whitehead, *India: A People Partitioned*: Amjad Husain, interviewed in Lahore, 11 October 1995.
12. Whitehead, *India: A People Partitioned*: Saroj Pachauri interviewed Delhi, 28 January 1997.
13. Moon, *Divide and Quit*, p. 125.
14. *Times of India*, 12 August 1947.
15. Constituent Assembly of Pakistan debates, 11 August 1947, in: M. Rafique Afzal (1967) (Ed.) *Speeches and Statements of Quaid-i-Millat Liaquat Ali Khan (1941–1951)* (Lahore: University of Punjab), p. 117.
16. Bhalla, A. (2006) *Partition Dialogues: Memories of a Lost Home* (New Delhi: Oxford University Press), p. 162.
17. India Office Records, Fortnightly Reports, L/PJ/5/276, Wylie to Mountbatten, 10 August 1947.
18. Ayesha Jalal, Gyanendra Pandey and Mushiral Hasan have analysed these conflations and confusions which were worsened by setting up 'nationalism' as a binary to 'communalism.' See for instance, Jalal, A. 'Exploding Communalism: The Politics of Muslim Identity in South Asia', in: S. Bose and A. Jalal (Eds) (1997) *Nationalism, Democracy and Development: State and Politics in India* (Delhi: Oxford University Press); Pandey, G. (1999) Can a Muslim be an Indian?, *Comparative Studies in Society and History*, 41(4); and Hasan, M. (1997) *Legacy of a Divided Nation: India's Muslims Since Independence* (London: Oxford University Press).

19. Burke, S. M. (Ed.) (2000) *Jinnah: Speeches and Statements, 1947–8* (Karachi: Oxford University Press), p. 28. Speech to Constituent Assembly, 11 August 1947.
20. Abdul Quaiyum Khan to Syed Mahmud, 8/10 February 1948, in: V. N. Datta and B. E. Cleghorn (Eds) (1974) *A Nationalist Muslim and Indian Politics: Selected Letters of Syed Mahmud* (Delhi: Macmillan), p. 267.
21. Fazila-Yacoobali Zamindar, V. (2007) *The Long Partition and the Making of Modern South Asia: Refugees, Boundaries, Histories* (New York: Columbia University Press). See also Khan, Y. (2007) *The Great Partition: The Making of India and Pakistan* (London: Yale University Press).
22. For a discussion of this question see C. Fuller and Harriss, J. (2001) For an anthropology of the modern Indian state, in: C. Fuller and V. Beneii (Eds) (2001) *The Everyday State and Society in Modern India* (London: Hurst) and Chakrabarty, D., Majumdar, R. and Sartori, A. (2007) (Eds) *From the Colonial to the Postcolonial : India and Pakistan in Transition* (Delhi: Oxford University Press).

Casting "the Kingdome into another mold":[1] Ghana's Troubled Transition to Independence

RICHARD RATHBONE
Aberystwyth University, Wales

Independence days are intended to be joyful occasions and, like Tolstoy's happy families, they resemble one another; all of them appear to share similar quotients of military display, fireworks, pious sentimentality at midnight and the profoundly implausible pledges of eternal friendship between long-term antagonists. There can, however, be an inherently unhappy side to such celebrations which was tactfully if temporarily silenced by cheers, tears, military bands and newly—and mostly badly—composed national anthems. To return to Tolstoy, it is in this respect that independence days can all be unhappy in quite distinctive ways.

In some details the events of Ghana's Independence Day had been rehearsed elsewhere; the extent to which the events of March 1957 were actually conscious echoes of the much grander affair in Delhi ten years before is an interesting question which sadly remains unanswered in what follows. But it is clear that some elements of the Accra celebrations were to be copied throughout Africa and elsewhere again and again—and again—in the course of the relatively short period of imperial closure which followed. This paper has little to say about the fun, being much more concerned with the distinctive unhappiness which swirled around Ghana's last days as the British colonial territory of the Gold Coast; it is mainly about the mess which was for a short period outwardly forgotten because of the public concentration upon the more demanding business—the pomp and the partying—which ushered in the birth of a nation.

That forgetting, however, was a temporary forgetting, a momentary, tactful amnesia. The bitterness which accompanied the end of colonial rule has been largely ignored outside Ghana because international interest focused, and still focuses upon, the political struggle for independence from British rule rather than upon the internal struggles for the eventual domination of the post-colonial state. By contrast, within Ghana, the painful divisions which characterized pre-independence politics have had a remarkably long life. While most people apparently relished the excuse for a terrific party, the local celebrations of Ghana's 50th anniversary of independence from British colonial rule were haunted by a particular embarrassment. The anniversary was to be known as *Ghana@50*: tacky as it might seem, that playful title caught rather nicely modern urban Ghanaians' long-term and very visible—and all too audible—love affair with both modern communications technology and snappy show-biz language. For the vast majority of Ghana's more than 20 million inhabitants, the anniversary's combination of dignified ceremonies, grave seminars and noisy fun—accompanied by serious disruptions of normal life— were caused by a celebration of the culmination of some very distant events which had taken place way back in the personal prehistory of most Ghanaians; it all happened in a distant era of black and white photography, of men in suits and ties, and streets on which motor vehicles were rare. For the predominantly young population of this relatively young state, the last day of colonial rule was the ending of something, a way of life, a distinctive kind of order, that they could only have learnt about rather than have experienced; the vast majority of Ghanaians were born after that witching hour in March 1957. What most Ghanaians know about the colonial period, the 90 or so years in which the area had been ruled by Britain, has been derived for better or worse from a combination of school text-books and, nowadays, less and less frequently from the memories of the older surviving members of their families or villages.

In many societies which have undergone periods of alien over-rule, what is relayed or remembered about such conjunctures almost inevitably depends upon contemporary expectations and conventions; in some circumstances accurate, honest recall might seem to be potentially threatening; in some circumstances factual accuracy might impede careers and even put lives in hazard. In the France of my childhood for example, everyone of a certain age claimed to have had an active, indeed courageous career in the Resistance; one never, never met an enthusiast for Vichy or German occupation, although it is abundantly clear that many people of all sorts and conditions were supporters or beneficiaries of those regimes.[2] One might expect things to have been a little like that in modern Ghana; one might expect to encounter a solid phalanx of older men and women who claim to have 'been there', to have unimpeachable nationalist credentials, to have been founder members of the anti-colonial movement and to have enjoyed intimacy with its heroes. It is, however, the case that the years which led to Ghanaian independence have always been understood within at least two utterly irreconcilable master narratives; and since the mid 1960s[3] these understandings have been reasonably comfortably expressed in public. The most obvious of these epics is the one which is best known to the outside world; it is an undeniably exciting story of the triumphant reassertion of sovereignty achieved by a courageous, radical political party led by the internationally renowned, charismatic figure of Dr Kwame Nkrumah. Much the most memorable, if clichéd, illustration of this story remains a grainy, flash-lit midnight photograph of Nkrumah and his closest political colleagues wearing northern smocks[4] and jaunty 'Prison Graduate caps'[5] happily clustered around a flagpole flying the new flag of their only just independent country. For the vast majority of outsiders, this remains the *only* narrative, repeated as it is in short pieces in innumerable encyclopaedias, world histories and on websites again and again. Very much less well-known beyond Ghana's borders is what appears to be a losers' account; this is a much grimmer, considerably less romantic story of rapidly worsening post-colonial oppression; it is also an account which lacks an eye-catching pictorial record.[6] The first, heroic story was essentially a *southern* account, a capital city account; it was after all the south of Ghana which was the heartland of the triumphant nationalist party, the Convention Peoples' Party (CPP). And a southern version was also necessarily that which was most often heard by decades of visiting journalists and scholars who have tended not to stray too far away from the country's capital and the Atlantic shore. The alternative story has always been much more audible further north and off the main roads.

This second epic might have been of much less significance, might even have slowly diminished in volume and then died away, had the losers in 1957 been permanently destined to continue to lose. But these particular losers were to be the major beneficiaries[7] of the *coup d'état* which toppled Nkrumah's regime nine years after the celebration of independence. Those politicians who were appointed to 'advise' the military regime, the National Liberation Council, in the immediate aftermath of the 1966 coup were almost without exception survivors of an opposition which had been gradually extinguished as Nkrumah sequentially abandoned the beginnings of parliamentary democracy and assembled his exclusive One Party State.[8] After the military eventually returned to barracks, a subsequent general election, in which the rump of Nkrumah's CPP was formally prevented from participating, returned a government headed by the old leader of that opposition, the National Liberation Movement, Professor Kofi Busia who had recently returned from a long period in exile after the overthrow of Nkrumah. Under the military and then under Busia, an active campaign of political vilification through the agency of Commissions of Enquiry and rather fewer trials sought, somewhat heavy-handedly, to tarnish the reputation of Nkrumah and the CPP within Ghana although some of the faithful certainly kept the flame alight.[9] Busia's ultimately authoritarian and undemocratic regime[10] was short-lived interrupted as it was by another military intervention. Amongst other things this ended the Busia government's personalized, frequently gleeful and certainly *revanchiste* anti-CPP propaganda. The discrediting of the CPP and its Life Chairman, Kwame Nkrumah, achieved some success; it was genuinely iconoclastic as Nkrumah's once ubiquitous image had been largely expunged[11] and a sad collection of his toppled and now recumbent statues gradually became overgrown with weeds behind the National Museum in Accra. But from the early 1980s some of Ghana's governments, especially those of the long period of military and quasi-military rule under Flight Lieutenant J. J. Rawlings, have actively sought to rehabilitate the memory—and the myth—of Nkrumah. The reburial in 1992 of Nkrumah's remains in a pleasant memorial park dominated by a large, abstract commemorative monument on Accra's waterfront was a significant symbol of that.[12] It is hard to be sure whether this commemoration caught the public mood or helped to create it; but given that Ghanaians had—and have—endured a spectacular and painful decline in their standard of living since the 1950s, the surrounding public sentiments about the Nkrumah years bear some resemblance to the grimly but wittily named *Ostalgie* in the old German Democratic Republic about which Anna Funder writes so movingly.[13] In Ghana this is not just based, so to speak, upon any largely spurious claim that the trains ran on time 45 years ago but, rather, a communal sadness about the fact that there *actually was* a functioning railway system in that long-lost world and that there are no trains today.[14] Above all else in that long-lost world, Ghana cast a much larger shadow than its geo-political significance might have suggested it possessed. Ghanaians had yet to be consigned to the margins by an indifferent world by the mere fact of their being Africans; nor, in those days before the discovery of massive oil reserves, was Ghana consistently internationally dwarfed by a future regional super-power, Nigeria, as it is today. Ghana was temporarily the cynosure of the world's gaze as a pioneer state, as a progressive state and as a harbinger of a new world order in which the ex-colonial world would be fully represented and powerful. It was a good time to be a Ghanaian—so long as one did not attract the malign attention of the government.

But the rehabilitation of Nkrumah and his party has been partial, tempered as it has been by political reality. For our purposes it is especially significant that Ghana's government since 2001[15] has been in many respects the linear descendant of the political parties that were so comprehensively defeated by Kwame Nkrumah's party in the last two pre-independence elections and were then to be outlawed and repressed in the first three years of the independence era. The families of several of the ministers in the current Ghanaian Cabinet, including that of the Prime Minister, John Agyekum Kufuor had variously suffered imprisonment without trial, harassment and exile in the years after March 1957.

This anniversary was accordingly an awkward conjuncture. Fifty years of independence is no slight anniversary; half-centuries are big occasions. And this one had to be celebrated not least because of its potential significance for Ghana's vital tourist industry. But that celebration was inevitably, inescapably linked with the name of Kwame Nkrumah, undoubtedly the most famous African in history before the arrival on the world stage of Nelson Mandela. Nkrumah and his party had unquestionably led and then dominated the struggle against the colonial power and, deservedly, have been given credit by history for the attainment of independence and in Ghana only the most eccentric critics of the CPP actually challenged the evident virtues of being independent of colonial rule. That seems to have been seen as a largely unquestioned good;[16] irrespective of whether his memory conjured devoted love or undying hate, he *was* the father of the nation. His reputation was magnified by a number of matters. Amongst other things, his position in world history has been buttressed by the fact that his triumph was the first of many reassertions of independence in sub-Saharan Africa and that his achievements had clearly inspired others in Africa and most especially in the United States in the course of the civil-rights campaigns. Additionally, he had acquired a name as a radical thinker even if much of his writing is unrealistically idealistic, inescapably derivative, confusing and often turgid.[17] Despite much that suggests feet of clay as well as great courage, remarkable political skills and abundant energy, he or perhaps his myth casts a long shadow and no other modern Ghanaian comes close to the national and international fame that he enjoys. While the excesses and failures[18] of his period in office can be acknowledged albeit somewhat grudgingly by those who use his name as a descriptor of their political leanings, these failings are usually ascribed to the corruption or wickedness of his followers and lieutenants or to the malign machinations of the imperialist world; for his enthusiasts[19] Nkrumah remains the austere Incorruptible, the single-minded, self-denying ultimate patriot. There was no way in which he could have been excluded from a celebration of the anniversary of that victory, *his* victory 50 years before without making those celebrations meaningless and even ridiculous. Hence one of the most frequently fly-posted images of *Ghana@50* in Accra was a poster showing the juxtaposed heads of John Kufuor and Kwame Nkrumah; in the context of Ghanaian political history, this incongruous pictorial shot-gun marriage of men so profoundly divided by experience, ideology and, very importantly ethnicity, was truly remarkable. Searching for comparisons, combinations of Lafayette and Robespierre or Charles I and Protector Cromwell seemed to fit.

So 'real' history—as opposed to comfortable or convenient history—risked getting in the way of all the fun in March 2007. In some respects that was an echo; 50 years earlier politics had profoundly threatened the celebrations of independence. To begin with Independence Day, 6 March 1957, was not, despite its historical resonance, the date of independence originally intended by either the British or Ghanaian governments.[20] There is no doubt that the announcement of that date of independence on 18 September 1956 emerged only after some hectic and complex politics. The documentary record shows that the Gold Coast's second general election of 1954 was understood in both London and Accra to be the last electoral test before the final grant of independence. It was to be a last step "before the attainment of full self-government within the Commonwealth". What was anticipated in 1954 by the new government of the Gold Coast, the Governor and the Colonial Office was further constitutional development, that is to say further constitutional negotiation both within the Gold Coast and between London and Accra, which would "ensure the smoothest possible transition from the present constitutional position to the status of independence" as the Governor wrote to W. L. Gorell Barnes in the Colonial Office.[21]

The 1954 election, the Gold Coast's first direct general election held on the basis of full adult suffrage, had returned Kwame Nkrumah's CPP with a massive majority of seats.[22] The resulting government was to enjoy something very close to full internal self-government with only law and order remaining the most significant "reserved" portfolios. The Governor no longer sat in Cabinet and the Cabinet Secretary was now an African, for example. It now became of considerable political importance for that government to work within a timetable which included an early projected date for independence itself; once that date was announced it would constitute the first instalment of the final delivery of the CPP's best-known slogan, "Self government NOW". It is hard to exaggerate the huge political importance for the CPP of the announcement of what was to be their crowning achievement; delivering independence was what the CPP was about.

We know that the date initially adopted in London and Accra for planning purposes was December 1956.[23] In April 1955 Sir Thomas Lloyd was to set out the methodology for the drafting of an independence constitution and an official letter of his suggested that the entire process might take 12 months.[24] In his initial exchange with Gorell Barnes, Arden-Clarke had however warned of the possibility of "some sudden twist of events which will postpone the attainment of full independence"[25]. That twist was, of course, to be the consequence of the emergence very shortly after the 1954 election of vehement, then violent and extra-parliamentary regional oppositions which eventually came together as the National Liberation Movement. Significantly, that opposition was to refuse to co-operate in the process of constructing a draft constitution for the eventual blessing of Westminster. Boycotting attempts to resolve a variety of issues was a potentially powerful weapon as Westminster and Whitehall had stressed the significance of an "agreed" constitution without ever specifying clearly what they meant by that. The NLM's weapon was accordingly a weapon that could be and was used in London; the CPP government had to secure "agreement" and until it had met that goal, a goal to be defined in London, all bets were off. So the timetable slipped. By June 1955 Gordon Hadow, writing to Sir Thomas Lloyd recognized this by suggesting that: "While I appreciate the anxiety of Ministers [in the Gold Coast] that nothing should stand in the way of the grant of independence by the end of 1956 ... the timetable which they favour is very tightly drawn ... it seems unlikely that independence could be granted before some time in the first quarter of 1957."[26] That this realistic if cagily expressed prediction was not shared by some members of the Gold Coast Government as late as mid 1956 is evident from a sad Cabinet minute in the National Archives in Accra. This recorded agreement on the planned installation of an inscription reading "A.D.1956" on a plaque to be placed upon the commemorative independence arch which today stands on Accra's Black Star Square.[27]

The particular "twist of events" which prolonged this colonial endgame was complex. At one level its proximate cause was an unusually intractable opposition which obdurately refused negotiation.[28] Its unwillingness to consent to a variety of forms of mediation might in other circumstances have invited a greater use of force had the Gold Coast not become an object of considerable interest for the world's press; however much some of their actions might have merited it, the temptation to "go in hard" had to be resisted as risking playing right into the hands of the propagandists of the NLM and their British supporters. The fact that the opposition enjoyed considerable support from right-wing British politicians and some business interests guaranteed them newspaper coverage and questions in the Houses of Parliament; the National Liberation Movement which sprang into being *after* the 1954 election, punched well above its weight not least because of its contacts in London amongst whom its intractability was consistently and misleadingly presented as evidence of massive local popular support. That portrayal owed a good deal to the scepticism of some and maybe many Tory politicians about what Arden-Clarke was to describe approvingly as "this liberal experiment".[29] These sorts of factors were vital to the drawing of first blood by the National Liberation Movement which undoubtedly pushed both governments towards the contemplation and then conduct of a third general election to resolve matters. This unsurprisingly attracted the fury of the fairly and very recently elected government of the Gold Coast. By managing that, amongst other things, the NLM had delayed both the announcement of a date for independence and of independence itself.

In order to forestall radical criticism within the CPP, the mutually agreed resort to a further election was presented as a result of the British government's demands. In announcing that decision, the secretary of state for the colonies in effect promised the House of Commons on 11 May 1956 that the election would lead to the announcement of a date for independence. The election was held on the basis of an understanding between London and Accra that, to quote a letter from Nkrumah to Lennox-Boyd: "HMG are fully prepared to accept a motion calling for independence ... passed by a reasonable majority in a newly elected legislature ... that HMG will be prepared to declare a firm date for the attainment of independence ... on or before 6th March, 1957".[30]

Those who claimed or expected that a third and last colonial election would reveal the extensive nature of serious opposition to the CPP were to be disappointed. It actually saw the CPP increase its national majority of seats[31] although it was in a minority in the two regions in which the NLM was strongest.[32] Although the election was designed to resolve an impasse, to be a tie-breaker, the opposition now refused to read the results as any kind of mandate for the CPP rapidly to lead the country into independence, despite the fact that the CPP had succeeded in going through the stipulated hoops.

Opposition obduracy and government despair continued to be played-out in street violence, the occasional bombing, threats of secession and, less visibly, a continual and not especially subtle playing upon the suspicions of some British politicians and officials who continued to regard the CPP government as, amongst other things, an authoritarian, corrupt catspaw of Moscow.[33] That negative argument was then strengthened by the findings of a Commission of Enquiry which showed that the CPP had been illegally raiding the coffers of an agency of the country's major statutory board, the Cocoa Marketing Board and had partly funded its election campaign in 1956 from that source. Colonial officials were still discussing whether these revelations constituted a case for the deferral of the announcement of the date of independence as late as August 1956. Much of that discussion was huff and puff; but by the 16th August it was recognized by officials that while they:

> were too far committed to be able to justify actually deferring the grant of independence ... we should have seriously to consider the public announcement of the date of Independence until we received some ... assurances from Dr. Nkrumah about the action which he proposed to take on the Cocoa Report ...[34]

The position of the secretary of state seems to have meandered. Although it was agreed in the Colonial Office that whatever response Nkrumah was likely to make would almost certainly fail to entirely satisfy them and their political masters, Lennox-Boyd seems to have sought every excuse for delaying the announcement of the date.[35] Nkrumah complained with some justification that delay was causing him political difficulties with his restive back-benchers but Lennox-Boyd's response to this complaint to the Governor was a dismissive masterpiece: "Surely you could explain to Nkrumah that matters other than Suez however important must take a back seat for the next few days."[36] A letter from the Governor to his wife suggests that well into mid-September, Lennox-Boyd "was doing a wobble and wanting to defer announcing a firm date for Independence ... Yesterday the S of S surrendered with the words 'I feel you have left me with no alternative'".[37]

Nkrumah and Arden Clarke remembered the moment when they shared the news of London's nomination of a date for independence. "'Prime Minister', the Governor said, 'this is a great day for you. It is the end of what you have struggled for.' 'It is the end of what *we* have been struggling for, Sir Charles', I corrected him" Nkrumah recalled.[38] Arden Clarke remembered that "After he [Nkrumah] had read the text of the despatch, he looked up and said in a rather awed voice 'H. E., that's nice ... We must have a party to celebrate this' ... It was a rather solemn and subdued little man that left my office."[39] And it was only on 18 September that the date was finally announced in both Westminster and Accra; the announcement in Accra ironically interrupted an extremely rancorous debate on an opposition motion demanding the resignation of the Prime Minister.

The radiant iconography of this and perhaps other independence days tends to conceal the bitterness of the struggles that surrounded such apparently bland issues as the timing of announcements of intended dates. Granting and withholding are of course powerful negotiating tools when one party controls the gift and the other desperately wishes for this, the most glittering of political prizes for a nationalist movement. The announcement of the Gold Coast's Independence Day initially afforded Nkrumah and his ministers—and the Governor—considerable pleasure:

> They all turned up [to Christiansborg Castle, the Governor's residence] ... and we repaired outside under the tower and stood in a cluster while a bottle of whisky was opened, a tumbler of neat spirit was filled and Gbedemah poured a libation to the Gods of Ghana ... This over, I gave them all champagne, and we laughed and chatted for a while ...[40]

But the opposition remained unreconciled to what now became a rapidly changing situation. The date of independence now became for them, as it had been for the British government, a significant negotiating weapon not least because the Secretary of State for the Colonies, and others in the British government, tended to somewhat sympathize with them. Along with demands for partition and threats of secession, their intransigence including a refusal to vote for the motion for self-government in the Accra Assembly and to meet with the Gold Coast government to agree a constitution began to create a threatening delay. A long letter from Lennox-Boyd to the British Government's Chief Whip, Edward Heath, brings out the sense of crisis over timetabling a legislative programme allowing the transfer of power to happen in the following March, a crisis almost entirely provoked by opposition intransigence.[41] It was not merely the legislative programme but the independence day celebrations that were now at risk; Lennox-Boyd wrote "there cannot help being an element of uncertainty until the Independence Act has received the Royal Assent; and we shall need an appreciable interval after that in order to make the firm and final arrangements for the Royal visit"[42].

The constitutional impasse was to lead to a visit by the Secretary of State to the Gold Coast between 24 and 30 January. Arden-Clarke was, he said in a telegram of 2 January, "counting heavily on [the visit] as affording the last chance of reaching a peaceful solution of local difficulties".[43] The contentious elements of the constitution were rapidly drafted into blandness almost literally on the backs of envelopes in the course of this visit. The aim was to draft something "which we can say we are confident will provide a framework within which all parties will be content to start their independent life".[44] As is well known, the elements of constitution designed to provide safeguards which would satisfy the apprehensions of the opposition in the form of Regional Assemblies were blown away quickly and quite legally in the immediate post-independence period.[45] Drafting under such pressure rarely produces respected, durable texts. In some respects the hastily drafted independence constitution was a Potemkin village.

The story so far takes us to the eve of independence itself. As we have seen, many of those who were to be on parade were privately nursing severely bruised egos. The surviving iconography is somewhat reminiscent of wedding photographs: large numbers of people who loathe one another can be forced to smile when faced by a camera and the implications of a permanent record. The attenuated process which led to Independence Day meant that away from the photographers' lenses, government and opposition remained utterly unreconciled,[46] an impasse which was soon to be addressed by the CPP government in draconian ways—imprisonment, exile, deportation—in the first years after independence. But the more obvious rifts were only part of the story. The Governor and the Secretary of State of the Colonies had continued to disagree with one another, a mutual distaste which culminated when these two large, hard-drinking men had a blazing row on a DC3 aircraft taking them back from Kumase to Accra. Arden-Clarke, it is convincingly alleged by some of his supporters, forfeited his otherwise fairly automatic elevation to the House of Lords in the course of this screaming match. The Colonial Office and the Commonwealth Relations Office (CRO) had fallen out over the diametrically different readings of the political and economic entrails. Colonial Office officials continued to follow Arden Clarke's fond but inescapably paternalist interpretation[47] which, roughly, suggested that Ghana's future was on the rosier side of shaky; officials in the Commonwealth Relations Office were more inclined to take the much gloomier view developed by Francis Cumming-Bruce during his period as adviser on external affairs to the government of the Gold Coast/Ghana from 1955 to 1957. This divergence of views led to friction between Lennox-Boyd and Lord Home inside and outside the Cabinet room.

The numerous uncertainties could not delay the planning of the celebrations. Planning, however, opened up other areas of bitter disagreement. An element of the military spectacle was to include a fly-past of 4 Valiant aircraft. This was initially turned down by the Chancellor of the Exchequer, Peter Thorneycroft, as it would involve an additional expenditure of £35 000 above the original UK contribution of £55 000 for the celebrations. A Cabinet discussion of the issue suggests some of the intentions of such grand theatre. Thorneycroft was reminded that the USA and the USSR would be sending "their most modern kinds of aircraft [and] it would be embarrassing if the UK was not represented on a comparable scale".[48] But the Treasury remained implacable; if the Air Force were to go, the cost must be met within the overall initial allocation and, they insisted, other things would have to be sacrificed. In a telegram from Accra to Lord Home, Lennox Boyd lamented the explicit meanness: "we should send effective air contribution too.[49] Celebrations will undoubtedly be a big occasion with representatives from all over the world present.

Many have lately come to doubt our strength.[50] Surely it would be madness to miss this wonderful opportunity of demonstrating outstanding qualities of our Air Arm on a particularly impressionable occasion".[51] A compromise of sorts ensued in which the Treasury was prevailed upon to find a little more cash for the event.

The costs to Britain were dwarfed by those of the infrastructural developments taking place in Accra, which were designed to be functional by 6 March 1957 and most of which survive in somewhat moth-eaten form to this day. These included the new residence for the Governor General,[52] the building of the impressive new sports stadium, the Independence Arch on what was to become Accra's huge parade ground, Black Star Square[53] and, in response to the lack of decent hotel accommodation for the numerous delegated dignitaries in Accra, the imposing but, for many years derelict, Ambassador Hotel. The Assembly building underwent an urgent make-over as the state opening of the first session of the Parliament of Ghana by the Queen's representative, the Duchess of Kent was, constitutionally at least, to be the high spot of the celebrations. The Gold Coast Regiment of the Royal West African Frontier Force, soon to become the Ghanaian Army, drilled and drilled and laid on demonstrations of their competence. These were not entirely ceremonial in intent. Arden-Clarke reported that: "On Wednesday the Army gave a demonstration for the benefit of the members of the Legislative Assembly designed to show the firing power of a company of infantry ... the demonstration was well-timed[54] as there has been a lot of loose talk among the Ashantis that they would go to war if they did not get the constitution they wanted".[55] Less belligerently, some members of the armed forces tested out the safety of the seating around the parade ground by jumping up and down on the chairs in their hob-nailed boots.[56]

The Duchess of Kent arrived on the 3 March on a chartered BOAC airliner which was significantly larger than those usually flying into the airport in Accra.[57] There followed the usual airport excitements—a 21-gun salute, an inspection of a guard of honour followed by a march-past and then a finger-crunching orgy of hand-shaking with a variety of notables. In the city of Accra, the Duchess was then given an extended official welcome by the extremely numerous chiefs of the Ga, the indigenous people of Accra. And of course the sequence of events was accompanied by drumming and played out against a backdrop of gorgeous traditional dress.

These few days of celebration were a splendid triumph of two quite distinct kinds of ornamentalism[58] which blended exceptionally well. The whole show, partly orchestrated by the Ghanaian Assembly's Speaker, Sir Emmanuel Quist, was a combination of two wonderful sets of invented regal traditions. Ghanaian fancy dress, sumptuous woven cloth, seriously heavyweight gold bling and ornamented sandals met its British equivalents, tiaras, anachronistic feathered hats and appliquéd braid. Rams' horns vied with trumpet fanfares, libations to the ancestors matched loyal toasts. Such grandiose displays were not entirely new to the Gold Coast; after all, the country had not so long ago successfully celebrated the end of the Second World War, and the coronation of Elizabeth II less than four years before.

The Duchess of Kent was not the only big name on the guest list. R. A. Butler[59] represented the British government and other official guests included Richard Nixon, the US Vice-President, François Mitterand, Minister of Justice, and the representative of the USSR, I. A. Benediktov.[60] Over the next day the Duchess was to lay a wreath on Accra's major war memorial, open the new museum in Accra, chat to and glad-hand innumerable beautifully turned-out schoolchildren, attend Convocation on the newly built Great Hall of the University College on top of Legon Hill and carry out the obligatory visit to some wards of the teaching hospital at Korle Bu. Then there was a regatta dominated by races between wonderfully painted surf boats, the only way of off-loading goods and people from ocean going ships before the completion of Ghana's only deep-water port in Tema. And despite the Treasury's earlier unwillingness, the Duchess was flown-past by three Valiant bombers and three Neptunes. After opening the Independence Monument, she, Nkrumah and the Governor, all smiles throughout, climbed the many stairs to the top of the arch from where they watched a firework display. This was followed by the last meeting of the old Legislative Council. Here the Speaker read the Governor's speech proroguing the Assembly and just after midnight, members of the government chaired Nkrumah[61] to the Old Polo Ground, a meeting place with a long resonant history in Ghana. It was here that the ex-servicemen's rally which preceded the outbreak of the riots of 1948 had been held before embarking on their march towards the Secretariat or Christiansborg castle.[62] Nine years later, however, exuberance gave way to a quieter more reflective happiness as Nkrumah made a short speech in which he affirmed that "our beloved Ghana is free now for ever".

On 6 March, Arden-Clark was sworn in as the country's new Governor-General. He was to remain in post until May 1957, leading "a rather futile existence" until he was replaced by Lord Listowel.[63] There followed a state opening of Ghana's Parliament, the successor to the Gold Coast's Legislative Assembly. The ceremonial followed almost exactly the procedures of a British state opening of parliament including the ritual carrying of a mace and the imperious door-knocking. The Assembly members had decided to wear traditional dress for this occasion and the few colour photographs which survive suggest that it was, as the cliché has it, a riot of colour. And then the Duchess of Kent read the Speech from the Throne which concluded with a personal message from her niece.

It was all very dignified and, as intended, it made a big impression upon those of the world's press who were covering these events. The press were handled with great flair by the Gold Coast's Director of Information Services, the larger-than-life figure of Jimmie Moxon.[64] It was a media event in more than the limited sense of news coverage. Nkrumah's publishers, Thomas Nelson and Sons, had cleverly timed the publication of Nkrumah's autobiography, *Ghana*, for Independence Day itself; Nkrumah and his secretary Erica Powell had no less cleverly submitted the completed manuscript of this enormously successful book in good time for Nelson to bring this off. As Nelson must have hoped, the book was widely noted and reviewed at length throughout the English-speaking world and has since been reprinted and translated many times. And this endearing, persuasive text has played huge part in laying out the master narrative with which this brief account began. It reinforced the positive, and some would claim intentionally misleading, impression given by Nkrumah to an avid outside world. He was throughout these exhausting days notably modest, utterly devoid of the stridency popularly associated with authoritarian leaders. He was graceful, statesmanlike, moderate and, above all, rather good-looking. His speech at the state dinner for the Duchess on 4 March was a masterpiece of mature and genial blandness which cleverly pressed all the right buttons: "We are most anxious to establish friendly and cordial relations with all countries." So far as relations with the old imperialist enemy were concerned "we part with the warmest feelings of goodwill. With the ending of the old relationship we shall establish our new position as a fellow-member of the Commonwealth". In 1957 Independence Day was a triumph for Nkrumah and a disaster for his opponents. He was on the cover of *Time* magazine, his biography was being read throughout the world and his name was both globally familiar and, as the title of his biography suggested, synonymous with the name of the country he now ruled; in Nkrumah's case l'*état* was most assuredly *moi*. Despite the discomfort of Ghana's ruling party, 6 March 1957 had been *his* day and 50 years later in 2007 it remained his day.

Notes

1. The quotation is from Andrew Marvell, *Cromwel's* [sic] *Return from Ireland*. Composed 1650 or 1651 but not published until 1681.
2. For more on this theme see Robert Gildea's excellent *Marianne in Chains: In Search of the German Occupation of France, 1940–45* (Basingstoke: MacMillan, 2002).
3. Following the military *coup d'etat* of February 1966. Before this the ousted Convention Peoples' Party (CPP) regime was not notable for its tolerance.
4. The wearing of these extremely comfortable tunics, *fugu*, was an attempt to assert the Party's credentials as being a party of the 'workers and peasants', a party of the *sans culottes;* these smocks were intended to symbolize the 'working man' as a large percentage of manual labour in both urban and rural southern Ghana was drawn from the relatively poor Northern Territories where they are customarily worn. This inherent populism was not to be followed by John Kufuor, who seems to have worn immaculately tailored western style suits throughout the celebrations in 2007.
5. These 'fore and aft' caps could be worn by Party members who had been detained by the police in the colonial period. They were obviously copied from the caps worn—and still worn—by supporters of the Indian Congress Party.
6. This account is critically chronicled in my *Nkrumah and Chiefs: The Politics of Chieftaincy in Ghana, 1951–60* (Oxford: James Currey, 2000).
7. There is, however, no serious evidence which suggests that they were involved in the organization of the military coup.
8. Some of them, such as Reginald Amponsah and Modesto Apaloo, had been imprisoned for much of the period following the gaining of independence. Others had sat out the Nkrumah period in exile.
9. That flame has been kept more vividly alight in Europe and North America, and especially within the diaspora, where Nkrumah's reputation has been regarded less ambiguously and much more romantically.
10. This was certainly ironic; in exile Busia had written a book called *Africa in Search of Democracy* (London: Routledge and Kegan Paul, 1968). That search assuredly did not end with his period in office.
11. From, for example, postage stamps and the currency, although his likeness was to be found on shirts and women's wrapper cloths for years afterwards, almost certainly suggesting the continuing ready availability of bolts of this cheaply produced material rather than political opinion.
12. Nkrumah died while undergoing medical treatment for cancer in Bucharest on 27 April 1972; he had previously been interred in May 1972 in Conakry, Guinea (where he had lived in exile after the coup) and later in the village of his birth, Nkroful, in south western Ghana.
13. See her recent *Stasiland* (London: Granta, 2003).
14. There is no question that many aspects of everyday life were state-supported, free and apparently more efficient in those days. For example, Ghana once boasted a decent mass transport system, including a functioning, albeit loss-making, railroad, state airline and merchant fleet, and many older Ghanaians claim that educational and medical provisions were of higher quality. One can, of course, hear similar claims in any British pub.
15. Elections took place in 2000.

16. What was much more closely questioned at the time was the nature of the post-colonial state. In his speech of welcome to the British Secretary of State for the Colonies on 24 January 1956, the Asantehene, the figurehead leader of the National Liberation Movement (NLM) said: "Everyone in this country wants independence, but Ashanti does not want independence at any cost. We want our liberties and freedom preserved."
17. There is an inescapable sense of condescension in some of the applause which accompanies the frequently uncritical readings of Nkrumah's work, which uncomfortably reminds me of Dr Samuel Johnson's comments about women preachers.
18. These were not slight matters and included imprisonment without trial, gerrymandering, denial of press freedom and economic collapse.
19. They frequently describe themselves as "Nkrumahists" and are a broad church. Ideologically Nkrumahists are so eclectic that seeking a precise definition of modern "Nkrumahism" in Ghana is a profitless enterprise.
20. 6 March was the day in 1844 on which some Fante chiefs and the British Government signed the famous Bond, the first of a succession of treaties in which some coastal chiefs acknowledged the jurisdiction of the British crown.
21. See National Archives, Kew (NA) CO 554/805, no 1 of 2 September 1954. Gorell Barnes was an Assistant Under-Secretary of State in the Colonial Office.
22. The CPP won 72 of the 104 seats in the single-chamber Assembly.
23. See NA CO 554/1162, no 9 of 22 December 1954.
24. See letter from Lloyd to Arden-Clarke of 16 April 1955, NA 554/888, no 1. Lloyd was permanent Under-Secretary of State in the Colonial Office.
25. CO 554/805, no 1 of 2 September 1954.
26. See NA DO 35/6170, no 3 of 21 June 1955. Gordon Hadow was writing as Deputy Governor.
27. Ghana National Archives (GNA) ADM 13/141, 1 May 1956. Nkrumah, it seems, had already privately conceded the enforced delay by February 1956 and is reported to have advocated 6 March as Independence Day. See NA CO 554/806, no 199, 5 February 1956. I continue to be puzzled by this apparent contradiction.
28. Nkrumah's nonchalant, almost Macmillanesque, reference to this crisis as "odd spots of bother" in a letter to Lennox-Boyd would have fooled nobody; this was a real and substantial mess. NA CO 554/806, no 140, 21 November 1955.
29. NA. DO 35/6178, no 10b. Inward telegram no 32, from Arden-Clarke to the Secretary of State for the Colonies on 22 July 1956. He was quoting a leading article in *The Observer* of 8 July 1956.
30. NA CO 554/807, no 269A of 20 April 1956.
31. With 73 out of the 104 seats.
32. In Ashanti region the CPP won 8 of the 21 seats and in the Northern Territories 11 of the 25 seats.
33. There is no doubt that some senior figures in the local civil service supported the NLM; there is, for example, ample evidence of a serious rift between Arden Clarke and the Chief Regional Commissioner for Ashanti, the heartland of the opposition. An outspoken opponent of the CPP, A. C. Russell was pressured to retire early immediately after independence and did so on 22 May.
34. NA CO 554/807. Minute by M.Z. Terry, 16 August, 1956. Zoe Terry was a Principal in the West African department in the Colonial Office, one of the *very* few senior women in the CO.
35. See especially paragraphs 4 and 5 of an outward un-numbered telegram from the Secretary of State to the Governor. NA CO 554/807, no 363, 18 August 1956.
36. NA CO554/808, no 383 of 12 September 1956. Outward un-numbered telegram to the Governor.
37. Letter from Arden-Clarke to his wife, 16 September 1956. In another attempt to excuse the prevarication Lennox-Boyd repeated to Arden Clarke that "preoccupation of Government over Suez" was an element in the delay of the announcement. See NA CO554/808, no. 383, 12 September 1956.
38. *Ghana: The Autobiography of Kwame Nkrumah* (London: Nelson, 1957), p. 282.
39. Letter from Arden Clarke to his wife, 18 September 1956. Arden Clarke Papers.
40. *Ibid.*, 19 September 1956.
41. NA DO 35/6180, no 18, 22 November 1956.
42. DO 35/6180, no 18, 22 November 1956.
43. NA PREM 11/1859, 2 January 1957.
44. NA CO 554/823, no 95, 25 January 1957. Letter from C. G. Eastwood (who had accompanied Alan Lennox-Boyd on this trip) to J. S. Bennett.

45. For more on this see my *Nkrumah and the Chiefs*.
46. The Asantehene and his council decided to send by way of protest only a token delegation of two people to the celebrations, although 12 had been invited.
47. He was, for example, to describe the relationship between the UK and Ghana as being like that "between pupil and teacher ... the pupil has safely left the school to begin adult life" in his farewell speech at Cape Coast on 23 March 1957. Less publicly he wrote to his wife on the 16 September 1956: "I shall have to see to it that my children [sic] do not smirch [sic] the record or throw their 'Freedom' away between now and Independence Day". Arden Clarke Papers.
48. NA CAB 128/31/1, CC 7(57)4.
49. The "too" is a reference to the fact that a Royal Navy cruiser and a frigate were to represent the British armed forces in Accra on Independence Day.
50. A reference surely to the still smarting wounds of the disastrous Suez adventure.
51. NA CO 554/1388, no 22. 25 January 1957.
52. Nkrumah was to move into Christiansborg Castle, until he decided that it was insufficiently secure. He eventually lived in more defensible Flagstaff House.
53. Built close to the spot at which two ex-servicemen had been killed on the first day of the riots of 1948.
54. It *was* well-timed. On 3 March a company of infantry was sent to the south east as there were apprehensions about violence being organized to disrupt the independence celebrations.
55. Arden-Clarke to Family, 27 January 1957. Arden-Clarke papers.
56. One of the companies to do this was commanded by a young seconded National Service lieutenant, A. D. Roberts, who went on to be a most distinguished historian of Africa.
57. Her itinerary had been rehearsed on the spot by her private secretary, Philip Hay, who flew to Accra in January 1957.
58. To adopt David Cannadine's nice neologism. See his book of the same name (London: Allen Lane, 2001).
59. Then the Lord Privy Seal.
60. At the time Benediktov was the Soviet Minister of State Farms.
61. And nearly brained him on the lintel of the Assembly's doors.
62. The destination of the march was contested by protagonists when the Watson Commission sought to establish what had happened on that fateful day.
63. Arden-Clarke to family, 28 April 1957. Arden-Clarke Papers.
64. He had been District Commissioner of Accra at the time of the 1948 riots and was one of the several British officers who was to stay on in Ghana after independence.

Whose Freedom at Midnight? Machinations towards Guyana's Independence, May 1966

CLEM SEECHARAN
Professor of Caribbean History and Head of Caribbean Studies, London Metropolitan University

Guyana (formerly British Guiana), the only British colony on the mainland of South America, became independent at midnight on 26 May 1966. But whose freedom was it? For nearly 20 years the Marxist leader of the People's Progressive Party (PPP), Cheddi Jagan (1918–97), of Indian extraction, buoyed by the independence of India and obsessed with the dominance of the British company, Booker, in the colony's plantation economy, had championed Guyana's 'struggle' for independence. Yet, on the big night it was the African leader of the People's National Congress (PNC), L. F. S. Burnham (1923–85), who was the recipient of the prize. His politics, though left-wing, were characterized by a cultivated pragmatism, strategic ambiguity—the facility to "tack and turn as advantage seems to dictate ... his whole political approach is opportunistic", as a British politician had assessed him in 1954.[1] With the aid of the Portuguese and Coloured (mixed race) political party, the United Force (UF), led by a Portuguese businessman, Peter D'Aguiar, a rabid anti-communist, in conjunction with the decisive intervention of US President John F. Kennedy himself and the CIA, in 1962–63, the PNC resorted to violence to make British Guiana ungovernable. The latter proved effective: it delayed independence, while Anglo-American collusion brought a Burnham-D'Aguiar coalition to power in December 1964 and independence in May 1966. Cheddi Jagan was a virtual spectator to the celebrations of the country's 'freedom'.

Speaking in the National Assembly on Independence Day, Jagan made it clear that this was not his freedom day. That had to be struggled for: foreign control of the economy had to be eliminated; only his party, the PPP, could achieve real liberation for the country. He meant disengagement from 'imperialism' and the capitalist system—the building of the communist utopia, following the path of the glorious Soviet Union. It was not an auspicious beginning for this troubled land:

> [P]olitical independence has been attained under the continuation and consolidation of foreign economic control and the maintenance of the colonial type economy, based on primary production and extraction. This has already detracted from the living standards of the working people ... The PPP, the vanguard of Guyana's struggle for national liberation, is convinced that liberty is achieved only when it has been struggled for and won. It cannot be a gift of charity. For the people of Guyana, real freedom is still a prize to be won, and win it we will—as a reunited free people.[2]

Jagan and Burnham, founder-members of the PPP in 1950, had won the first general elections under universal adult suffrage in April 1953. But after 133 days the British suspended the constitution and evicted the PPP government from office, convinced that Jagan was a pro-Moscow communist bent on subverting liberal democracy.[3] His politics were anathema to the Fabian socialism of the British West Indies. The tenuous coalition, suggestive of African-Indian unity in the PPP, did not survive the report of the Robertson Commission sent by the Colonial Office to British Guiana in early 1954, following the suspension of the constitution. It sought to make a distinction between the 'communism' of Cheddi Jagan and the moderate 'socialism' of Forbes Burnham. But this was not merely a 'divide and rule' tactic; it was an astute exploitation of the seeds of ethnic division, immanent in the society, and marked by a tendency towards Indian triumphalism and African apprehension, since the freedom of 'Mother India' in 1947. They argued:

> Mr Burnham (chairman of the Party) was generally recognised as the leader of the socialists in the PPP and as such to be in rivalry with Dr Jagan for the moral leadership of the Party as a whole ... [T]here were many who thought that as the recognised leader of the socialists ... Mr Burnham ought to have taken a much stronger line than he did in opposition to the more blatantly communist activities of the Jagans and their supporters. We came to the conclusion that ... the ambiguous Mr Burnham ... and a number of its less prominent leaders were socialists ... We doubt, however, if they had the wit to see the essential difference between themselves and their communist colleagues or the ability to avoid being out-manoeuvred by them.[4]

As early as the elections of April 1953, 30-year old Burnham, a brilliant lawyer with considerable oratorical gifts and already identified as the premier African leader in the colony, had endeavoured to wrest the leadership of the PPP from the Indian leader, Cheddi Jagan. The mutual African-Indian suspicion permeating the wider colonial environment was reproduced in the Party, Jagan's Marxist dogmas on the primacy of the class struggle notwithstanding. It was so bedevilling a feature of the

PPP, in its so-called golden phase of racial unity, that Eusi Kwayana (formerly Sydney King), another founder-member of the Party, an African school teacher from the historic village of Buxton, fearing the escalation of racial rivalry if the assumption of power were to be confronted precipitately, had counselled that they should not contest more than eight seats. The Party should focus on forging a degree of genuine ethnic unity. He had advised Jagan and Burnham that they should seek **not** to win in 1953:

> Some people like to ignore reality. I had moved in the PPP Executive **that we should not win a majority**, and my reason was that the country was not sufficiently united. I think only Martin Carter [the poet] and I supported the motion that we should **not** go for a majority. I knew we would win a majority, but I didn't think the Party was prepared for it because although the racial unity was there—it was a kind of coalition—it was not well-grounded; it was tenuous. I told Jagan and Burnham we would win the elections. They didn't believe it; they thought we would win about eight seats [out of 24]. I moved a motion that we fight about eight seats and try to do, in a multiple of eight, what Jagan alone had done [since 1947], and really try to unite the country [emphasis added].[5]

Kwayana was correct. African and Indians are separated by a cultural chasm that breeds mutual incomprehension. Indians were not a clear majority, but they constituted the largest group. Africans were afraid that with growing economic and cultural self-assurance, coupled with their demographic superiority, Indians under Cheddi Jagan's leadership would soon lead British Guiana to 'freedom' from British rule. They were therefore apprehensive that independence would herald their permanent subjugation by a wily people. Indian rule was infinitely less tolerable than British colonialism. Indeed, African Guyanese would have opted for remaining colonials indefinitely rather than support independence under a party led by an Indian. The instinct to categorize and calibrate everything on the basis of ethnicity is chronic in this polyglot, incoherent place.

Kwayana is a rare example of an individual at the heart of these seminal events in Guyana's meandering path to independence, speaking frankly on racism in the colony. He contends that Jagan failed to address the fundamental fact of African insecurity in the early 1950s. Jagan thought that his Marxist truth, 'scientific socialism', the source of 'total understanding', would dissolve the question of race: a false problem in any case. He failed to comprehend, in Kwayana's evocative phrase, "the hinterland of suspicion" in the African community. Kwayana explains why the PPP split into two factions in 1955, one Indian (led by Jagan); the other African (led by Forbes Burnham:

> The two major groups have stereotypes of each other. Africans tended to see Indians as clannish, as having more money, having an interest in land—a lot of them were selling out their lands to Indians when they went broke. Although they were doing it voluntarily, it also alarmed them. Then there was this rumour that someone from India had come and said who owned the land owned the country ... A lot of Africans were unable to go beyond that. They would look

at the behaviour of Indians near to them in judging the PPP (the PPP does not understand this until now).

He elaborates:

If there is an aggressive [racist] member of the PPP in their district, this is how Africans see the PPP. Jagan never ... [dealt] with these things at the subjective level, although he ha[d] a lot of rage against Imperialism. That problem was never dealt with; that's one of the reasons why I left the PPP [in 1956, the year after Burnham]. The psychology of the leader is crucial. We had to fight to get Africans to accept an Indian leader [Jagan]. He didn't have that problem. He never had to accept a leader of another race so he didn't know what it is. He talks about revolution, but the personal revolution—nothing. He had a cultural problem. Having rejected colonialism and its intellectual and cultural baggage he had to take something from somewhere else [Russian communism]; he didn't rely on his own personality. If he had Hinduism, it would have made him a different person.[6]

There were no intellectual or cultural foundations to Cheddi Jagan's ideology. He had rejected his Indian cultural antecedents, so he absorbed the received Marxist dogmas uncritically. They took the place of the eclectic Hinduism of his boyhood. Yet, imprisoned by the intractability of racial identities in Guyana, Jagan was discernibly adept at garnering Indian loyalty—and keeping it, manipulating crucial Indo-Guyanese idioms with dexterity. That was why he was able to survive the split in the PPP in 1955, with the departure of Forbes Burnham, as well as that of Eusi Kwayana and Martin Carter in 1956, and proceed, on the basis of Indo-Guyanese invincibility under the first-past-the-post electoral system, to gain re-election in August 1957. Burnham's faction of the PPP was vanquished, so he decided to form a party with a less ambiguous identity, the predominantly African, People's National Congress (PNC), in late 1957. Africans were demoralized. This was exacerbated by the fact that in 1960 the Conservative government of Harold Macmillan granted Jagan self-government with virtual assurance of independence, in a couple of years, after fresh general elections. Burnham was rudderless and his African supporters clueless (like their contemporary situation in Guyana). For Cheddi Jagan, independence was there for the take. He just had to know how to wait. **He did not**.

Fidel Castro's revolution of 1959 dazzled him. The circumspection and moderation he strained to project in 1957–59, since his re-election, did not sit easily with him. His rehearsed Marxist dogmas, the source of 'total knowledge', were battling within him for release. In 1991 he explained for V. S. Naipaul the illumination that was given him by some Marxist primers:

It was Janet [his American-born wife] who, when she came here [British Guiana] in 1943, brought me Little Lenin Library books—little tracts, pamphlets. It was the first time I read Marxist literature. And then ... I began reading Marxist books like mad. I read *Das Kapital* after the Little Lenin series. And that helped me to have a total understanding of the development of society. Until then, all the various struggles—Indians, blacks, the American people—had been disjointed experiences. To put it in a way that was totally related to a socio-economic system came from the reading of Marxist literature. For instance, the women question was dealt with in Engels's book, *The Origins of the Family*. The Marxist theory of surplus value brought a totally new understanding of the struggle of the working class—not only that they were exploited. It was exciting to me, an intellectual excitement because a whole new world opened to me, **a total understanding of the world** [emphasis added].[7]

Such was the mesmerizing spell of the received dogmas! He got the chance to break out of his brief, but stressful, play at moderation, in early 1960, when it became clear that Fidel Castro was a communist, and that the new Cuba would be guided by Marxism-Leninism. Cheddi was over the moon. He would not play ball with the 'imperialists' any longer. Even Ian Macleod, the liberal Secretary of State for the Colonies, who had defied several right-wingers in the Tory Party and committed himself to granting Jagan independence by 1962, would be construed as just another imperialist by Cheddi. After the constitutional conference in London, where it had become transparent that no 'struggle' was really necessary for independence, Jagan proceeded to Cuba, his new Mecca, twice in 1960. He was certain that Marxism-Leninism, the purest form of governance devised by humankind, was inevitable. Fidel had vindicated this. The days of capitalism were numbered—the communist utopia was around the next bend. He pontificated:

> I completely support the Revolutionary Government of Cuba ... [It] has the support of most of the Cuban people. I have no doubt the revolution will achieve all its objectives. Any revolutionary movement such as this which is tending towards social and economic emancipation will obviously have enemies both inside and outside the country, but if we take into account the times in which we are living, the speed with which the progressive forces of the world are advancing [the communist bloc], and the great support of the majority of the Cuban people, I have no doubts about the Cuban Revolution.[8]

Cheddi boasted in September 1960 that "the only Government in Latin America which was openly supporting the Cuban Revolution was ours". He was confident that time was on the side of communism, guided by the Soviet Union and the so-called people's democracies of Eastern Europe. He added that Marxism-Leninism was bound to win; Suez (1956) was a "turning point in the history of imperialism which is now on the defensive and is losing more and more positions every day. The process will grow not in arithmetic, but in geometric progression". He predicted that the communist utopia was unstoppable: it would "emerge triumphant", as capitalism was "becoming a moribund system". Communism represented the logic of history; the Cuban Revolution was the watershed in the Western Hemisphere. He could not contain himself: "Fidel Castro is not only the liberator of the American continent but also the liberator of the century".[9]

It is arguable that without Castro's Revolution and Cheddi's consuming infatuation, he might have kept his head, his circumspection of 1957–59; he would not have stirred the Cold War venom of the United States. He would also have deprived his local enemies—Burnham's PNC and the rabidly anti-communist UF and their allies, the Catholic Church—of the desperate ammunition that would resurrect their seemingly terminal fortunes. In spite of Jagan's folly, in early 1961 Ian Macleod genuinely sought to persuade President Kennedy that Jagan was not a communist; he was more of a Laskiite radical (Kennedy was taught by Harold Laski at the London School of Economics): there was no need to be afraid of his political outlook. Meanwhile, the Fabian socialist-oriented head of Booker in Guyana (owner of most of the sugar plantations), Jock Campbell (a friend of Macleod), also, endeavoured to play down Jagan's fatal attraction to communism. This, however, was not easy for Kennedy to take. After the failure to overthrow Castro—the Bay of Pigs debacle of April 1961—the President became preoccupied that he would be seen as being too soft on communism. Therefore, he still harboured apprehensions about Jagan's ideology, wary that an independent Guyana would become a Soviet beachhead for spreading the virus into the continent.

But Jagan was re-elected in August 1961, and it seemed as if the Kennedy administration could be persuaded to follow the British and put up with him, hoping that power would breed responsibility and moderation. However, Jagan organized a tawdry triumphalist parade to celebrate his victory. His jubilant Indian supporters repeatedly behaved in a manner humiliating to African bystanders: they dragged the symbol of the PNC, the broom, behind their vehicles; some displayed small coffins marked 'PNC'. Africans were demoralized by another electoral defeat and deeply apprehensive that Indians were about to collect the big prize: 'freedom' for Guyana. Jagan's pretext for the parade was that it would dispel whatever doubts the imperialists had of the strength of his support. This was unnecessary: independence was there for the taking—whoever won the elections had earned the right to collect the prize. The meretricious display, the perceived arrogance of Indians, magnified the fears of Africans that dark times were ahead when Jagan got independence, which the British were committed to granting. Africans viewed independence with foreboding: freedom for the 'coolies'; slavery for them.

In August 1961 Jagan had all the trumps; few envisaged that he would pull defeat from the jaws of victory. Ever a fantasist, he believed passionately that Marxism-Leninism was superior in comprehending the laws of development—it constituted a science of society—and that the mighty United States was in line for the fall. So his meeting with President Kennedy in the Oval Office, in October 1961, to procure aid for development, was potentially fatal. He was going to see the President precisely at a time when he was buoyed by the Cuban Revolution and impatient to create the communist utopia on which he thought Fidel had embarked. The British Embassy in Washington had sought to counsel Jagan to moderate his stance when he met the President, eschewing words or expressions that Americans tended to construe as synonymous with communism. This proved futile. A little before he met Kennedy, Jagan explained his political philosophy to the Washington Press Club:

> I believe ... that the economic theories of scientific socialism [Marxism] hold out the promise of a dynamic social discipline which can transform an underdeveloped country into a developed one in a far shorter time than any other system. We may [therefore] differ from you in the way we [choose to] organise our economic life.[10]

He could not comprehend that it was not simply a matter of differential approaches to economic development; it was a deeply contentious question, with implications for the Cold War. He had taken his little country into it, on the side the Americans deemed abominable—a peril to 'freedom' in the Western Hemisphere. British Guiana was on the verge of becoming another Cuba.

Jagan did not excel either, in his appearance on 'Meet the Press' on 15 October 1961. The President was watching the programme, and the moderator had asked Jagan whether there was freedom in the Soviet Union and China. He waffled:

> All I can say—I haven't been to China, I haven't been to Russia, but the experts who have been there have said—for instance, you have this chap who is a writer on the question, an expert apparently, who writes for the London *Observer*, I can't recall his name right now. But he has said in his latest book that life in the Soviet Union is growing day by day better and better. The standards of living are improving, and as such, we are concerned. We want to know how this is done.[11]

When he met President Kennedy on 25 October 1961, he virtually committed political suicide by leaving the President with no doubt whatsoever that he was a communist. No aid would be forthcoming, and in view of Kennedy's apprehension that he was being perceived as soft on hemispheric subversion, he soon became obsessed with the future of little British Guiana. The British must not give independence to Jagan; a second Cuba must not emerge. By early 1962, therefore, Jagan's enemies in the colony were aware that the American President was on their side. The PNC and UF therefore used the budget of February 1962 as a pretext for fomenting trouble: they mobilized African, Coloured and Portuguese resistance to Jagan's government in the capital Georgetown. A vast section of the commercial district was burnt down. It is noteworthy that Burnham was in favour of independence before the elections of August 1961; by early 1962, with the Americans on his side, he had changed his mind. He was prepared to use violence to make the place ungovernable. His aim was to delay a date for independence, which many had anticipated as forthcoming in May 1962. In fact, Jagan's government had printed a stamp for official documents that read: 'Freedom Year, 1962'.

Burnham's socialist pretensions and his craving for Third World credibility, however, had inhibited his capacity to initiate any form of subversion of Jagan's government. In late 1961 he was floundering. He was saved by the United Force and the Catholic Church, which were closely aligned and had been propagating a rabidly anti-communist crusade against Jagan. They did not prevaricate. Although their support base was smaller, they had a consistency of focus engendered by a hatred of Castro and 'godless communism'—the 'red peril'. In May 1961, for instance, the *Catholic Standard* observed that Jagan's government had never "uttered one breath of criticism of any of Castro's doings—to them, he is apparently perfect. It means that ... they support all of Castro's methods (as well as aims) in Cuba. Among these are: the denial of freedom; the destruction of free trade unions; suppression of the free press; mass arrests."[12] They also deemed Jagan an enemy of freedom of worship, as the paper cited, week after week, incidents of persecution of the Catholic Church in Cuba. The organ of the United Force, the *Sun*, and a daily newspaper largely owned by Peter D'Aguiar, leader of the Party, the *Daily Chronicle*, sustained a veritable ant-communist crusade against Jagan. They were clearly sustained by Jagan's declared admiration for Castro; they were also energized by the presence in the White House of the first Catholic President. This was the context, in early 1962, in which Burnham was resurrected. His socialist rhetoric notwithstanding, he dexterously exploited the virulent anti-communist passions of the Portuguese and Coloured minority in order to make British Guiana ungovernable. In the process, the Kennedy administration settled on him as their man. President Kennedy himself would put relentless pressure on Harold Macmillan to ensure that independence was not granted to Cheddi Jagan.

As Kennedy's chief political assistant, Professor Arthur Schlesinger, documented:

> [I]n May 1962 Burnham came to Washington. He appeared an intelligent, self-possessed, reasonable man, insisting quite firmly on his 'socialism' and 'neutralism' but stoutly anti-communist ... In the meantime, events had convinced us that Jagan though perhaps not a disciplined communist had that kind of deep pro-communist emotion ... [that] the United States could not afford ... when it involved a quasi-communist regime on the mainland of Latin America. Burnham's visit left the feeling, as I reported to the President [on 21 June 1962], that 'an independent British Guiana under Burnham ... would cause us many fewer problems than an independent British Guiana under Jagan'. And a way was open to bring it about because Jagan's parliamentary strength was larger than his popular strength ... An obvious solution would be to establish a system of proportional representation [PR]. This, after prolonged discussion, the British Government finally did in October 1963; and elections held ... at the end of 1964 produced a coalition government under Burnham. With much unhappiness and turbulence, British Guiana seemed to have passed safely out of the communist orbit.[13]

But Schlesinger had not told the whole tale: the machinations of the President and the CIA to ensure that their man, Forbes Burnham, would take Guyana to independence. Burnham, with the priceless support, also, of the Portuguese leader, Peter D'Aguiar, was now on the road to eclipsing Cheddi Jagan. By 1963 the CIA had got into the act, providing funds through diverse front organizations, to fight Jagan Government's Labour Relations Bill. It was a measure to empower the Minister of Labour to recommend a poll to resolve jurisdictional disputes between contending trade unions. The main reason, of course, was that although the overwhelming majority of the workers in the sugar industry were Indians, Jagan's supporters, they were still represented by a union, the Manpower Citizens' Association (MPCA), which the PPP deemed a company union that was collaborating with Burnham in subverting their government. They had founded their own union, the Guyana Agricultural Workers' Union (GAWU), and were seeking to get it recognized by a poll in the strategic sugar industry. If the Bill were passed, they would require two-thirds of the workers' votes to unseat the MPCA. The PNC and UF had found another issue for galvanizing more resistance to Jagan and delay independence. The Labour Relations Bill was framed as a pernicious measure to eliminate unions deemed enemies of the PPP—a threat to free trade unions. The first half of 1963 was marked by an 80-day general strike ostensibly against the Bill; it was sustained primarily with money from the CIA.[14]

The constitutional conference held in October 1962 had collapsed because the PNC and UF had stalled on all the contentious issues, knowing that the US was on their side. As in 1962 the aim was to delay independence further. The general strike of 1963 degenerated into racial violence throughout the colony. Apart from economic disaster, Africans and Indians were consumed by racial hatred and violence, even perpetrating 'ethnic cleansing' in some districts. This, in conjunction with the destruction of most of the commercial section of Georgetown the previous year, provided President Kennedy with the ammunition he needed to pressure the British to delay independence and to change the electoral system to proportional representation, which, as Schlesinger had argued, was bound to secure the defeat of Jagan.

Kennedy met Macmillan in England on 30 June 1963: the destruction of Cheddi Jagan was the principal item on the agenda. The President made his case forthrightly:

> It was obvious if the UK were to get rid of British Guiana now it would become a communist state. He thought the thing to do was to look for ways to drag the thing out [no immediate independence] ... He [argued] that Latin America was the most dangerous area in the world. The effect of having a communist state in British Guiana in addition to Cuba in 1964 [the Presidential elections], would be to create irresistible pressures on the United States to strike militarily at Cuba.[15]

Coming after the Cuban missiles crisis of October 1962 and the consuming fear that the world was on the brink of nuclear war, Kennedy's pressure to get rid of Jagan, which the British had hitherto sought to deflect with much conviction, now carried the force of a moral imperative.

In delaying independence, Kennedy counselled that they should rationalize it as a necessity to prevent the "unleashing of racial war", not because of the "danger of British Guiana becoming communist". The President was adamant that Cuba would be the major issue in the elections of 1964; and that "adding British Guiana to Cuba could well tip the scales, and someone would be elected who would take military action against Cuba".[16] He was alluding to Barry Goldwater, known for his ultra right-wing views on communism. The British acquiesced: they would delay independence and impose a solution changing the electoral system to proportional representation. But, having suspended the constitution in 1953, they were wary about repeating the exercise ten years later. They therefore decided to hatch a plot, knowing that Jagan's enemies would again stall on all the outstanding issues. In fact, Duncan Sandys, Secretary of State for the Colonies, was anxious for Burnham to spurn Jagan's initiative to get him to enter a coalition, prior to the conference. Burnham was an astute politician; Sandys need not have worried.

Prior to the convening of the constitutional conference in October 1963, Burnham left no stone unturned. He sought to allay whatever lingering doubts the Catholic Church and the UF still harboured about his socialist rhetoric. In August 1963 the *Catholic Standard* felt reassured that there was blue water between Burnham's PNC and Jagan's PPP: "The statement by the PNC that the Party's brand of socialism is very different from the communism of the PPP is welcome indeed. There has, to our mind, been a distressing ambiguity in the past about the PNC's policy, and we are very glad they have come out with a forthright statement."[17]

At the second constitutional conference, in October 1963, after the predicted deadlock had eventuated, Jagan was tricked into signing a document prepared by Sandys, empowering him to be the sole adjudicator on all the outstanding issues. Sandys persuaded Jagan to go to the conference alone on the fatal day when the trick would be perpetrated. He complied and although he encountered Burnham and D'Aguiar at the conference venue—with their teams of advisers intact—an undiscerning Jagan thought nothing was untoward. He was the first to sign the deceptive document, lured by the illusion that even if he did not win on the electoral system (staving off proportional representation [PR]) and the voting age (he wanted it reduced to 18), a date for independence would surely be fixed as a quid pro quo.

The illusion of a commitment to early independence was not detected by Jagan because of the skilful construction of the sentence in the second paragraph of the document below, dated 25 October 1963 (I cite it with emphasis.) Read quickly, and bereft of legal scrutiny, it lends itself to the interpretation that an imposition by Sandys would **not** delay independence. It is arguable, too, that the fact that Jagan certainly had no part in its composition and therefore warranted his circumspection, was diluted by the phrase: 'we are agreed'—**not** 'we have agreed'. Jagan was ignorant of Kennedy's machinations and the fact that the British were now unreservedly committed to his removal before independence:

TO THE SECRETARY OF STATE FOR THE COLONIES

At your request we have made further efforts to resolve the differences between us on the constitutional issues which require to be settled before British Guiana secures independence, in particular the electoral system, the voting age and the question of whether fresh elections should be held before independence.

We regret to have to report to you that we have not succeeded in reaching agreement; and we have reluctantly come to the conclusion that there is no prospect of an agreed solution. **Another adjournment of the Conference for further discussions between ourselves would therefore serve no useful purpose and would result in further delaying British Guiana's independence and in continued uncertainty in the country**.

In these circumstances **we are agreed** to ask the British Government to settle on their authority all outstanding constitutional issues, and we undertake to accept these decisions [emphasis added].[18]

Jagan was the first to sign because, as he explained before Sandys announced his decision, he was "assuming that independence was obviously forthcoming". He had found the PNC and UF "very unreasonable", and faced with the futility of the situation—broken by the unrelenting chaos of 1962–63—he had opted for an imposition. Even among his supporters, it was rumoured that the alleged infidelity of his wife, Janet, had undermined his capacity for rational judgement—not one of his strengths in any case, entranced as he was by his Marxist certainties. (She had said: "I am surprised they agreed to sign.")[19] Yet he trusted the evil imperialists: "I have put my confidence in the hands of the British Government and I hope decisions will be taken on the basis of constitutional principles, on British and Commonwealth precedents and conventions ... Independence is absolutely necessary ... for the country cannot get anywhere without it." He noted, without grasping the subtlety of the Machiavellian mind, that Burnham had initially refused to sign but fell in after D'Aguiar had done so.[20]

Jagan would soon be bitterly disappointed. Adhering to Kennedy's request, Duncan Sandys changed the electoral system to proportional representation, just under a month before the President was assassinated. He kept the voting age at 21, and stated that a date for independence **would not** be fixed until new elections were held under PR.

Burnham was the victor. Violence had paid off. Jagan's end was assured. There was no way he could secure a majority under PR. He called for "a hurricane of protests" to get the British to revoke their iniquitous decision. He argued that he was not bound to abide by Sandys's ruling "because independence was a condition of his imposing a solution". It was a "betrayal of trust". Belatedly, he recognized the foundation of the trick for which he had fallen: "It is clear that the decision is in keeping with the wishes of the American Government and is subservient to it ... The machinations of the Imperialists cannot destroy the PPP. I call upon the people of Guyana to stand firm in this hour of betrayal."[21] He realized that his enemies were rewarded for their violence; he would now seek to retaliate, to stall new elections scheduled for late 1964 from being held. It was a step inspired by despair. He knew that freedom would soon be the gift of his enemies.

Burnham, ever the slick manipulator, pretended that he was offended by their having asked their colonial masters to adjudicate on the unresolved issues. He claimed that this was an abrogation of the spirit of independence. Having drawn victory out of the jaws of defeat, he was basking in his good luck with feigned regret, while dancing on Jagan's humiliation: "I am pleased about nothing. A nationalist can never be pleased over the indignity of an imposition. We find no reason for jubilation because British Guiana is without a firm date for independence ... Perhaps ... [Jagan] should rethink his naïve statement in which he expressed great confidence in the British sense of fair-play and justice ... I agree with Dr Jagan that the people of British Guiana should stand firm in this hour of betrayal—of them by him."[22] It was, indeed, a magnificent "indignity"!

Then, typically, gloating from his self-assured intellectual and political stature over Jagan, he mocked him, noting that he had told the BBC he reposed "great faith in the sense of justice and fair-play of the British". He rubbed it in, assuming his legal persona:

> If the Premier is the expert on the wicked machinations of the Imperialists, why did he concede this *volte-face*? ... Let me concede, as a lawyer would, that the proposition is correct and that the US Government was particularly interested in the outcome of the conference and preferred a particular outcome so far as the electoral system is concerned. Is it not naïve of the same Dr Jagan who says that the US Government would be interested in a particular outcome, to entrust

the political future and the destiny of this country to the greatest friend of the US Government?[23]

I have written elsewhere of Burnham's mockery of Jagan's ignominy—of the Indians' impending fall:

> More of this studied ridicule was to emanate from the sagacious brain of this master manipulator. In February 1964 he told a mammoth crowd in Georgetown of his efforts (a spurious ... [claim]) to reach an agreement with Jagan, 'before the fateful document was signed'. He jeered: '[S]ome people have learnt to write ... they had a pen and there was ink!' This was especially galling—provocatively evocative of the barely lettered Indian, the *arriviste* 'coolie' pitted against the African scribe.[24]

Jagan launched a well-publicized march by his Indian supporters throughout the coastland of Guyana, to protest the British trickery. He then called a strike for recognition of his union, the GAWU, as the sole bargaining agent for sugar workers. It soon degenerated into virtual civil war between Africans and Indians. Nothing could change the fact that Burnham was on the way to gaining the prize that Jagan thought was rightly his. D'Aguiar tagged along with Burnham, reluctantly: he was the lesser of two evils. Both he and Jagan were on a journey to nowhere: the exodus of the Portuguese and Coloureds had begun; so too the Indians.

Jagan, in despair, bemoaned in a radio broadcast on 30 May 1964 that the Opposition had been "recompensed" by the British. He who had toiled for freedom had it stolen from him. Their "illegal and unconstitutional activities yielded them rich rewards"; all he had fought for "now hangs in the balance":

> Factional strife strides the land and our movement lies divided and weak. For many years, while others spent their time and leisure in the pursuit of wealth or pleasure and frivolity, I tread every nook and cranny of our wide country preaching the gospel of nationalism and freedom and seeking to infuse in our diverse groups a Guyanese consciousness which would transcend the bonds of race and creed ... Today ... my hopes of national unity have been cast in the dust ... I wish to appeal for the end of racial strife. Racial antagonism is not deeply rooted in this country. But it can easily become so if it is not promptly removed.[25]

He did not know his country's history; very little had been written at the time. Racial insecurity was endemic, and with the ascendancy of Indians after the Second World War, of which his own rise was symptomatic, African suspicion of the motives of Indians was chronic. It was the major factor inhibiting the pursuit of a national identity. Jagan's Marxism was deeply rooted in his aversion to Booker's dominance of the colony's plantation economy. Jagan was an Indian from the plantation. His whole anti-colonial stance, inspired by the nationalist movement in India, had blossomed in this soil of hatred for the 'sugar gods'. It had no resonance, however, with the African people in British Guiana. They were, strangely, not anti-colonial because they thought the end of colonialism would open the floodgates to Indian domination.

Eusi Kwayana elaborates on the pitfalls of a national consciousness in this polyglot colony:

> I lived among very poor [African] people all my life. They were very political. I knew they had a lot of ethnic suspicion although nobody wanted any racial confrontation; that was not there then, not mature enough. **But I knew [also] that they hadn't strong feelings against colonialism—no strong feelings against colonialism—or against Booker because of their monopoly or their treatment of people ... The whole idea of rejecting Britain was not very firm.** Indians had it a lot firmer because of the Indian nationalist movement. They had a kind of ideological and cultural resentment against colonialism ... [They were exposed to] people coming from India to lecture. Africans did not have this. The link was broken [emphasis added].[26]

Jagan lost the elections under PR on 7 December 1964. Burnham and D'Aguiar formed a coalition government, as expected. The communist Jagan, as the Americans had planned it, was now ousted. He was impotent; he had squandered his trumps, having been lavished with them up to the end of 1961. Relieved of responsibility, he embarked on a regime of nihilistic tactics, characterized by the boycotting of crucial events. He refused to enter the House of Assembly because several of his Party's members were still in detention, Burnham's pretext being that this was in the interest of national security. He boycotted the International Commission of Jurists in 1965, on grounds that their terms of reference were too broad. He had asked for the redressing of racial imbalance in the security forces; the government decided that the question of racial imbalance would be explored in all its dimensions. He boycotted the crucial constitutional conference in November 1965 when the British government duly granted independence to the Burnham-D'Aguiar coalition. Jagan explained his absence as a protest against the violence and deceit fomented to ensure that the prize was awarded to the lackeys of imperialism. He told the BBC: "I do not wish to lend support to the formal promulgation of decisions already taken [independence] which are gravely inimical to the interests of the Guianese people."[27] The date for independence was fixed for 26 May 1966. Jagan also boycotted the visit of the Queen to Guyana in February 1966. The reason: "solidarity with the 4,000,000 Africans in Rhodesia ... now suffering from white minority rule" under Ian Smith. The PPP accused Her Majesty's Government of "lacking in its duty to Africans to crush the rebellion [Smith's unilateral declaration of independence]".[28]

Percy Armstrong, a veteran anti-PPP columnist, reflected on the implications of the boycotts. His views were congruent with those of Burnham:

> All this means that the forthcoming celebrations, like those of the Queen's visit, will be largely a celebration of Africans, while people of the Indian community will perhaps huddle themselves in their homes, peeping through creases and cracks and giving furtive glances over their shoulders to see whether terrorists from amongst them ... are lurking in the rear ... The main aim behind all these

boycotts is to convert the Indian community into a dissident group which will become an irritant in the body politic of the newly independent state of Guyana, to be used like putty by the Communist international organisations.[29]

Jagan's reaction to Burnham's winning the prize of freedom was to veer outrageously to the left, claiming the ideological high ground—authentic Marxism, which in the long run was bound to supersede the moribund pro-imperialist and capitalist stance of the PNC-UF coalition. Jagan was setting himself up for terminal marginalization: long-term irrelevance and exclusion from power. He had boycotted the Independence Conference in London, but he attended the Tri-continental Conference in Havana, from 3–15 January 1966, where long-term revolutionary tactics against American imperialism were debated. In March 1966 the organ of the PPP, *Thunder*, made it clear that they were combatants in the Cold War and that America was not only Cuba's enemy, it was theirs also. Kennedy and Sandys were vindicated:

> The delegates had, above all, a clear-cut objective—how in the face of a ruthless and immoral enemy to unite all the progressive forces for simultaneous confrontation ... The establishment of a tri-continental organisation with provisional headquarters in Havana, Cuba, and a continental (Latin American) organisation was a stunning blow to US imperialism. Cuba represents to the national liberation movements two symbols. Firstly, the symbol of a small country successfully confronting the giant colossus of the north and exploding the myth of US omnipotence and invincibility. Secondly, a symbol of ideological unity. The Cuban Revolution encompasses in a brief period revolutionary nationalism, socialism and communism.[30]

Jagan had played into Burnham's hands. He kept 17 PPP activists in detention, arguing, erroneously, that they were agents of communist subversion trained in Cuba. The Burnham government continually renewed the state of emergency on grounds that it was an imperative necessitated by the subversive programme of Jagan's PPP. In fact Guyana became independent in May 1966 with the state of emergency still in place. In January of that year Dr P. A. Reid, the Deputy Prime Minister, speaking in the House of Assembly on the rationale for extending the emergency, observed: "We want to make it known that this Government has no one detained for political reasons. They are not political detainees. If we lift the emergency, we have no control over the movement of explosives which is the basis of the trouble." He was astutely defining them as terrorists precisely at the time Jagan was attending the Tri-continental Conference.[31]

In April 1966 Prime Minister Burnham sought to reinforce the government's projection of the PPP as an organization committed to subversion: "When lawlessness prevails Government must exercise control of the source from which senseless and irresponsible acts are inspired ... PPP member Dr Ramsahoye ... described the extension of the emergency as a disgrace for a country going into independence ... It is not for those who participated in Tri-continental conferences to criticise actions by the state, permitted by the constitution and aimed at protecting the community at large."[32]

Shortly afterwards, Jagan announced that the slogan of the PPP for the Independence celebrations was: "Independence Yes! Celebrations No!" He explained the rationale:

The PPP opposed the fraudulent constitutional arrangements which resulted in its removal from the government in 1964. It did not take part in the rigged constitutional talks in London in November 1965. And it was not consulted on the date for independence. The party's attitude to the independence celebrations is therefore coupled with mixed feelings. On the one hand it is happy that on May 26 our Guyana flag will replace the Union Jack, that we will have our own national anthem and coat-of-arms. But independence has meaning for us not only in symbolic terms. Above all we want also the substance of independence. The substance has been denied the Guyanese people. For the following reasons, we cannot celebrate independence. Firstly, full powers have been transferred to the puppets of the imperialists [the PNC and the UF] by a rigged constitutional arrangement. Secondly, the imperialists who have a stranglehold on our economy are being further strengthened. Thirdly, independence is being ushered in under a state of emergency. The main purpose is to silence the political opposition and to intimidate the working class. Fourthly, on independence day comrades who have fought vigorously for independence during the course of several years will be in detention.[33]

Jagan and his son did attend the flag-raising ceremony at midnight on 26 May 1966. That was the totality of their participation. But they certainly were not planning to subvert the government. The truth is they were clueless. They would now seek the moral high ground, claiming that they were the true practitioners of a pure Marxism: the source of genuine liberation and independence. But it was indicative of their impotence rather than their commitment to revolution. Even the anti-communist *Weekend Post and Sunday Argosy* observed that the tendency to project on to the PPP subversive motives after Independence was an exaggeration; it was beyond their capacity even when they were in power.[34] But Burnham would return continually to the question of violence and the PPP, using the 'Tricontinental stick' to give credence to his assertions, in the absence of concrete evidence that they were fomenting revolution. Jagan's revolutionary rhetoric notwithstanding, the accusation against the PPP had a ring of fantasy. In June 1966 Burnham addressed Jagan:

If ... [he] genuinely wishes to unify our peoples and insure their future happiness and well-being, he can readily do this by openly renouncing, once and for all, his penchant for looking outside our borders for solutions to the nation's problems: by renouncing violence, subversion and armed conflict which he affirmed in his recent utterances at the Tri-continental Conference in Havana; by henceforth ceasing to send his supporters and representatives abroad for 'ideological orientation' and financial assistance; by halting the training of his followers in guerrilla warfare, the manufacture of bombs and by openly giving up his ambitions as an international communist leader.[35]

Jagan had been in office for seven years, from 1957 to 1964. If he were not imprisoned by his communist dogmas, Burnham could never have got anywhere near the big prize. Jagan was an honest man, but a poor politician. He published his autobiography on the eve of Guyana's independence in May 1966. It was grandiloquently titled: *The West on Trial: My Fight for Guyana's Freedom*. Richard Gott, reviewing it for the *Guardian*, wrote: "Unfortunately for him, his arrogance, intolerance and political misjudgement made him an easy target for criticism ... [even] from those who were not predisposed to believe that he was a communist". David Holden, reviewing it in the *Sunday Times*, was less charitable: "[I]ts author is an inept politician, with an inflated sense of his own importance, a garrulous pen (and tongue) and a thoroughly woolly mind."[36]

Jagan would remain in opposition for 28 years as Burnham, having got rid of the United Force, proceeded to rig all the elections between 1968 and 1985, with the connivance of the United States. Meanwhile he had stolen all Jagan's clothes: he adopted the bulk of what Jagan considered his Marxist programme, including nationalisation of 80% of the economy, an anti-American posture and "fraternal relations" with Cuba and the USSR. Yet Jagan remained loyal to his comrades in the Kremlin. Confronted with a choice between Jagan and Burnham, the United States still opted for the latter, even if its aid dried up. Yet Jagan could not see the folly of his actions. On the 25th anniversary of the PPP, in 1975, he revisited his years in government, between 1957 and 1964. What he had to say was pure fantasy:

[O]nly fools who do nothing make no mistakes. The main burden of their attack is that we should not have openly espoused Marxism and given support to the Cuban Revolution. What they fail to note is that had we not taken a firm patriotic position, a world-view [Marxism-Leninism] ... we would not have been able to win over the masses [presumably Africans: a fantasy!] from the traitors and collaborators [Burnham's PNC] ... The mistake we made was not the espousal of Marxism; it was that we did not fully implement it in practice. The PPP was a party geared to winning elections ... It was not until 1961 that we established an ideological school, and only in 1969 that we took a decision to transform our loose mass party into a disciplined Marxist-Leninist party. One of the difficulties encountered was that ... there was not enough personnel to man both the government and party administration at the same time. The result was that party work suffered while we were marking time in government without power and being sabotaged at the same time. The mistake we made was to have given priority to government rather than the party, staying in the government too long without independence, assuming responsibility without real power, and thereby undermining our influence, cutting the ground from under our feet.[37]

Burnham ensured that Jagan had 28 years, from 1964 to 1992, for nothing but 'party work'!

Forty-two years after Guyana was granted independence, it remains a poor, backward, racially polarized, country, its African and Indian peoples still defining themselves primarily by their ethnic identity. Guyana is still not a nation, and with more than half its population having migrated to the United States, Canada, the

UK, the islands of the Caribbean, anywhere that would have them, the country has lost its best and brightest: all the progressive Portuguese and the original Chinese communities, most of the able Indians and Africans. The population has, in fact, declined from the early 1970s, when it was estimated at about 815,000; today it is under 800,000. In my village in the East Canje district of Berbice, over 80% of the original inhabitants have gone. Of 60 or 70 of us who completed secondary school, at Queen's College in 1968, I am not aware of a single one who still resides there. The British had created a number of first-rate secondary schools, so it was common for people of a certain age in the former British West Indies, those born during the Second Word War or in the decade or so after it, to speak of their contemporaries from Guyana with awe: generally they were, intellectually, seen as a crop above others. The quality of the education was a prime factor, but the environmental hazards of the place, its daunting hydrological problems, were also a significant element in the shaping of its peoples. The difficulty of reclaiming the land bred a partiality for education; it also bred an instinct to escape: geographical and psychological. This was exacerbated by its racial and political futility. The fatal fantasies of Jagan and Burnham are of a piece. As V. S. Naipaul pointed out in 1991: "Guyana has always been a land of fantasy. It was the land of El Dorado." (see note 7)

As early as midnight 26 May 1966, with most Indo-Guyanese, at the behest of Cheddi Jagan, boycotting the Independence celebrations, it was clear that while Guyana was terminating its colonial links with Britain a nation was still to be born. A Guyanese nation remains elusive.

Notes

1. This quote is from the Labour Party's Patrick Gordon Walker, cited in Cheddi Jagan, *The West on Trial: My Fight for Guyana's Freedom* (London: Michael Joseph, 1966), p. 202.
2. See http://jagan.org/articles: US declassified documents 1964–8.
3. See Cary Fraser, *Ambivalent Anti-Colonialism: The United States and the Genesis of West Indian Independence, 1940–64* (Westport, CT: Greenwood Press, 1994); Cheddi Jagan, *The West on Trial*; my *Sweetening 'Bitter Sugar': Jock Campbell, the Booker Reformer in British Guiana, 1934–66* (Kingston, Jamaica: Ian Randle Publishers, 2005); Thomas J. Spinner, *A Political and Social History of Guyana, 1945–83* (Boulder, CO: Westview Press, 1983); and Maurice St Pierre, *Anatomy of Resistance: Anti-Colonialism in Guyana, 1823–1966* (London; Macmillan, 1999).
4. *Report of the British Guiana Constitutional Commission, 1954* (Sir James Robertson, chairman), Cmd. 9274 (London: Her Majesty's Stationery Office, 1954), p. 37.
5. Interview with Eusi Kwayana, Georgetown, Guyana, 22 September 1992.
6. *Ibid.*
7. V. S. Naipaul, 'A Handful of Dust: Return to Guiana', *New York Review of Books*, 11 April 1991, p. 18.
8. CO1031/3907 [National Archives], Copy of a translation of the interview of Dr Cheddi Jagan with the newspaper, *Revolucion* [Havana], September 1960.
9. *Ibid.*
10. CO1031/4177 [National Archives], Cheddi Jagan, 'Towards Understanding ... ', Text of an Address to the National Press Club, Washington, DC, USA, 14 October 1961.
11. CO1031/4177 [National Archives], Cheddi Jagan on 'Meet the Press' [transcript of the interview], 15 October 1961.
12. Leader, *Catholic Standard*, 5 May 1961.
13. Arthur M. Schlesinger, *A Thousand Days: John F. Kennedy in the White House* (London: Andre Deutsch, 1965), pp. 668–669.

14. For the role of the CIA in British Guiana, see 'Foreign Relations, 1964–8, Vol. XXXII, Dominican Republic; Cuba; Haiti; Guyana'. It may be accessed from:http://www.guyana.org/govt/US-declassified-documents-1964–1968.html.
15. US Government [Department of State], Meeting of Kennedy and Macmillan, Birch Grove, England, 30 June 1963.
16. *Ibid.*
17. Leader, *Catholic Standard*, 23 August 1963.
18. *British Guiana Constitutional Conference, 1963,* Cmd. 2203, November 1963.
19. *Daily Chronicle*, 26 October 1963.
20. *Ibid.*
21. *Daily Chronicle*, 1 November 1963.
22. *Ibid.*
23. *Guiana Graphic*, 20 February 1964.
24. See my *Sweetening 'Bitter Sugar'*, p. 571. The quote from Burnham is taken from the *Guiana Graphic*, 9 February 1964.
25. *Mirror*, 31 May 1964.
26. Interview with Eusi Kwayana, Georgetown, Guyana, 22 September 1992. The quote is reproduced from my 'The Anatomy of Cheddi Jagan's Marxism', in John La Guerre and Ann Marie Bissessar (eds), *Calcutta to Caroni and the Indian Diaspora,* 3rd ed. (St Augustine, Trinidad: The University of the West Indies, School of Continuing Studies, 2005), p. 452.
27. *Mirror*, 5 November 1965.
28. *Mirror*, 26 January 1966.
29. *Weekend Post and Sunday Argosy*, 8 May 1966.
30. See 'The Havana Conference: New Stage in the Struggle against Colonialism, Neo-Colonialism and Imperialism', *Thunder*, March 1966.
31. *New Nation*, 16 January 1966.
32. *New Nation*, 3 April 1966.
33. See 'Message from Party Leader: Independence Yes! Celebrations No!', *Thunder*, April 1966.
34. *Weekend Post and Sunday Argosy*, 3 April 1966.
35. *Sunday Chronicle*, 5 June 1966.
36. *Sunday Chronicle*, 3 July 1966.
37. See 'Address Delivered to the 25th Anniversary Conference on behalf of the Central Committee of the People's Progressive Party, by the General Secretary, Dr Cheddi Jagan, 3 August 1975', *Thunder*, September–December, 1975, pp. 3–35.

Freedom at Midnight: A Microcosm of Zimbabwe's Hopes and Dreams at Independence, April 1980

SUE ONSLOW
International History Department, London School of Economics and Political Science, London, UK

"*You have given me the jewel of Africa.*" Robert Mugabe to Ian Smith, 3 March 1980

At midnight of 17–18 April 1980, in the Rufaro football stadium packed with foreign dignitaries, former Rhodesian civil servants and security personnel, government ministers, journalists and excited Zimbabweans, the Union Jack was lowered and the new flag of internationally recognised Zimbabwe was raised. Under the eyes of the international press, world leaders had gathered in Salisbury.[1] These representatives from over 100 countries included Indira Gandhi, the Prime Minister of India; the Presidents of Pakistan and Nigeria; Seretse Kharma of Botswana, Kenneth Kaunda of Zambia; a leading and sizeable Soviet and Cuban delegation; Andrew Young, US President Jimmy Carter's envoy to the United Nations 1977–79; Kurt Waldheim, the UN Secretary General (before the scandal of the revelations of his Austrian SS past); Lord Carrington, and, representing the Queen, Prince Charles. Who was not there? Mrs Thatcher and the South African Prime Minister, P. W. Botha.

As Robert Mugabe, the newly elected Prime Minister (representing ZANU(PF)), went forward to receive the insignia of office from Prince Charles, a mighty roar went up from the crowd. It was an extraordinarily emotional moment: those there laughingly recall that if the stadium had had a roof, it would have been blown off. This was the culmination of the long and tortuous path to independence: from the arrival of Cecil Rhodes' Pioneer column in the 1890s, the period of settler capitalism of the quasi-autonomous colony of Southern Rhodesia from 1923 to 1953, participation in the ill-fated Central African Federation, the era of the Rhodesian unilateral declaration of independence (UDI) rebellion, and the short-lived Internal Settlement of 1978, which had seen the election of Bishop Abel Muzorewa as Zimbabwe/Rhodesia's first black premier. Lord Carrington and his team, and the understated governorship of Christopher Soames and his aides, appeared to have done the impossible: Britain had overseen the final peaceful transition of her former colony to internationally recognized independence, based on universal franchise in freely contested elections. The hope was that the long and bloody civil war which had cost so many lives, wounded many more, deeply traumatised Rhodesian/Zimbabwean society, and poisoned regional peace and stability, was finally over. The dream was a multiracial, prosperous and peaceful society for all. This, then, to my mind, encapsulates that moment at Midnight for Zimbabwe:

Appearances, Hopes and Dreams

Appearances

What HAD finally led to that moment? Understanding the immediate historical hinterland helps to explain the intensity and swirl of emotions in that football stadium on that night of 17–18 April. First, there is the background of the civil war in Rhodesia/Zimbabwe. By 1979 all sides in the civil war—Robert Mugabe and radical elements in Zimbabwe African National Union (ZANU(PF)) and its military wing, Zimbabwe African National Liberation Army (ZANLA), Nkomo's Zimbabwe African People's Union (ZAPU) and Zimbabwe Independent People's Revolutionary Army (ZIPRA) and the Rhodesian Security Forces (now the official army of Bishop Abel Muzorewa's United African National Congress (UANC), through the Government of National Unity, GNU)—honestly believed that military victory was possible. But their external patrons were weary—particularly South Africa, Zambia and Mozambique. Bishop Muzorewa's attempt at indigenous nationalist rule through collaboration with Ian Smith's Rhodesia Front regime had manifestly failed either to secure domestic tranquillity, or international acceptance.[2] This was despite concerted efforts by the GNU to solicit support from American private and Congressional opinion, and associated British Conservative backbench pressure on the minority government of James Callaghan, for the lifting of international economic sanctions. President Carter's resolute refusal to give in to Congressional opinion (spearheaded by Senator Jesse Helmes) that sanctions should be lifted was an important consideration for the incoming Thatcher government in May 1979. The new Foreign Secretary, Peter Carrington, also recognised the need to broaden the base of the Rhodesian/Zimbabwe peace settlement—otherwise the civil war would simply continue, with disastrous consequences for regional stability.

Furthermore, despite increasing financial, military logistical and material support from the South Africans[3] with whom it had signed a Total National Strategy document in March 1979, the GNU had failed to resolve the deepening security crisis in the country—although the Rhodesian security forces were convinced they could still win. With ZIPRA forces being trained in Angola, Botswana and Zambia (using Cuban training, and sophisticated weaponry from the Soviet Union), ZANLA fighters infiltrating the eastern districts from neighbouring Mozambique (using Maoist three tier strategy techniques), by August 1979 the Rhodesian Security forces had lost control of most of the rural districts. Although the Conservatives' election manifesto had raised hopes that a Conservative government would extend crucial recognition to the GNU as it had been based on the election process (even if the Patriotic Front had not participated in the Rhodesian election in April 1979), Carrington came to see the Rhodesia situation as a fundamentally negative drain on British foreign policy and political standing; and crucially, marshalling all his charm and political and foreign-policy experience, managed to persuade his Prime Minister of the logic of his reasoning.

The final transition to negotiated armistice, then renewed elections, had been achieved in stages: first at the Lusaka Conference in August 1979, where there had been initial fears for the safety of the Queen, then for the personal safety of Mrs Thatcher (who arrived wearing dark glasses as she fully expected acid to be thrown in her face). This Commonwealth Heads of Government Meeting (CHOGM) was an extraordinary, and unlikely, triumph. This was thanks to a key caucus of Commonwealth leaders, principally Commonwealth Secretary-General 'Sonny' Ramphal, Kenneth Kaunda, Malcolm Fraser of Australia and Michael Manley of Jamaica, who supported Britain's willingness to hold a constitutional conference and secure a negotiated transfer to recognised independence. Mrs Thatcher's acceptance of this approach, which went against her emotional judgement, and sustained political support for Carrington's subsequent negotiations, was a key element in containing vociferous Conservative backbench criticism back in London. Then pressure behind the scenes from President Machel of Mozambique and his extremely able spokesperson, Fernando Honwara, and the Cuban government, persuaded the Patriotic Front to attend the London discussions. The process of hard-fought negotiations at Lancaster House, between the various delegations, and Peter Carrington's small and dedicated negotiating team, survived the three great crises of the conference: the constitution; the transitional arrangements; and finally, the ceasefire itself. The crucial land question was deliberately excluded from the Lancaster House deliberations; here again the good offices of 'Sonny' Ramphal (much to Carrington's irritation) were of vital importance in reaching agreement on the phrasing of the relevant clauses, which allowed for the degree of necessary ambiguity. Key financial backing for land restitution (although the exact sum could not be specified for fear of antagonising Congress) was promised by the Carter administration. Final acceptance of the ceasefire arrangements was only finally resolved when Carrington and Thatcher were en route to the United States, and Christopher Soames, the newly appointed Governor of Rhodesia/Zimbabwe, was in the air on his way to Zimbabwe/Rhodesia.

Lancaster House had been possible because each political party, with its own sizeable army, believed it could triumph through the ballot box. So, equally important in the process of final transference of independence, was the period of the Soames' governorship and the arrangement of new elections. The signs were not promising: there was the death of Josiah Tongogara, the ZANLA military commander, on Christmas Day in a car crash in Mozambique.[4] Then the Governor and his small team discovered that "far from being over, the war had developed a new intensity as ZIPRA and ZANLA tried to get the bulk of their forces in Zambia and Mozambique into Rhodesia and the Rhodesians responded with ferocious cross-border raids".[5] (The British estimated that approximately 2–3000 ZANLA combatants remained in the field, but in reality, ZANLA kept approximately 7000 men outside the assembly points.[6]) There was detailed knowledge of the extent of violence and intimidation in the run up to the March elections—threats, mutilation, abduction, murder (one ZAPU parliamentary candidate was last seen having red-hot coals forced down his throat, whilst Mugabe survived an assassination attempt, undoubtedly organized by Rhodesian security forces, and their South African counterparts, who also used explosions/attacks on civilian targets to discredit ZANU(PF). Mutterings about the widespread intimidation of rural constituencies by Mugabe's militants, who had used the lightly guarded assembly points as bases to target the surrounding communities, were matched by knowledge of atrocities by the Rhodesian security forces to discredit ZANU(PF). There were no innocents. Soames was faced with the unenviable task of turning a blind eye to the scale of ZANU(PF) election abuses, for barring Mugabe's party from participating in the forthcoming poll would destroy the chances of final peace and ensure the civil war continued.[7]

Against British expectations, Robert Mugabe won a landslide victory. The British had anticipated—indeed, expected—a victory by Joshua Nkomo, or at least a Nkomo-Muzorewa bloc. Peter Carrington's office in the Foreign Office in London operated an unofficial sweepstake. But only one person had predicted Mugabe's triumph, and the winner was a junior Foreign Office official with responsibility for Europe. Carrington's apocryphal comment was: "Bloody typical. The person who knows the least about Rhodesia!" As Sonny Ramphal had warned, the Zimbabwean people had voted for self-government, not good government.

This was the moment of maximum danger. Most in the Rhodesian white community were stunned. As soon as the evidence started to accumulate of a substantial poll for Mugabe, "attempts began to be made among the other parties to form some kind of anti-ZANU coalition".[8] But it became evident that ZANU(PF) had an absolute majority of the 80 African seats, and the host of international observers felt that the elections had been overwhelmingly fair. Although all election observers felt that the degree of intimidation did not invalidate the result, the Rhodesian military did not agree: Government House in Salisbury was all too aware of the sense of outrage among middle-ranking officers, and the dangers of a military coup. There were indeed those in the Rhodesian security forces who were actively planning for a coup should Mugabe win. With the pass word 'Tally Ho the Fox', the plan was to attack and destroy the main combatant assembly points—lightly guarded by a token Commonwealth force. (There were ominous, lurid instances of slaughtering of cocks—the insignia of ZANU(PF)—and their blood being daubed on the walls). These plans were scotched by a crucial lack of support by the Rhodesian police leadership, the lack of South African political backing, and General Walls himself, who clearly saw that it would be suicide as Rhodesia would be completely isolated in the international community. Walls had attempted to get the election result disavowed—and sent a telegram to Thatcher asking her to overturn the election result. He did not get the result he wanted. Walls had also visited Mozambique the day before the poll began—at the instigation of Fernando Honwara, Machel's crucial spokesman at the Lancaster House period. Thanks to the mediation of the Mozambique government, Walls and Mugabe also began the process of integration of the three military forces: the decision to begin training of a ZIPRA and ZANLA battalion by the Rhodesian Army at Essexvale Barracks outside Bulawayo, was taken immediately before the general election, specifically to initiate the imperative process of military integration. For their part, these

Rhodesian officers believed that Britain had embarked on a deliberate campaign of psychological profiling to ensure that the three key personalities in the Rhodesian armed forces were effectively neutralized. Ken Flower, the Director of the Central Intelligence Organization, strongly advised against a military coup; and the feeling was that Smith strongly disapproved—although this was hearsay, it was very important in containing the situation.

The other vital consideration was that the Rhodesian middle-ranking officers, and Walls, did not have South African backing. Indeed, woven all through the tale of Rhodesian/Zimbabwean independence is the attitude and behaviour of Pretoria: it is fair to say that South Africa was 'Banquo's ghost' at the independence celebrations. The British government was very well aware of the presence of substantial numbers of South African troops still in Rhodesia. The South Africans, who had invested heavily in terms of Muzorewa's electioneering expenses, training for Rhodesian auxiliary forces, and weaponry, had approximately 6000 troops in the country—although the South African Government was also spreading its bets to cover financial support for the veteran nationalist leader, Reverend Ndabaningi Sithole. Botha and his colleagues were stunned by the poll result. The State Security Council minutes make this clear. But the 'securocrats' in Pretoria—the military/intelligence nexus that dominated South African foreign policy by the beginning of the 1980s—realized that overt military intervention was simply a non-starter. But an immediate offer was made to the Rhodesian Selous Scouts of positions in the South African counter-insurgency forces/intelligence. Most accepted this.

So this was the very volatile, indeed explosive situation in Zimbabwe/Rhodesia in mid-March and mid-April 1980, and that moment at midnight was 'a close run thing'. The failure of the putschists' plans, did not mean plain sailing between March and April 1980. Mugabe's reception at Government House by Soames the day after the announcement of the election result, was an important gesture of reconciliation. So too was Mugabe's request to Soames to stay on as Governor until official Independence Day. Mugabe's meeting with Smith similarly impressed the veteran Rhodesian political leader, whose views percolated down through the white community of hope of non-retribution and mature government.

The sense of palpable relief that the Rhodesian military had not intervened, that the South African forces (and their weaponry) were withdrawing, together with Mugabe's gestures of reconciliation (Walls was asked to stay on as Commander of the new Zimbabwean Army, and to oversee the process of integration), helps to explain the particular intensity of feeling at the moment of transition to independence.

For Christopher Soames and his small entourage, Anthony Duff (Deputy Governor) Nick Fenn (Press Secretary), Robin Renwick, Major General Acland (Commander of the Commonwealth Monitoring Force), Sir John Boynton (Election Commissioner), Robert Jackson, as well as Lord Carrington, and his delegation, the sensation as midnight approached was one of overwhelming relief. Against the odds, Britain had pulled it off. Soames had set off to Salisbury "with understandable misgivings".[9] Within Rhodesia, as well as outside, it was far from clear whether Soames' mission had any chance of success. In Britain some of the newspapers, recalling what had happened in Saigon, wondered if he might not have to make his exit in a helicopter from the grounds of Government House. Cartoons had depicted

Soames standing in a river full of crocodiles,[10] and it was suggested, that the best place for the Governor to announce the election results would be by megaphone from a departing aircraft.[11] As I have shown, this sense of trepidation was well-founded. However, although British officials and army officers in the football stadium might be mightily relieved, the feeling among many young white Rhodesians was a mixture of anger and confusion. As one young Rhodesian army conscript put it, it was not "Britain has pulled it off", rather, "You Traitors. You have sold us out." Then with the relatively peaceful transition, the sense was one of unreality:

> By the moment of independence, we could not believe it had happened; that we had actually done it. NONE of us had thought it would be peaceful. In the Army, we had been brainwashed into thinking that we were fighting communists, not against the blacks; then we didn't think Mugabe had enough control over his troops that they would gather at the assembly points, and hand over their weapons. We had thought of Mugabe as a monster, the Enemy; suddenly thanks to the elections, he was the Leader. We predicted a bloodbath, yet that month to full independence was peaceful, and (at the time) it seemed he wasn't that bad after all.[12]

A degree of bemusement then. This was the appearance as midnight approached: three warring armies reconciled and integrated:

> To roars of approval from the packed terraces of the football stadium, 100 soldiers marched past side by side. As the khaki-clad troops presented arms blazing floodlights illuminated their sweating faces—black and white, drilling together with absolute precision. Barely four months earlier, these men had been killing each other. For the euphoric crowd ... witnessing the birth of independent Zimbabwe, it seemed almost too good to be true. Soldiers from three opposing armies formed the ranks of the guard of honour. Now they marched as one—winners and losers, in perfect step. The victors had served in two black guerrilla forces and the leader of the largest was at the centre of attention on this joyous night.[13]

Hopes and Dreams

Outside the stadium, the city was teeming with people. Thousands had converged on the capital to take part in the independence celebrations, and the crowd outside the stadium itself was huge, and febrile with excitement. Inside the stadium were an extraordinary cross section of Rhodesia's past. The audience included Wilf Mbanga, a young black Zimbabwean journalist.[14] At that point, Mbanga was based in Salisbury, but travelling on a British passport and working for the liberal South African Argus Press Group. In 1974 he had secured an extraordinary journalist coup, with his exclusive series of interviews with the Zimbabwean nationalist political leadership—Nkomo, Muzorewa, and the then almost unknown Robert Mugabe. These series of interviews in the column 'The Zimbabweans' were syndicated and published across Southern Africa. Mbanga had told a sceptical

Mike Nicholson, an immensely experienced and influential reporter for ITN, that Mugabe was the political personality to watch and took Nicholson to meet Mugabe, who had recently been released from prison. This interview still exists in the ITN archives. The footage shows Nicholson quizzing Mugabe: Was he bitter? No. Did he hate the white man, for what they had done to him? "No", came the reply, "We are fighting a system that is wrong. We don't hate the whites. We will have no racial discrimination in an independent Zimbabwe."[15]

This point had made an enormous personal impact on Mbanga—married to a white Rhodesian/Zimbabwean, with two children. Because of the urban residential segregation legislation, Mbanga and his wife Trisha lived on a farm outside the capital, from which Mbanga commuted to work every day. In February 1980, Trisha's and Wilf's third child, Matthew, was born. He was given the middle name 'Tongai'— meaning 'Rule Well' in Shona—a deliberate and conscious endorsement of their faith and hope in Mugabe as their future leader. The February 1980 election was the first time Mbanga had ever voted. Out of principle, he had refused to vote in the era of qualified franchise, even though he satisfied the education and income criteria for African voters, for the allocated 16 seats for African MPs. On 17 April, Mbanga conducted a personal interview with Mugabe, which was published the following day, formal Independence Day: "Mugabe could put his argument very lucidly, very persuasively, very clearly. I thought he was different, especially at the time compared to the other regional leaders. He was a giant, intellectually head and shoulders above them." Recalling his sense of euphoria as midnight approached, Mbanga laughingly recounted that Bob Marley and the Wailers had performed free of charge. After local bands (in particular, the voice of Chimurenga—also known as 'the Lion of Zimbabwe'—Thomas Mapfumo and his Halleluiah Chicken Run Band), Marley came on stage. "You must know Marley had written the song 'Free Zimbabwe'. It was extraordinary! Even Marley's most avid fans felt he hadn't written great lyrics, but the beat was fantastic! And he sang it that night." Outside the stadium, in a frantic bid to disperse the press of people, the police had let off teargas canisters. Unfortunately, because of a change in wind direction, the gas promptly wafted into the stadium, bringing even more tears to the eyes of the emotional crowd. It did nothing to dull their sense of anticipation. When Mugabe went forward to receive the insignia of office from Prince Charles, Mbanga too was shouting with the rest of the crowd. "I was not an objective journalist at that moment. Yes, tears were rolling down my cheeks, but not just because of the tear gas!" As the new flag of Zimbabwe was raised, Mbanga admits that he had "a lump in his throat". It was everything Mbanga had hoped and dreamed of: he was a proud, young Zimbabwean, who felt as if he had just been given $30m. "I was now a human being. An adult." He shared Mugabe's declared vision of reconciliation, and a genuinely non-racial society. This was the moment of realization of everything Mbanga had lived for: the end of segregated living, the chance of his children to attend any school he chose, his chance to make it to the top in the profession of his choice through merit, not colour of skin. It was a question of his very identity and sense of self: "In the old era of Rhodesian UDI, when Africans were killed *The Rhodesian Herald* did not use surnames. Now, if I died, they would."[16] This reflects the sense of final recognition of equality of status, and their individual humanity. That night Mbanga drove back to his farm outside Harare, where Trisha and his newborn son were, and wrote an impassioned piece for *The Johannesburg Star* which was syndicated in the Argus Press through out the region.

Sitting behind Prince Charles that night were a very different type of new Zimbabweans: Brian Oliver and his wife, Avril, sitting in the balcony above Prince Charles and the other dignitaries, in the section allocated for invited guests. Oliver had emigrated from Britain in the late 1940s, and worked as the Assistant Secretary in the Prime Minister's office in the 1960s, furthermore, Oliver had attended the *Tiger* and *Fearless* talks between 1966 and 1968. In the 1970s he had joined Rhodesian military intelligence as part of his compulsory military service, whilst still working as a civil servant in Harare. Oliver had never endorsed the hard-line racial attitudes of the extreme element of the Rhodesia Front movement, but had believed that the majority African population had to be educated in their responsibilities of economic and political development—in the need for maintaining 'European' civilized standards. Oliver had been among those who were trenchantly critical of Soames' refusal to disbar ZANU (PF) from participating in the February poll, on the grounds that violence and intimidation in the rural areas had distorted the election result. But he had accepted—to him—the imperfect outcome, and was determined to stay and help participate in a new multi-racial Zimbabwe:

> The rest of the stadium was packed and the Africans were very excited. But our section, which was reserved for invited guests was relatively empty (It had a mixture of Europeans, coloureds and Africans.) Many of the whites who had been invited stayed away. They were anti-the new regime. So there were comparatively few Europeans there. Most of the Europeans were not as philosophical as I was. They were more apprehensive, although they did not openly express their feelings. We all knew how Mugabe had come to power—through widespread intimidation—but Mugabe's conciliatory speech softened the general feeling to a great extent. It gave us hope. But there was a sense of unreality about the whole evening: one of very mixed emotions indeed. Happily, we weren't affected by the tear gas. But it was profoundly sad that it was not the old flag of Rhodesia that was lowered, rather than the Union Jack.[17]

Not everyone in that football stadium was ecstatic, or hoping against hope. I have alluded to the feelings of the senior members of the Rhodesian security forces who had agreed to serve under Mugabe. There were also those who had failed to secure the crown of leadership. Most notably, these included Joshua Nkomo and his wife maFuyana. This was a case of 'Dreams Shattered'. Nkomo had long regarded himself as "the senior political leader" in the Patriotic Front, but he and his wife found themselves "relegated to seats for the lower ranking guests":

> Behind the saluting base were the benches for the junior minister, the party officials and the supporting cast. At the back of those rows, in the dark by the radio commentator's box, where the television cameras could not see us and our supporters in the crowd could not single us out for their applause, places were reserved for maFuyana and myself. In the stadiums of Zimbabwe I had so often stood up to address the crowds, and found the words to express what they wished to say but had not yet articulated. Now I was hidden away like

something to be scared of. My wife could scarcely restrain her tears at this symbolic humiliation.[18]

The other end of the spectrum was his arch rival in the Patriotic Front:

> Robert Mugabe took the oath of office. His nerves showed. His fingers shook as he snapped off his glasses, before reading: 'I, Robert Gabriel Mugabe, do solemnly swear that I will faithfully serve Zimbabwe in the office of Prime Minister of the government'. To those deafening cheers from the crowd shouting their approval, the dignitaries politely applauded.
>
> Midnight. The Union Jack was lowered to the sound of 'God Save the Queen.' Up went the new flag of Zimbabwe—and the stadium exploded, a crowd of some 40 000 people. It was an extraordinary moment of innocent, intoxicating euphoria.[19]

Sixteen years after the independence of Northern Rhodesia (Zambia), this was the new nation: the image of the all-night celebrations (which were called Independence Pungwes, a reference to the political rallies) lasting the entire holiday weekend, but which contrasts sharply with the parallel spectacle of the departure of a sizeable element of the white community (particularly the security and intelligence services.) A nation born into such hope. Where the new Zimbababwe $1 = £1.00.

"*You have inherited a jewel in Africa. Don't tarnish it.*" (President Julius Nyerere of Tanzania, to Robert Mugabe, April 1980)

Notes

1. On the second anniversary of independence (in April 1982) Salisbury was officially renamed Harare—the name of the city's designated African residential area of the Rhodesia era.
2. David Owen had tried while Foreign Secretary to broaden the Internal Settlement to include Joshua Nkomo's ZAPU party, using the good offices of Nigeria; but this clandestine diplomacy had failed because of rivalries within the African nationalist movement. See Owen, D. (1984) *Time to Declare* (London: Michael Joseph).
3. The country was increasingly dependent upon South African economic support, military personnel (especially in the Rhodesian Air Force and helicopter fleet) and weaponry.
4. The public British line was that this was a tragic accident. M16 felt the evidence of foul play was inconclusive, whilst Rhodesian and South African intelligence reports pointed to an East German contract killing on behalf of disaffected elements within ZANU/ZANLA, irate at Tongogara's moderate stance at Lancaster House.
5. Renwick, R. (1997) *Unconventional Diplomacy in Southern Africa* (Basingstoke: Macmillan Press), p. 63.
6. *Ibid.*, p. 86.
7. See *ibid.*, pp. 88–95. Also Hudson, M. (1981) *Triumph or Tragedy: Rhodesia to Zimbabwe* (London: Picador).
8. Renwick, *Unconventional Diplomacy*, p. 96.
9. *Ibid.*, p. 63.
10. Coincidentally, Robert Mugabe's clan insignia is a crocodile. See Godwin, P. (2007) *When A Crocodile Eats the Sun: a Memoir* (London: Picador).
11. Renwick, *Unconventional Diplomacy*, p. 64.
12. Sue Onslow telephone interview with Kevin Barnes, (Rhodesian Light Infantry) (1976–1977), 16 May 2007.

13. Blair, D. (2003) *Degrees in Violence. Robert Mugabe and the Struggle for Power in Zimbabwe* (London: Continuum), p. 9.
14. Mbanga became Robert Mugabe's first head of the Zimbabwe Independent News Agency in 1981. Later he was appointed editor of *The Daily News*, and is now proprietor of the exiled newspaper, *The Zimbabwean*.
15. Sue Onslow telephone interview with Wilf Mbanga, 17 May 2007.
16. Mbanga interview with author.
17. Sue Onslow telephone interview with Brian Oliver, 26 June 2007.
18. Quoted in Meredith, M. (2002) *Mugabe: Power and Plunder in Zimbabwe* (Oxford: Public Affairs), p. 40.
19. Blair, *Degrees in Violence*, p. 10.

References

Barber, J. (1983) *The Uneasy Relationship. Britain and South Africa* (London: Heinemann for the Royal Institute of International Affairs), pp. 11–13.
Barber, J. and Barratt, J. (1990) *South Africa's Foreign Policy. The Search for Status and Security 1945–1988* (Cambridge: Cambridge University Press).
Carrington, Lord (1988) *Reflect on Things Past* (London: Collins).
Charlton, I. (1990) *The Last Colony in Africa: Diplomacy and the Independence of Rhodesia* (Oxford: Blackwell).
Davidow, J. (1984) *A Peace in Southern Africa: The Lancaster House Conference on Rhodesia, 1979* (Boulder, CO: Westview Press).
Deroche, A. (2001) *Black, White and Chrome: The United States and Zimbabwe 1953–1998* (Trenton, NJ: Africa World Press).
Geldenhuys, D. (1984) *The Diplomacy of Isolation. South African Foreign Policy Making* (Johannesburg: Macmillan South Africa).
Martin, D. and Johnson, P. (1981) *The Struggle for Zimbabwe. The Chimurenga War* (Harare Publishing House/London: Faber).
Meredith, M. (1979) *The Past is Another Country: Rhodesia 1890–1979* (London: André Deutsch).
Renwick, R. (1997) *Unconventional Diplomacy in Southern Africa* (Macmillan: Basingstoke, 1997).
Stedman, S. (1991) *Peacemaking in Civil War. International Mediation in Zimbabwe 1974–1980* (Boulder, CO: Lynne Rienner).
Tamarkin, M. (1990) *The Making of Zimbabwe: Decolonisation in Regional and International Politics.* (London: Frank Cass).
Thatcher, M. (1993) *The Downing Street Years* (London: Harper Collins).
Verrier, A. (2001) *The Road to Zimbabwe 1890–1980* (London: Jonathan Cape).

'Transfer of Destinies', or Business as Usual? Republican Invented Tradition and the Problem of 'Independence' at the End of the French Empire

MARTIN SHIPWAY
School of Languages, Linguistics and Culture, Birkbeck, University of London

At midnight on 12–13 August 1960, on the banks of the Ubangi river at Bangui, the Central African Republic was ushered into sovereign existence in a curiously muted ceremony. André Malraux, poet, adventurer and travel-writer, Resistance fighter, 'Aristotle' to de Gaulle's 'Alexander',[1] and Minister of Culture in the first governments of de Gaulle's Fifth Republic, spoke for France. Delivered "in his lyrical style, his tone breathless and declamatory", Malraux's speech carries unmistakeable echoes of the more famous pronouncement of his friend, Jawarharlal Nehru, 13 years before almost to the day:

> An era comes to an end as night falls ... This is not merely a transfer of attributions, but a transfer of destinies.[2]

This is a rare glimpse in the published record of a supposedly climactic moment (or rather, series of moments) in this 'Year of Africa', in the course of which, starting with Cameroun on 1 January, Madagascar and all sub-Saharan African members of the French *Communauté* gained their independence (leaving Djibouti, which only gained its independence in 1977). Of course, a far more momentous process of decolonization was approaching its climax north of the Sahara; the first official talks between the French government and the self-proclaimed Provisional Government of the Algerian Republic had taken place, and rapidly stalled, at Melun in June 1960. Even so, details of what actually took place in these African independence ceremonies are surprisingly sparse, hazy and ill-remembered by French actors. Malraux himself makes no mention of them in his not-inaptly named *Anti-memoirs*.[3] Jacques Foccart, who, as de Gaulle's legendary African *éminence grise*, may or may not have been present, did not trouble to mention it in his informative published interviews.[4] Pierre Messmer's 1992 account only implies that he was present to hear Malraux, and as de Gaulle's loyal Minister of Armies he may well have been, but he placed Bangui on the Congo, rather than its tributary (which becomes an anonymous 'river' in his 1998 volume), and slipped the date forward to 14 August. As it happens, at midnight on 14–15 August, Malraux spoke at a similar ceremony at Brazzaville (on the banks of the Congo). If Messmer was indeed present, he may be excused the confusion: at midnight two days before Bangui, the French government delegation was in Fort-Lamy (Ndjamena) for Chad's independence celebrations, and precisely 48 hours after Brazzaville, the ceremony was repeated at Libreville, capital of Gabon.[5] According to one account, Jean Foyer, Secretary of State for Relations with the *Communauté*, had wanted the ceremonies for all four former members of the Federation of French Equatorial Africa (AEF) to take place on the same day, but this was made impossible by plane timetables;[6] at least this way, the symbolism of the 'midnight hour' could be repeated at will.

One figure was notable by his physical absence, and yet was omnipresent: General de Gaulle was mentioned in every speech, including Malraux's and those of Presidents Tombalbaye (Chad) and Youlou (Republic of Congo) and Prime Ministers David Dacko (CAR) and Léon M'Ba (Gabon). Perhaps also the performances of the looming, big-nosed dancing figures of the Congo Basin, called *ngol*, took on particular intensity.[7] The significance of de Gaulle's immanent presence was twofold. First, former AEF in general, and Fort-Lamy and Brazzaville in particular, constituted a formidable cluster of Gaullist *lieux de mémoire* going back to the *ralliements* of August 1940, which had given the leader of Free France his first territorial base. Here, on 30 January 1944, de Gaulle had made his first *discours de Brazzaville*, the myths surrounding which long overshadowed the record of the ensuing eight-day conference.[8] Secondly, it was perhaps unthinkable that de Gaulle should attend these hurried and grudging ceremonies, having already delivered himself, less than two years before, of his second *discours de Brazzaville*, in which he set out the intended course of France's future relations with the African and Malagasy members of the newly conceived *Communauté*. As in 1944, de Gaulle had arrived in Brazzaville as part of a triumphal tour of French Africa, although this time he came with the specific agenda of preparing African electorates for the forthcoming referendum on the new Constitution and on the French *Communauté* which it enshrined. Thus, on 24 August 1958, two days after he had been rapturously acclaimed in Tananarive (Antananarivo), he was welcomed to the Brazzaville football stadium which, in 1944, he had dedicated to Félix Eboué, Brazzaville's wartime Governor-General and Gaullist 'of the first hour'. Here, Barthélemy

Boganda, President of the Council of Government of Oubangui-Chari (subsequently the CAR), and President of the Grand Council of AEF, gave his own convoluted twist to the myth of the 'Man of Brazzaville':

> We are sure that you have come here today in order to bring to term the work started at the Brazzaville Conference, and to give your blessing to [*consacrer*] an AEF marching towards independence, but forever united with an independent and immortal France.[9]

De Gaulle replied in kind, playing up the myth, and further muddying international legal waters, by claiming that "it was at Brazzaville that France, through my voice, set our African territories along the road which has led them to self-determination [*la libre disposition d'eux-mêmes*]".[10] We return below to de Gaulle's August 1958 African tour, in its way as important as Macmillan's 'wind of change' tour 16 months later, not least because at its next leg but one, in Conakry, it went badly wrong.

In a volume centred on the ceremonial of British independence celebrations, it is difficult to avoid responding to the obvious contrasts with the French experience in these matters with the rhetorical equivalent of a Gallic shrug. There may be several reasons why, beyond the tribute paid by Malraux and his colleagues in serially plagiarizing the trope of the 'midnight hour' (which anyway derives from Nehru's sense of theatre rather than Mountbatten's), France felt no need to borrow the newly invented traditions of the British empire in retreat. First, as in the life of the colonial empires, so in their death throes, Republican France was never going to indulge in anything remotely resembling British monarchist pageantry, and the ordered, hierarchical instincts of the British official mind—what we might now, following David Cannadine, call its 'ornamentalism'—had no place in French colonizing or decolonizing strategies. Secondly, one of the reasons French policy-makers—and after them historians and memoirists—ostensibly paid such scant attention to the staging of the 'transfer of power' is surely because the two most important such transfers for France took place in Vietnam, following the humiliating defeat at Dien Bien Phu, and in circumstances of almost unimaginable disorder in Algeria. Thirdly, it might be suggested that, in Africa at least, France had little interest in marking—much less celebrating—the transfer of power because it had no intention of making any such transfer. Thus, the true symbolism of the independence ceremonies of 1960 came, not on the riverbank at midnight, but in the conference chamber back in Paris, where bilateral 'co-operation' accords covering the cultural, economic and military arrangements of the post-colonial Franco-African relationship were signed, accords which the French government sought to impose on newly independent states as a condition of the granting of independence.[11]

The first instinct of the historian of French decolonization should perhaps therefore be to challenge the underlying premise of the implied frame of reference, or simply to turn it around: why is it that the British patterns and symbols of the end of empire are now taken so readily as the historiographical norm? Or more simply still: why *should* we interpret the end of French empire according to a British model? It is surely a measure of the symbolic appeal of those quirky, self-deluding, but ultimately rather comforting, rituals which marked British transfers of power that they loom so large in British accounts of the end of empire; indeed, the 'transfer of power' can seem almost synonymous with decolonization itself, thus implying decolonization as pre-planned endpoint, rather than as an often messy political process. Ronald Hyam, for example, over the first four pages of the 'Epilogue' to his recent study of 'the road to' British decolonization, discusses independence ceremonies (especially that of Swaziland) at length, before somewhat tendentiously contrasting Britain's numerous "relatively smooth and peaceful transfers of power" with the "scale of foreign chaos, often bitter, in Algeria, Indonesia, Belgian Congo, Western Sahara or Mozambique".[12] Of course, even where British counter-insurgency had not been deployed in order to render a dependency "safe for decolonization",[13] the formal transfer of power could serve to distance, or even to exculpate, the departing colonial power from incipient violence or ongoing political disorder and division. This was clearly so in India in 1947 or, as Richard Rathbone argues elsewhere in this volume, in Ghana in 1957; in both cases, the departing British in their ostrich plumes gave themselves—quite literally—an incontrovertible alibi. It is perhaps a pity that the French writer and academic, Roland Barthes, an occasional, somewhat dilettante critic of French colonialism, did not write on the subject of the British empire. Apart from delighting in the rich semiology of the event itself, he would no doubt have relished the British independence ceremony as a piece of myth-making, in that it 'naturalises' history; in other words, it makes what is historically contingent seem 'natural', translating urgent, political necessity into immutable, 'inevitable', myth.[14]

As already suggested, post-war France could draw on powerful myths of its own, not only those informing its sense of imperial mission, but also those generated by that 'incarnation' of French legitimacy, Charles de Gaulle.[15] On the whole, these myths did not readily lend themselves to preparing the end of empire, and indeed the confluence of both sources of myth made that eventuality seem even more remote. Thus, at Brazzaville in 1944, the Governors and Governors-General of French Africa deliberating in closed session, acting in de Gaulle's name but guided by the firm hand of French colonial traditions, explicitly ruled out a British-style evolution towards self-government, a concept so alien that it was rendered in a kind of *franglais*:

> The ends of the civilising mission accomplished in the colonies exclude any idea of autonomy, all possibility of evolution outside the French bloc; also excluded is the eventual establishment of *self governments* [sic, emphasis added] in the colonies, even in a distant future.[16]

As has been extensively argued elsewhere, the clumsy phrasing of this declaration has tended to deflect attention from the Conference's not unreasonable or, for 1944, unduly illiberal agenda.[17] Away from such categorical pronouncements, the Conference organizers laid the groundwork for an ambitious and ultimately rather quixotic project to create a Republican 'empire-state',[18] rejected at Brazzaville but enshrined in compromised form in the French Union articles of the 1946 Constitution. De Gaulle's Commissioner for the Colonies, René Pleven, in his opening speech at the 1944 Conference (the warm-up act for de Gaulle's main feature), not only sought to put an acceptable gloss on this modernist variant of France's traditional *mission civilisatrice*, but also made an explicit link between this and the problematic concept of 'independence' for a French Republic which, in

January 1944, had yet to be liberated, or rather (as subsequent Gaullist myth would have it) to liberate itself, from foreign occupation:

> In greater colonial France there are neither peoples to enfranchise nor racial discrimination to abolish ... There are populations which we intend to conduct, stage by stage, to a political personality, and for the more developed to political rights, but this will still mean that the only independence they will want will be the independence of France.[19]

In fact, this late colonial project was realized much more fully and concretely than Pleven or the *Corps colonial* could have anticipated: within a decade, French Africa had received billions of francs of development funding and, largely through the critical political engagement of the French African elites on whom Pleven had thought to bestow French favour, had achieved a substantial measure of social welfare reform and political development, including not least, universal suffrage within a single citizens' college.[20]

'Independence', on the other hand, remained no less problematic. We will return below to 1958, and to the French African political processes which culminated in the ceremonies evoked at the outset. First, however, we examine briefly an episode from the immediate post-war period which serves to underline some of the problems faced by French officialdom in confronting both the fact of imperial transitions and their overlaying symbolism.

Vietnam and the 'Bao Dai solution': Anything But Independence

Whereas in Africa, French officials in 1944 could still push any idea of self-government back over the receding horizon of 'a distant future', in Indochina, independence was declared—twice in Vietnam—before the French had even re-established a presence at the end of the Second World War. Following the *coup de force* of 9 March 1945, when the Japanese had finally overthrown Admiral Jean Decoux's Vichyste administration, the French presence had been "physically and intellectually wiped from the face of Vietnam", thus bringing to an end France's "celestial mandate" to rule.[21] The Japanese had encouraged declarations of independence by the sovereigns of Laos, Cambodia and Vietnam; and Vietnam was reunited with its southern province of Nam Ky which, as Cochinchina, was the only part of Indochina to have been annexed as a colony under French sovereignty (as opposed to various protectorates). In its August 1945 Revolution, the League for the Independence of Vietnam (*Viet Nam Doc Lap Dong Minh Hoi*, or Viet Minh) had replaced the imperial regime by the (Democratic) Republic of Vietnam, whose independence was further declared on 2 September by the Viet Minh's leader, by now known as Ho Chi Minh. Emperor Bao Dai, France's puppet on the throne of Annam since 1926, and still aged only 32 in 1945, elected to abdicate in favour of the person he thought of as "the famous revolutionary Nguyen Ai Quoc", and was appointed 'Supreme Counsellor' by Ho under his civilian name, Vinh Thuy; he soon retired to Chiang Kai-shek's temporary capital at Chongqing, and thence to Hong Kong, where he lived up to the sobriquet of the 'playboy emperor'.[22]

The period leading to the definitive outbreak in December 1946 of hostilities between the French and the Viet Minh has been extensively covered elsewhere. The increasingly fraught state of play between the French government and Ho's regime, centring on notions of Vietnamese independence and national unity, is surely reflected in the confused iconography of Franco-Vietnamese encounters, as French officials and ministers treated Ho variously as 'one of us', or as a head of state in waiting, even while officials increasingly regarded him, not without some justification, as the ruthless leader of a "brutal and puerile gang". The relaxed camaraderie of Ho's meetings with Jean Sainteny or General Leclerc following the signing of the Accords of 6 March 1946, or the highly charged exchange of the *tutoiement révolutionnaire* between French and Vietnamese delegates (i.e. calling each other *tu* as if they were comrades) at the follow-up Dalat Conference of April–May 1946, thus contrasted vividly with Ho's formal invitation aboard the cruiser *Emile Bertin* anchored in Along Bay on 24 March 1945, or again, aboard the *Dumont d'Urville* following his return from France in October, on both occasions to be given full naval honours by the frosty High Commissioner, Admiral Georges Thierry d'Argenlieu.[23]

Given that diplomatic, military and political realities were at least as confused as these mixed messages suggested, the breakdown of relations with Ho's regime brought a clarification of French purpose. Indeed, even before the events of Haiphong and Hanoi, which cut through the ambiguities of the March 1946 Accords, officials were already reaching for a more amenable solution: in November 1946, d'Argenlieu's political counsellor, Léon Pignon, who subsequently, as High Commissioner himself, would be called on to implement this idea, proposed what he described as "the French restoration by force of the Annamite monarchy, accompanied by the proclamation of Greater Vietnam and inspired by liberal, bourgeois socialist principles".[24] As he added, the alternative was "immediate recourse to the ultimate fallback position, which is the proclamation of independence". Events in Vietnam also coincided with the wearied agreement by referendum of the Constitution of the French Fourth Republic. Shaped by the course of Franco-Vietnamese negotiations, as well as by the backlash to communist manipulation of the first, failed, constitutional draft (a backlash ably remote-controlled by de Gaulle in his July 1946 speech at Bayeux), this set a fairly rigid framework for a French Union determining France's relations with its imperial dependencies, not least those which could aspire to the much-prized (but still vague) 'political personality' as Associated States: at stake here was not only the future of Vietnam, but also of Morocco and Tunisia, much closer to home and arguably also to the heart of French concerns.

From the outset, therefore, notwithstanding qualified French willingness to concede to Bao Dai the national unity that had been denied Ho Chi Minh, the so-called 'Bao Dai solution' was always envisaged as a way for France to maintain its position in Indochina, and by extension to avoid any dangerous precedents for Tunisian and Moroccan potential status as Associated States;[25] and also, crucially, to win the war against the Viet Minh. The transparency of this strategy goes some way to explaining Bao Dai's reluctance to be drawn into it, nor can it have helped that it took the best part of a year after December 1946, and the decisive shift of French politics to the right over the course of 1947, for French governments to turn their backs on Ho as a possible negotiating partner. Although Bao Dai insisted that his own prestige was such that even Ho had sought to draw on it by naming him

'Supreme Counsellor' (a title which Bao Dai still nominally retained),[26] he can have been in little doubt that he was a consolation prize.

Both the French and Bao Dai reached for their own interpretation of British models, but the comparison was clearly unfavourable: in contrast with Mountbatten's break-neck pace of negotiations, it took some two years to reach an agreement falling far short of the finality of the Indian settlement. The first move came from d'Argenlieu's successor as High Commissioner, Emile Bollaert, a centrist politician with a fine Resistance record, but whose main qualification for the job was his complete lack of Indochinese experience. Having failed to parley with Ho, his plan was for a big speech to be given on 15 August 1947 (a date already familiar to readers of this volume), in which he would compete for headlines with the forthcoming pomp and circumstance in Delhi. However, officials in Paris and local military commanders baulked at his proposed, hopelessly straightforward, offer of independence and of a conditional French ceasefire. In the end, he gave a less grandiose speech in the Hanoi suburb of Hadong on 11 September, for which someone in Paris hit upon the novel idea of uttering the contested word in Vietnamese. And so, Bollaert called on "all spiritual families of Vietnam" to rally around the banner of '*Doc Lap*'; although this was believed to denote an ambivalent grey area between 'liberty' and 'independence', it convinced no-one, not least because two years before, Bao Dai and Ho had both already declared *Doc Lap*, without ambiguity. Bollaert's speech was, however, the agreed signal for Bao Dai to respond, after a decent interval of a week, with a proclamation from Hong Kong on 18 September that he was "ready to make contact with French authorities".[27] It took the fall of the Socialist-led government of Paul Ramadier in late November to remove the last temptation to look to Ho Chi Minh as sole '*interlocuteur valable*', and on 6 December 1947 it was Bao Dai's turn to be welcomed aboard a French cruiser, the *Duguay-Trouin*, in Along Bay.

For his part, Bao Dai was seeking Dominion status, by which he understood effective independence for a united Vietnam, albeit within the framework of the French Union. Pierre Messmer, who as Bollaert's *directeur de cabinet* was close to the negotiations with Bao Dai, suggests that Bao Dai was uninterested in a restrictive interpretation of Dominion status, according to which he would not have been head of state; and indeed, Bao Dai later wrote that he might have accepted to be a vassal of the King of France, but not of the President of the Republic.[28] While neither Messmer nor Bao Dai allows for the suppleness of British constitutional practice in this matter, French practice was far from supple, as Bao Dai discovered on his two official visits aboard the *Duguay-Trouin*, the second on 5 June 1947. Although the latter occasion saw the solemn signature of the Along Bay declaration, in which France offered independence and the opportunity to seek national unification in return for Associated State status within the French Union, on both occasions, Bao Dai was presented with (but refused to sign) a secret protocol, subsequently a *modus vivendi*, in which France took back in detail what had been offered in principle. In Paris, also, Minister of Overseas France, Paul Coste-Floret, gave a highly restrictive interpretation of the declaration, particularly in respect of the (re)integration of Cochinchina, French sovereign territory, within Vietnam.[29]

Without the diplomatic (much less military) capacity for a fight with the French over their evasive obduracy on the issues of independence and national unity, Bao Dai's only recourse over this period, highly effective nonetheless, was flight, either to

Hong Kong or to his estate at Cannes. Indeed, 'flight' can be taken here in two senses, as without a succession of chartered Catalinas and DC4s (faithfully logged in his memoirs), Bao Dai would hardly been able to practice the early, and rather perverse, form of shuttle diplomacy of the coming months, when he drove French ministers and President Vincent Auriol to distraction in his refusal to undertake the symbolic return to Vietnam which they so urgently needed. Thus, Bollaert, whom Bao Dai had never trusted (not least because of his attempts to deal with Ho), stood down as High Commissioner in October 1948, following a scene in which he begged Bao Dai to return to his homeland; at about the same time, after Bao Dai had intrigued fruitlessly with the Gaullist opposition, Paul Ramadier lost his temper following lunch at the Elysée Palace, instructing Bao Dai in terms that might have been used to Louis XVI in 1791, to "take up your post in Vietnam in order to carry out your duties!"[30] Bollaert's replacement was Léon Pignon, whom Bao Dai appreciated for his 'courtesy' (*courtoisie*, a word carrying here its full *ancien régime* etymology), but who pursued the same line with Bao Dai into the New Year. It was the shifting geopolitics of the region, with Mao Zedong's troops closing on Vietnam's Yunnan frontier, which finally forced agreement upon the French government and Bao Dai. Even then, Bao Dai returned from signing the Elysée Accords, on 8 March 1949, to Cannes, prompting Vincent Auriol's exasperated (mis-)judgement that "Really, that man has no psychological sense."[31] And then, following a false start when the newly elected Cochinchinese Assembly failed to vote decisively for reunification, and was obliged by Pignon to vote again, Bao Dai returned finally to Vietnam. However, even then, "for reasons of courtesy", he chose to land, and to take up residence, at the pleasant but remote hill station of Dalat, as the Norodom Palace in Saigon was occupied by the High Commissioner.[32] Bao Dai's ambivalent approach to "taking up his post" was matched by the lukewarm welcome of his subjects: when he did visit Saigon, in June 1949, the crowds were so thin that the police were easily able to identify and arrest three would-be bomb-throwers.[33]

There was never any doubt that the 'Bao Dai experiment' was, as Bao Dai put it, a French experiment,[34] nor that the real issue was the war; and, quite aside from the patchwork pattern of political influences and authorities over whom he nominally ruled, even Bao Dai could not claim true independence when there was, as yet, no Vietnamese army to counter the Viet Minh, poised in 1949 to receive its first logistical support from the Chinese People's Army. As already suggested, the real transfer of French power did not come for another five years, following Dien Bien Phu and Geneva; until then the shadow play of French evasive semantics and Bao Dai's equally evasive intrigues had to stand substitute for the real thing.

French Africa After 1958: Independence for the Taking?

The eventual African legacy of the debates at Brazzaville in 1944 arguably came in the shape of the Framework Law (*Loi-Cadre*) passed by the Socialist Minister for Overseas France and long-term Mayor of Marseille, Gaston Defferre, in April 1956. This was an enabling law which allowed the establishment of an effective measure of autonomy for Madagascar and the territories (not yet states) of the two sub-Saharan Federations of AEF and AOF (French West Africa), which, as suggested above, had by this stage already achieved a degree of political participation in advance of their

British counterparts. Many years later, the Law served as a model for Defferre's Framework Law of 1982 ushering in French regional reforms. Although ambitiously liberal in scope, it was driven in part by anxieties about the likely emergence of a nationalist threat in sub-Saharan Africa to add to France's difficulties in Algeria, as well as concerns as to the future costs to France of its emerging African social welfare system. The system created by the Framework Law took a year to put in place, and was barely fully functioning by the time of de Gaulle's return to power in May 1958, and the subsequent shift to the *Communauté*.[35] Neither the French Union as reformed by the Framework Law nor the *Communauté* as set out in the 1958 Constitution were conceived as transitional institutions; rather, both were intended, as in the spirit of the 1944 declaration, as a definitive response, at least by implication, to the British challenge of *self governments* which was to be realized in Ghana in March 1957; as it turned out, however, the 'distant future' evoked in wartime Brazzaville was, by late 1958, countable in months.

As discussed in the weeks preceding de Gaulle's African tour, the *Communauté* represented a series of step-changes rather than a fundamental revision of the Framework Law. Thus, on 14 July, de Gaulle had summoned African leaders to announce that they would henceforth be Presidents of their Government Councils, rather than, as before, Vice-Presidents of a Council chaired by the High Commissioner (as territorial governors were now called).[36] It was also established that African *députés* would no longer be elected to the French National Assembly, thus marking the end of this distinctive feature of French late colonial rule. Both measures ostensibly moved French practice closer to British. A more contentious question was whether membership of the *Communauté* should be on a federal or a confederal model. On 18 July, a newly formed Party of African Regroupment (PRA), led by the arch-federalist Senegalese leader, Léopold Sédar Senghor, had joined together with elements of the rival African Democratic Assembly (RDA) in presenting a plan for federal membership of the *Communauté* based on the existing 'primary' federations of AOF and AEF. This, however, was rejected by Félix Houphouët-Boigny, leader of Côte-d'Ivoire, who feared that the prosperous Côte-d'Ivoire would thus retain its status as 'milch cow' of the federation; a similar position was held by Léon M'Ba, leader of Gabon, in respect of AEF. Unsurprisingly, it was Houphouët-Boigny, Minister of State in de Gaulle's government, member of the Constitutional Committee, and much else besides, who ostensibly carried the day on this issue. He also approved the restrictive interpretation which de Gaulle placed on the forthcoming constitutional referendum set for 28 September, according to which a 'no' vote by African voters would be interpreted as a wish for immediate independence; this, it was reasoned, would raise the stakes for any African leader campaigning for rejection of the (not yet finalized) constitutional text.[37] As the then High Commissioner of Gabon, Louis Sanmarco, has argued, this placed an anomalous and possibly discriminatory burden on African and Malagasy voters, who, unlike metropolitan French voters, thus had no option of simply rejecting the constitutional text, as such a rejection would trigger their departure from the *Communauté*.[38] This was the state of play when de Gaulle departed for his African tour on 21 August. However, on the eve of his departure, he was persuaded to make two potentially crucial concessions, both of which contradicted the Houphouët-Boigny argument: in his speeches at Tananarive and

Brazzaville, he thus proposed, first, that applications for membership of the *Communauté* might now be accepted from 'groups of territories', in other words the 'primary federations' championed by Senghor; and that, secondly, independence would be granted at a later date to members of the *Communauté* who demanded it.[39]

It is an open question as to just how much of what transpired in the Guinean capital, Conakry, on 25 August 1958, may be ascribed to a misunderstanding between powerful personalities, to a misreading of text and gesture, or to the spectacular backfiring of late colonial ceremonial. After Brazzaville, the stopover at Abidjan had been included in the itinerary as a reward for Félix Houphouët-Boigny, and was the occasion for another adulatory reception. The choice of Conakry (the only other non-federal capital to be visited) was more controversial, but Foccart and others had successfully argued, against the advice of Messmer, now High-Commissioner General for AOF, that de Gaulle's charisma might have a positive effect on the troublesome Sékou Touré.[40] The Guinean leader's speech was only vetted at the last moment by de Gaulle's entourage. They did not forewarn de Gaulle of its content, partly because the text of the speech was only produced at the last minute, but not least because it contained very few clues to alert them to the trap that had been set for them, and some rhetorical excess was expected: "c'est du Sékou".[41] Read as a whole, the speech is a not insubstantial essay on the virtues of Liberty, Dignity, Solidarity, Independence (whatever that meant), and, more specifically, the virtues of federation (explicitly *within* the *Communauté*) in allowing the expression of a properly African self-determination.[42] On this last point, Sékou Touré had clearly not paid attention to the content of de Gaulle's speeches, so was unaware that he was pushing against an open door. However, it was the tone of the speech, and the aggressive manner in which it was delivered, which were decisive, rather than its content: in short, the medium overwrote the apparent message. Thus, Ahmed Sékou Touré, eschewing a dark suit and tie in favour of the white robes and cap of a Muslim dignitary and putative descendant of the warrior Samory Touré, acknowledged the symbolism of de Gaulle's visit ("the first French head of government to tread on Guinean soil", etc.), but cancelled it out with his own strident, nationalist street theatre, broadcasting his words on loudspeakers to the waiting crowds, to chants of "Silly, silly!" (i.e. 'elephant', the emblem of Sékou Touré's mass party, the Democratic Party of Guinée, PDG). Even the oft-quoted sound-bite of the day, preferring "poverty in freedom to wealth in slavery", suggests the borrowed rhetoric of anglophone African nationalism—Kwame Nkrumah *circa* 1950, say—rather than its more accommodating francophone counterpart.

There is ample evidence to suggest that Sékou Touré had not intended to force a showdown, not least his repeated references on 25 August to continued Guinean membership of the *Communauté*, but there is no mistaking the consequences of the encounter with de Gaulle. De Gaulle's improvised response to his speech, guaranteeing independence if that was what Guineans voted for on 28 September, already suggested that the overlaid message had been received loud and clear. Afterwards, he warned Sékou Touré privately that "France lived for a long time without Guinée" and could continue to do so in future.[43] Those officials who understood de Gaulle, not least his capacity for identifying a personal insult as one directed at France, understood that the 'offer' of independence was now no longer for form's sake. Indeed, following the expected resounding 'no' vote in Guinée (contrasting with an almost equally resounding 'yes' everywhere else in sub-Saharan Africa), and despite Sékou Touré's repeated protests that "we wish to remain within the French and Western orbit, in every possible way", it fell to Pierre Messmer, as High Commissioner General for AOF, to prepare and execute one of the most abrupt and absolute of colonial withdrawals, starting on 29 September.[44] Thus it was that Sékou Touré became Head of State, on 2 October 1958, even before de Gaulle (who was only elected President of the Republic in December).

De Gaulle also said to Sékou Touré that the French Republic no longer, as in the past, "preferred scheming to decision making", and the harsh treatment of Guinée served its purpose in demonstrating that France would not, as Houphouët-Boigny put it approvingly, "show preferment to those choosing secession over those choosing the *Communauté*".[45] Paradoxically, however, in the wake of Guinée's departure from the French fold, independence became not only easier to obtain but also, by the same token, less intrinsically important. The prelude to the unassuming and rather derivative ceremonies evoked at the outset may thus be identified in two complementary symbolic gestures in December 1959. The first, on 13 December, was de Gaulle's characteristically grandiloquent, but nonetheless undramatic, acknowledgement of the right claimed by the Federation of Mali, and hence open to all other members of the *Communauté*, to independence. Secondly, on 22 December, Pierre Messmer left the Governor General's palace in Dakar, his mission at an end as the federation of AOF ceased to exist: in an impromptu ceremony entirely of his own devising, Messmer walked alone, in uniform, past guards of honour and silent, curious onlookers, "neither shouting nor clapping nor whistling", to the ship waiting to take him to Marseille.[46]

The short-lived Federation of Mali represented the last-ditch attempt by Senghor and others to create an independent statehood on some wider, more viable, basis than that dictated by colonial boundaries; rapidly reduced from four members to just two, the former territories of Senegal and French Soudan, its accession to independence in June 1960 prompted the break-up into separate independent states of Senegal and Mali in October 1960. An attempt to create a parallel federation based on former AEF, the Union of Central African Republics (URAC), similarly foundered on the refusal of Gabon to participate.[47] Even now, 'independence' did not imply, as it had for Guinée two years before, separation from France, merely a necessary concession to allow Franco-African relations to pass into a new, post- (or neo-) colonial phase. A vital transition point had nonetheless been passed, allowing de Gaulle to concede on the far more momentous Algerian question, as he did in April 1961, that "decolonization is in the French interest, and is therefore French policy".[48]

In conclusion, we may return to the earlier comparison with the British ceremonies of independence with which this volume is primarily concerned. The episodes examined in this chapter have a logic of their own, and yet, try as they might, French officials and politicians seeking to manage France's troubled end of empire could never quite resist the urge to borrow from the emerging British iconography of the end of empire, or more substantially, to finesse questions of independence and self-determination rooted in the 'Anglo-Saxon' constitutional tradition. It would surely be unfair to surmise, in the words of the 17th-century French aphorist, the Duc de la Rochefoucauld, that this was, like hypocrisy, the "tribute that vice pays to virtue". Rather, both in the case of Vietnam in 1948–49, and for sub-Saharan Africa after

1958, the French 'official mind' might be accorded some sympathy for seeking to deal as best it could with the momentous concerns which loom in the background of both episodes, namely, the worrying transformation of Vietnam into a front in the Cold War, and the intractable Franco-Algerian conflict.

Notes

1. Saint Robert, P. de (2006) André Malraux, in C. Andrieu, B. Philippe and G. Piketty (Eds) *Dictionnaire De Gaulle* (Paris: Robert Laffont), pp. 709–713.
2. Quoted in Messmer, P. (1998) *Après tant de batailles: Mémoires* (Paris: Albin Michel), p.247; idem (1998) *Les Blancs s'en vont: Récits de décolonisation* (Paris : Albin Michel), p. 158.
3. Malraux, A. (1968) *Anti-Memoirs*, trans T. Kilmartin (London: Hamish Hamilton).
4. Foccart, J. (1995) *Foccart parle 1: Entretiens avec Philippe Gaillard* (Paris: Fayard/Jeune Afrique); Chafer, T. (2002) *The End of the Empire in French West Africa: France's Successful Decolonization?* (Oxford: Berg), p. 184, includes a photograph of Foccart at the 'Accession of Mali to independence'; this is presumably the ceremony on 19–20 June, when the Federation of Mali was composed of Senegal and Soudan, before Senegal seceded in October. See *Keesing's Contemporary Archives* (London: Keesings), 1960, 17513, 17685–88 (Foccart is not mentioned for either occasion).
5. For a reliable record of dates and personalities, *Keesing's Contemporary Archives*, 1960, 17612A.
6. Bernard Lanne, interview in O. Colombani, *Mémoires coloniales* (Paris: La Découverte), 1991, p. 178.
7. See Bernault, F. (1996) *Démocraties ambiguës en Afrique Centrale: Congo-Brazzaville, Gabon, 1940–1965* (Paris: Karthala), pp. 187–195.
8. For a recent account, Shipway, M. (2008), 'Brazzaville, entre mythe et non-dit', in Fondation Charles de Gaulle, *De Gaulle Chef de Guerre : De l'appel de Londres à la libération de Paris 1940–1944* (Paris: Plon), pp. 392–404. At the 2006 *colloque* on which this volume is based, the author was assured, as it were *ex ore infantium*, by retired Admiral Philippe de Gaulle, that there was nothing mythical about his father's perennial commitment to decolonization. The 'Brazzaville myth' was explicitly evoked by Gaston Defferre in 1956 as a way of garnering Gaullist parliamentary support for the 1956 Framework Law (on which see below), as recalled by his *directeur du cabinet*, the ubiquitous Messmer, in *Les Blancs s'en vont* (note 2), pp. 139–140.
9. In Institut Charles-de-Gaulle and Institut d'Histoire du Temps Présent (1998) *Brazzaville, Janvier-Février 1944 : aux sources de la décolonisation* (Paris: Plon), p. 252; and see Shipway, 'Brazzaville' (note 8), pp. 392–393. Boganda died in office, in an air crash in early 1960.
10. This second Brazzaville speech is not included in standard series of the *Discours et Messages*, alongside the Tananarive and Dakar speeches on the same tour, but in a supplementary volume of De Gaulle, C. (1988) *Lettres, notes et carnets*, Vol. XII, *Compléments* (Paris: Plon), pp. 419–422.
11. See Chipman, J. (1989) *French Power in Africa* (Oxford: Blackwell), p. 108.
12. Hyam, R. (2006) *Britain's Declining Empire: The Road to Decolonisation, 1918–1968* (Cambridge: CUP), pp. 398–401, 403. The point of the list is presumably that it embraces all possible 'foreign' empires, French, Dutch, Belgian, Spanish and Portuguese; Hyam does then concede that, in the British empire, "there were too many examples of violent suppression of local disturbances".
13. 'Making Malaya Safe for decolonisation', in R. Holland (1985) *European Decolonization, 1918- 1981: An Introductory Survey* (Basingstoke: Macmillan).
14. See his *Mythologies* (Paris: Seuil, 1957), and especially the concluding essay, 'Le Mythe aujourd'hui'.
15. '... in the name of the legitimacy that I have embodied (*que j'incarne*) for twenty years', speech of 29 January 1960, in De Gaulle, C. (1970), *Discours et messages* (Paris: Plon), vol. 3, p. 166.
16. Ministère des Colonies, *La Conférence Africaine Française: Brazzaville 30 Janvier-8 Février 1944* (Paris: Ministère des Colonies, 1945).
17. Shipway, M. (2008), *Decolonization and its Impact: A Comparative Approach to the End of the Colonial Empires* (Oxford: Wiley-Blackwell), pp. 88–90, pp. 127–130.
18. Frederick Cooper's phrase, in Cooper, F. (2005) *Colonialism in Question: Theory, Knowledge, History* (Berkeley and London: University of California Press), pp. 154, 200.
19. *La Conférence Africaine Française* (note 16); quoted in Chipman, *French Power* (note 11), p. 91. On the 'resistancialist' myth of a home-grown liberation, see H. Rousso (1991) *The Vichy Syndrome: History and Memory in France Since 1944* (Cambridge, MA: Harvard University Press).

20. For a fuller account, Shipway, *Decolonization* (note 17), pp. 130–135, 185–191.
21. Pierre Messmer, interview with the author and Philippe Oulmont, 12 March 2007, relating to Messmer's two-month imprisonment at the hands of the Viet Minh in Tonkin, August–October 1945.
22. Marr, D. G. (1995) *Vietnam 1945: The Quest for Power* (Berkeley: University of California Press); Antlöv, H. (1995) 'Rulers in imperial policy. Sultan Ibrahim, Emperor Bao Dai and Sultan Hamengku Buwono IX', in H. Antlöv and S. Tønnesson (Eds), *Imperial Policy and Southeast Asian Nationalism* (London: Curzon), pp. 227–20; and for a summary, Shipway, *Decolonization* (note 17), pp. 73–75.
23. Ho does not appear to have been intimidated by this latter ritual, remarking on the first occasion to Sainteny, on the Catalina flying-boat that took him back to Hanoi, that large naval vessels could not navigate the river to Hanoi Sainteny, J. (1967) *Une paix manqué*, rev. ed. (Paris: Fayard); and see Shipway, M. (1996) *The Road to War: France and Vietnam, 1944–1947* (Oxford: Berghahn), pp. 182, 185, 236.
24. In Shipway, *Road to War* (note 23), p. 231.
25. The latter was never achieved: see 'Comment le Maroc et la Tunisie n'entrèrent pas dans l'Union française', in G. Chaffard (1967) *Les Carnets secrets de la décolonisation* (Paris: Calmann-Lévy).
26. See Bao Dai (1990) *Le Dragon d'Annam* (Paris: Plon), pp. 207, 213.
27. Folin, J. de (1993) *Indochine 1940–1955: La fin d'un rêve* (Paris: Perrin), p. 193; Messmer, *Après tant de batailles* (note 2), pp. 185–186.
28. Messmer, loc.cit.; Bao Dai, *Dragon d'Annam* (note 26), p. 219.
29. Bao Dai, *Dragon d'Annam* (note 26), pp. 208–209.
30. *Ibid.*, pp. 210–211, 216. According to Auriol, Ramadier was "rather brutal, but it is no bad thing if Bao Dai grasps that we are firm and united", Auriol, V. *Journal du Septennat*, Vol. II, *1948* (Paris: Armand Colin, 1970–71; 25 Oct. 1948), p. 498.
31. Auriol, *Journal du Septennat* (note 30), Vol. III, *1949*, pp. 147–148.
32. Bao Dai, *Dragon d'Annam* (note 26), p. 225.
33. Antlöv, 'Rulers in imperial policy' (note 22), p. 249.
34. Bao Dai, *Dragon d'Annam* (note 26), p. 246.
35. Shipway, *Decolonization* (note 17), pp. 185–191.
36. Chafer, *End of Empire* (note 4), p. 174.
37. Foccart, *Foccart parle I* (note 4), p. 159.
38. Sanmarco, L. (1983) *Le colonial colonisé* (Paris: Editions ABC), p. 212.
39. Foccart, *Foccart parle I* (note 4), p. 161.
40. *Ibid.*, p. 165; Messmer, *Après tant de batailles* (note 2), p. 233. Foccart had, however, successfully argued against de Gaulle's original itinerary, which placed Dakar and Conakry first, and which might thus have had an even more disastrous impact on the turn of events.
41. Foccart, *Foccart parle I*, (note 4), p. 163; Messmer, *Après tant de batailles* (note 2), p. 235.
42. http://www.sakho.com/discours.html (accessed 15 August 2008).
43. Messmer, *Après tant de batailles* (note 2), p. 235.
44. Indeed, even before the referendum, on 25 September, Messmer, in defiance of orders from Paris urging caution, sent a detachment of commandos to Conakry to recover a regular consignment of CFA francs which had recently been delivered to the Guinean capital: see *ibid.*, p. 241; idem, *Les Blancs s'en vont* (note 2), pp. 14–18.
45. Messmer, *Après tant de batailles* (note 2), p. 242.
46. *Ibid.*, pp. 246–247. Messmer goes on to claim inspiration for Malraux's speeches six months later, presumably for the symbolism of France returning to the seas whence it came.
47. See Lanne, B. (1995) 'Comparaison de deux formes possibles de décolonisation. Le projet d'Union des Républiques d'Afrique Centrale (URAC), 1960', in Institut d'Histoire Comparée des Civilisations and Institut d'Histoire du Temps Présent, *Décolonisations comparées: Actes du Colloque international "Décolonisations comparées"* (Aix-en-Provence: Publications de l'Université de Provence,), pp. 163–173.
48. De Gaulle, *Discours et messages* (note 15), vol. 3, 11 April 1961, p. 288.

Merdeka! Looking Back at Independence Day in Malaya, 31 August 1957[1]

A.J. STOCKWELL

National celebration and Malay tradition

In later life Tunku Abdul Rahman would frequently reminisce about independence day. After a career that included leadership of the United Malays National Organisation and the creation of the Alliance (UMNO, the Malayan Chinese Association and Malayan Indian Congress), this genial son of the Sultan of Kedah and Malaysia's first prime minister would relive the scene in Kuala Lumpur as his Malay supporters crowded onto the *padang* to witness, as he put it, a new star rising in the eastern sky. On the stroke of midnight, the union flag was lowered and that of the Federation hoisted to cries of '*Merdeka!*' (Freedom!). Then Sardon Jubir, leader of UMNO Youth, stepped forward to adorn the Tunku with a golden medallion inscribed '*Bapa Merdeka*' (father of independence). Later the same day, after a cloudburst that prolonged British rule by an hour, the formal transfer of power took place in the brand-new Merdeka Stadium witnessed by, amongst others, the Malay rulers, members of the Tunku's Cabinet, delegations from British and Commonwealth governments, colonial and former colonial officials, and

---

This article was first published in *Indonesia and the Malay World* 36, 106 (November 2008) and I thank the editor and publisher for permission to reproduce it here. It is a revised version of a lecture delivered at the international seminar on 'Britain and the Malay World' held at the Royal Asiatic Society, 17-18 May 2007. A shorter version was given as a paper to the one-day symposium on 'Freedoms at Midnight: The Iconography of Independence' at the Institute of Commonwealth Studies, University of London, 28 June 2007.

citizens of the new Malaya. Dressed in the tropical whites of a field-marshal, the Duke of Gloucester presented the Tunku, who was himself arrayed in the finery of a Malay prince, with the constitutional instruments transferring British jurisdiction. When the Tunku completed the proclamation of independence, shouts of Merdeka once again rent the air, guns boomed, the new national anthem played and the Malayan flag was raised aloft. As a week of international games got underway in the stadium, dignitaries withdrew for a farewell lunch in honour of the outgoing colonial high commissioner, Sir Donald MacGillivray, who left the country before the evening's state banquet and firework display (Abdul Rahman 1977: 69–72; Miller 1959: 207–09).[2]

The next round of ceremonies in a week-long programme centred upon the Yang di-Pertuan Agong, the Federation's recently-created constitutional monarch. The Agong's origins and purpose require some explanation. Throughout their imperial history the British had had bitter-sweet relations with the kings and princes of their dependencies. They had treated some as enemies, others as allies and yet others as agents who were required to acknowledge the over-arching majesty of the crown imperial. As they struck deals with nationalist politicians at empire's end, however, the British were frequently embarrassed by their own close connections with indigenous rulers. For example, under pressure to transfer power as soon as possible in the Indian subcontinent, Mountbatten had little option but to abandon British commitments to the princes and urge them to join either independent India or Pakistan. As they surrendered power elsewhere, they exploited the mystique of monarchical tradition to foster national identity and deployed the regalia of pre-colonial kingdoms to enhance the legitimacy of new states. Thus they returned to Ceylon the throne of the last king of Kandy and to Burma the ornate ivory chair which had been looted during the sack of Mandalay in 1885 (de Silva 1997: II, 358–59; Ashton 2005: 82). In the case of Ceylon, which, unlike Burma, remained within the Commonwealth and acknowledged King George VI as head of state, an eminent Commonwealth jurist observed that, while 'a good deal of ingenuity' was required 'to prove the apostolic succession from Prince Vijaya' to the House of Windsor, it 'was important that the first Prime Minister could claim to be the representative of the oldest monarchy in the Commonwealth and that, when she visited Ceylon [in 1954], the Queen could sit on the Kandyan throne in the Assembly Hall of the Kandyan kings' (Jennings 1956: 137).

Relations with the Malay rulers had a similarly chequered past, involving deposition and interference in the royal succession. The legitimacy of Britain's presence in the Malay states, however, rested on recognition of the sultans' sovereignty which it challenged at its peril, as was demonstrated most powerfully during the Malayan Union crisis in 1945–46. Subsequent moves towards decolonisation required the agreement of the Malay rulers who could hamstring the process were they to fall out with each other or with Alliance politicians whose ambitions they mistrusted. The differences between nationalist leaders and rulers' representatives were more or less resolved during their leisurely journey to London for constitutional talks in early 1956 when the office of Yang di-Pertuan Agong took shape (Smith 1995: 149). Elected on a five-year basis and in rotation by and from among the hereditary Malay rulers, the Agong was intended not only to preserve royal interests but also, by rising above state allegiances and communal ties, to provide a focus of national

---

[2] See also *The Times* (London), 31 August 1957.

loyalty. It is a rare example of an elective monarchy and set Malaya apart from other Commonwealth countries. When, from the late 1940s onwards, territories left the empire to join the Commonwealth as free and equal members, they either acknowledged the British monarch as head of state or became republics with their own presidents. Malaya was exceptional in having not only its own monarchy but a monarchy that was elected and rotated.[3]

The nature of the office perplexed Whitehall civil servants and courtiers at Buckingham Palace who puzzled over such matters as the correct style of address. They wondered whether the form 'Sir, My Brother' (which was used for foreign sovereigns) or 'Our Good Friend' (customarily applied to presidents) should be preferred in letters from the Queen to the Agong. After much consultation, a compromise was reached whereby both His Majesty and the presidential 'Our Good Friend' were adopted.[4] Although it was essentially ornamental, the role of the Agong was untested and by no means straightforward. The first incumbent would have no precedents to guide him. Nor could he yet draw upon an inherited fund of loyalty outside his own state. More immediately for the Merdeka ceremony, the presence of a Malayan head of state raised procedural issues which the British had not encountered in either Ceylon or Ghana where members of the British royal family had opened the parliaments of the new nations.

Since the first Agong would have as much scope to tarnish his office as to add lustre to it, his selection was a matter of great sensitivity. The most senior ruler, and the one to be offered first refusal, was Ibrahim of Johore who was 83 years of age and had reigned since 1895. Autocratic and unpredictable, he had regularly clashed with his brother rulers and Malay politicians. He had vainly urged the British to retain an adviser in Johore after independence so as to insulate his state from the Alliance government. There was considerable relief in both British and Malayan circles when Ibrahim declined to be considered. The next in line was Abu Bakar of Pahang whose 'good record' during the Japanese occupation and the communist insurrection found favour with the British. On the other hand, he was heavily in debt and had recently lost the approval of his peers and 'shocked public opinion' by absconding to Hong Kong with a 'taxi girl'.[5] In the end the Yang di-Pertuan Besar of Negri Sembilan, who had been a student with Tunku Abdul Rahman in Britain during the 1930s, accepted the position. In a reign cut short by untimely death, he would do much to raise the status of the Agong above that of the other rulers and 'fix it in the popular understanding as the focus of national loyalty'.[6]

Two days after Merdeka, the first Yang di-Pertuan Agong was installed.[7] This was a theatrical ceremony reminiscent of the coronation of Queen Elizabeth four years earlier which had been attended by representatives from the Federation including three Malay

---

[3]Malaya was later joined in the Commonwealth by the monarchies of Lesotho (1966), Swaziland (1968), Tonga (1970) and Brunei (1984).
[4]Minutes in DO 35/9958.
[5]J. Chadwick, 24 July 1957, DO 35/9958.
[6]Sir Geofroy Tory (British high commissioner, Malaya) to Lord Home (secretary of state, Commonwealth Relations Office), 23 April 1960, DO 35/10036.
[7]Press reports, e.g. *The Times*, 3 September 1957; see also CO 1030/764, DO 35/9958, DO 35/10013.

rulers.[8] Like the Queen's coronation, which brightened up post-war Britain, the Agong's installation glorified the start of a new era in the history of Malaya. It was designed to be an expression of national unity and a declaration of obligations. Its form and ornamentation derived from the traditions of the kingdom of Melaka as handed down through the *Sejarah Melayu* and modified by the practice of the royal house of Kedah, of which the Tunku was a scion and which claimed a direct and unbroken descent from the Melaka sultanate. In the historic world-view of Malays, the ruler occupied not merely the apex of government (*kerajaan*) but the centre of the cosmos (Brown 1952; Milner 1982). The raja was responsible to Almighty God and had inviolable ties with the *ra'ayat* (people). The acquisition of sovereignty, as distinct from its inheritance by birth, required an installation ceremony in the presence of regalia which, like the ampulla, swords, sceptre, orb and crown of the British coronation, was held in great awe. Indeed, Malay regalia had traditionally been endowed with magical properties (Gullick 1965: 45–46). The very act of seizing regalia had often been enough to win acceptance as king (Heine-Geldern 1942: 26–27).[9] That the position of Yang di-Pertuan Agong was a recent confection by no means demeaned the rites of his installation. On the contrary, as Clifford Geertz has observed, because 'majesty is made, not born', its artifice is 'the very thing that the elaborate mystique of court ceremonial is supposed to conceal' (Geertz 1983: 124). In 1957, as in the past, regalia endorsed the ruler's legitimacy.

So it was that on 2 September 1957 HRH Tuanku Abdul Rahman ibni Almarhum Tuanku Muhammad, Yang di-Pertuan Besar of Negri Sembilan, entered the audience hall, which had been specially built in the grounds of the *istana* (palace) in Kuala Lumpur. He was accompanied by his consort and by *panglima* (chiefs) bearing yellow umbrellas (the seat of a protective spirit), *pedang* (ceremonial swords), the *chogan alam* (the mace symbolising temporal power), the *chogan ugama* (symbolic of spiritual authority) and the royal *nobat* (drums).[10] After the Agong and his consort had been ushered to thrones on the canopied dais, the Grand Chamberlain led a procession bearing a gold-bound copy of the Koran, the gold kris of state, the proclamation and

---

[8]The sultans of Johore, Kelantan and Selangor were allotted different carriages in the procession. Physically slight, His Highness Ibrahim of Kelantan was overshadowed by his travelling companion, the statuesque and ebullient Queen Salote of Tonga, who endeared herself to the London crowd by refusing to close the canopy against torrential rain. In the coronation honours, the Sultan of Pahang was awarded an honorary GCMG, and Dato Onn bin Jaafar and Raja Uda bin Raja Muhammad (Mentri Besar of Selangor) received honorary knighthoods. Representatives of Malay royal houses had also attended the coronations of Edward VII (1902), George V (1911) and George VI (1937). For the significance of grand spectacles for reinforcing imperial hierarchies and connections, see Cannadine 2001.

[9]For example, in the contest for the throne of Perak in the 1870s, Raja Ismail had the weakest claim by birth and was passed over in favour of Abdullah at the meeting of chiefs convened by the British at Pangkor in January 1874, but Ismail's standing was strengthened and the legitimacy of the agreement was undermined by his possession of the regalia which he refused to surrender (Cowan 1961: 182–85, 187–89, 218).

[10]For centuries court orchestras of the Malay sultanates of Sumatra and West Malaysia had played at a sultan's installation and on other significant occasions such as royal births but, with a few exceptions, the practice died out in post-revolutionary Indonesia (Kartomi 1997: 3–15).

oath of office. Having read the proclamation, the Grand Chamberlain offered the kris to the Agong who unsheathed it and, as a sign of loyalty to the nation, kissed the blade which had been blended from eleven blades given by the nine states and two settlements of the Federation. He next took the oath promising 'justly and faithfully to perform our duties in the administration of the Federation of Malaya in accordance with its laws and constitution'. Then the assembly shouted *'daulat!'* (majesty) three times, musicians played and outside a 21-gun salute was fired. Finally the chief *kathi* recited a prayer.[11] Although no more than 600 attended the installation (and most of these were British and Malayan dignitaries), it was regarded as a collective affirmation of the new nation. The following day the Yang di-Pertuan Agong opened the federal parliament. On this occasion ritual was shaped by the Westminster, rather than the Malay, tradition as the Agong read his ministers' words and outlined the legislative programme of his government.

These four ceremonies – the political rally on the *padang*; the formal transfer of British jurisdiction in the stadium; the installation of the Agong in the *istana*; the opening of parliament by the paramount ruler – together formed a rite of passage designed both to endorse the colonial legacy and legitimate the new state. Though they may have approached independence celebrations with varying degrees of enthusiasm, neither the British nor the Malayans doubted the importance of the ornamental aspects of the transfer of power. All accepted that even a minor setback might be regarded as a bad omen for the future of the nation.

The protocol and pageantry of imperial recessional

Britain's imperial recessional from 1947 to 1997 was marked by pageantry in one territory after another. By the time it was the turn of small islands in the 1970s, routine had become well-established:

> There is a check-list of about eighty points under ten main headings. They are ticked off in a bureaucratic way one by one – relevant or not – it is as simple as that. Only one or two will be so controversial as to require substantial negotiation. It has all been done, over forty times before![12]

Indeed, the pattern followed a more or less standard form of flag ceremonies, military tattoos, firework spectacles and state banquets. The first of these took place in India in August 1947 when the British attempted to present the transfer of power as the fulfilment of their historic mission. While there was no ceremonial lowering of the union flag in Delhi, Mountbatten himself choreographed a scene in which the last viceroy and his

---

[11] All this was new to Lord Kilmuir who was on his first visit to Malaya as leader of the British government delegation. He felt that the 'weird jungly music restored the feeling of the East which had been slightly diluted by the British robes of the judges and the European dress of the spectators'. His lord chancellor's costume consisted of a wig, knee-breeches, a heavy tail-coat and a gold robe (Maxwell Fyfe 1964: 305–7).

[12] Sir Colin Allan, governor of the Seychelles (1973–76) and the Solomons (1976–78) quoted in Hyam (2006: 399–400).

staff would salute the Indian flag when it unfurled. But the Indian crowd upset his plans; it 'surged into the specially prepared arena and threw the display into turmoil' providing 'perhaps the only moment of real comedy in a tragic summer' of communal bloodshed (Bayly and Harper 2007: 292). There were minor hitches on other occasions, too. In Ceylon there was some talk about independence martyrs and a man in the crowd produced a placard urging the king's representative to go home (de Silva 1997: II, 366). At the inauguration of Malaysia in September 1963, Sarawak's head of state fainted (Stockwell 2004: 578). Sometimes the weather threatened proceedings: on Kenya's day of independence (12 December 1963) heavy rain caused such chaos on the route to the stadium in Nairobi that the British secretary of state missed the ceremony (Devonshire 2004: 78; Sanger 1995: 3).

In planning the transfer great care was taken to anticipate and prevent solecisms. Thus, soothsayers meditated over propitious dates and bureaucrats pondered upon protocols. As ritual was devised and tradition invented, they were scrupulously checked against precedent and etiquette. Local superstition was always taken into account; seers in India pronounced that freedom should come at midnight on 14 August 1947 (Ziegler 1986: 422). During the preparations for Malayan Merdeka, regular reference was made to procedures adopted in Ceylon, Ghana and even the hapless Burma where the choice of the most auspicious moment for the transfer – 4.20 am on 4 January 1948 – failed to secure a peaceful future for the Union or its lasting friendship with Britain. Indeed, the British regularly cited their withdrawal from Burma as a lesson and a warning; on the eve of independence 'there was a governor: but no British administration'. At least the governor departed with all due honours. After making 'a nostalgic farewell trip down the Irrawaddy' and inscribing a message of peace in the visitors' book of the Shwe Dagon, Sir Hubert Rance embarked on the cruiser *HMS Birmingham* (Tinker 1984: II, xxxvi–xxxvii, 799, 837). When Rance reached London, Sir Gilbert Laithwaite of the Burma Office rewarded him with a pair of tickets for *Annie Get Your Gun* which had been pulling in audiences at the Coliseum since June (Bayly and Harper 2007: 323). Far worse than Burma was the debacle in Palestine which the British left in May 1948 without reaching a settlement or retaining their dignity. The high commissioner, Sir Alan Cunningham, ran the gauntlet of Jewish and Arab irregular troops as he was driven in a bullet-proof car from Jerusalem to the port of Haifa, while his chief secretary, Henry Gurney, allegedly told journalists at the King David Hotel that he would leave the keys of government 'under the mat' for anyone who might chance to find them (Hyam 2006: 399; Hennessy 1993: 242). Nearly 20 years later, Sir Humphrey Trevelyan agreed to go to Aden as its last high commissioner on condition that the Cabinet would not let the country collapse into 'another Palestine'. Nevertheless, within a few months of his arrival, Trevelyan was briskly escorted from government house to the harbour accompanied by a military band playing 'Fings ain't what they used to be' (Thornhill 2004).

Thirty years after Aden, the eyes of the world were upon Hong Kong. Advances in technology by this time meant that pictures of its formal retrocession to China were instantly beamed round the world. The occasion was attended by Prime Minister Blair, former Prime Minister Major, Prince Charles and Chinese officials from Beijing whom His Royal Highness, writing in a diary that he mistakenly thought would remain confidential, described as 'appalling old waxworks'. Tearful and drenched by rain, the last governor gathered the union flag and embarked on the royal yacht. *Britannia* sailed through a storm of fireworks out of the harbour to join 'the largest fleet assembled by Britain east of Suez since the closure of the naval base in Singapore'. When they reached Manila the Pattens boarded a plane for Britain. For the last governor and his family the empire ended with a bump as they joined the queue for a taxi at Heathrow airport (Patten 2006: 59–60). Yet, however much post-colonial *tristesse* might afflict them, the British were determined to put on a show when decolonisation reached its climax. Even when they transferred responsibility for Basra province to Iraqi forces in December 2007, 'they did so with a precision of language and ceremonial perfected over more than half a century as a contracting colonial power ... The Foreign Secretary represented the British government. Iraq's National Security Adviser thanked British forces and hailed a "victory for Iraq". Flags were raised and lowered; a memorandum was signed'.[13] In Malaya, as elsewhere, they endeavoured to strike a balance between the bland and the brilliant, and orchestrate a withdrawal that would both reflect and reinforce the fundamental strength of the independence arrangements, or at least disguise their fragility.

Tunku Abdul Rahman took a keen interest in the rituals of independence, although, as he did with so much else, he left his loyal lieutenant, Dato Abdul Razak, to take care of the details. Razak chaired the Merdeka Celebrations Committee one of whose members was sent to Accra to learn from the Ghanaian experience in March.[14] By nature intensely superstitious, the Tunku scrutinised the calendar for favourable dates for the transfer of power.[15] He was advised by a wise man of Penang, grandfather of a later prime minister, that 31 August would be an opportune time for the inauguration of the new nation-state and he was reassured when this date was publicly announced on his fifty-third birthday, 8 February 1956.[16] He took it upon himself to design a special uniform which, much to their embarrassment, his ministers were instructed to wear on Merdeka Day. He was also the driving force behind the construction of the Merdeka Stadium and chaired the search committee for a national anthem which eventually decided to adapt a new song, *Negaraku* ('My country'), to the tune of Perak's state anthem. In addition he insisted that the Queen should be represented at the handover and hoped for Princess Margaret.

The request for what British officials referred to as a 'Royal Personage' was a sensitive issue in London. Ministers were wary of over-using top-ranking royals at high-profile occasions marking empire's end, since, as they put it somewhat ruefully, 'this sort of ceremony is likely to become a recurring one over the years

---

[13] *The Independent* (London), editorial, 17 December 2007.

[14] 'Merdeka comes to the Federation of Malaya', despatch from John M. Farrior (second secretary, US Embassy, Kuala Lumpur) to the US State Department, 17 September 1957, RG 59: 797.00/9-1757. Farrior had been US consul-general in Kuala Lumpur immediately before independence.

[15] The Tunku admitted freely that he was careful to plan important events in his life so that they fell between propitious dates or happened in some mysterious harmony with lucky numbers. In 1962 he was delighted that the Malaysia agreement was signed on 1 August, his lucky day, but must have been discomforted the following year when its inauguration was postponed from 31 August to 16 September, Lee Kuan Yew's fortieth birthday. See biographical note, 27 June 1958, DO 35/9997; Miller (1959: 211); Lee (1998: 440–44).

[16] For this background I am grateful to participants at the international seminar on 'Britain and the Malay World' and particularly to Ms Shuhaimi Baba, director of the film docudrama, '1957 Hati Malaya' (Heart of Malaya), Pesona Pictures, 2007.

ahead'.[17] Moreover, aware that whoever represented Her Majesty would be playing second fiddle to Malaya's own monarch, they needed to forestall any confusion over protocol. They therefore turned to the second tier of royals and, since the Duchess of Kent (widow of one of the Queen's uncles) had already been lined up for independence celebrations in the Gold Coast/Ghana, another royal uncle, the Duke of Gloucester, was invited to do the honours in Malaya. This news 'was greeted with only faintly disguised disappointment' by Malayans who felt they deserved better.[18] The Duke was shy, lacking in self-confidence and had a volatile temper. To his credit he had visited Malaya before the war, served as governor-general of Australia after it, presided over Ceylon's independence ceremony in February 1948, and, but for the intervention of a constitutional conference, would have attended the unveiling of the war memorial in Singapore earlier in 1957.[19]

Harold Macmillan, who became the British prime minister in January 1957, was much less closely involved than the Tunku in planning celebrations for what would be, after all, *Malaya's* day. Yet even Macmillan was drawn into the selection of British representatives, decisions on commemorative gifts and the drafting of goodwill messages. As regards the ministerial delegation, Alan Lennox-Boyd, the secretary of state for the colonies, would have been its leader had he not been indisposed and Duncan Sandys would have taken his place had it not been pointed out that the presence of the minister of defence might appear gratuitously neo-colonial. Macmillan then turned to Lord Kilmuir, the lord chancellor. Unlike the Duke of Gloucester, Kilmuir had never been to Southeast Asia but he had gravitas appropriate to the occasion and a wife who was on friendly terms with the Duchess. It was agreed that both Lord and Lady Kilmuir would go at public expense, though Lord Kilmuir would pay for his valet.[20] In an expansive mood, and until the Cabinet secretary reminded him of the principles governing ministerial conduct, Macmillan maintained that the public purse should cover the costs of the wives of other ministers too, 'just as if', he commented, 'they were the wives of tycoons' whose expenses would be set against profits.[21] There were all manner of other guests, many of them invited by the federal government, such as Sir Gerald Templer, who was credited with winning the battle for Malayan hearts and minds during the war on communist terrorism. Also present were Lady Gent and Lady Gurney, widows of high commissioners killed while in Malayan service, and a young woman who had been the Tunku's driver during the London constitutional talks and 'was billed as a representative of the British working class'.[22] The Duke and his retinue were installed in 'Swettenham's palace', Carcosa. King's House, which the MacGillvrays were preparing to vacate, became a hostel for other

---

[17] Lord Home (secretary of state, Commonwealth Relations Office) and Lord Perth (minister, Colonial Office) to Macmillan, PM(57)7, 21 February 1957, DO 35/9747 and PREM 11/2068.
[18] 'Merdeka comes to the Federation of Malaya', RG 59: 797.00/9-1757.
[19] For the selection of the Duke of Gloucester as Her Majesty's representative, see CO 1030/841, 848, 851; DO 35/9747; PREM 11/2068.
[20] For Kilmuir's role, see CO 1030/842 and LCO 2/5829, TNA; Maxwell Fyfe 1964: 305–7.
[21] F.A. Bishop (principal private secretary to the prime minister) to J.B. Hunt (Cabinet Office), 24 June 1957; Sir Norman Brook (Cabinet secretary) to F.A. Bishop, 20 July 1957, PREM 11/1925.
[22] 'Merdeka comes to the Federation of Malaya', RG 59: 797.00/9-1757.

VIPs.[23] Space was at a premium and there were worries about how far the cutlery, crockery and linen would stretch and whether the air conditioning would be adequate.

The Duke of Gloucester brought with him cordial greetings from the Queen, and Lord Kilmuir had a similar message from the prime minister. There were gifts, too: the Grand Cross of the Royal Victorian Order (GCVO) from Her Majesty the Queen to His Majesty the Yang di-Pertuan Agong; a speaker's chair from the mother of parliaments, as had been presented to Ghana; a postgraduate scholarship from the British people. The suggestion of a scholarship tickled Macmillan's fancy. It was, he wrote, 'the sort of thing Cabinet delight in'. Its cost would be no greater than the fly-past in Ghana and probably a good deal cheaper than the mock battle staged for Nigeria's celebrations three years later when, it was said, 'sufficient thunderflashes were exploded to last the British Army of the Rhine for a year'.[24] The Malayan scholarship fund would provide for one postgraduate studying in the United Kingdom for two years every two years. A recipient in the early 1960s was the historian Kernial Singh Sandhu, who went on to become Director of the Institute of Southeast Asian Studies in Singapore.[25] For his part, the Tunku presented the British government with the deeds of Carcosa, the former residency and finest colonial house in Kuala Lumpur, which after independence was home to a succession of post-colonial British high commissioners until 1984 when Margaret Thatcher agreed to return it to Malaysia.[26]

The road to independence was paved with good intentions but there were potholes on the way. Had the Tunku gone ahead, as many in his party wished him to do, and issued invitations to the governments of Egypt, Syria and Saudi Arabia, he would have caused considerable embarrassment for the British government which had severed diplomatic relations with these countries following the Suez crisis the previous year.[27] Further controversy was triggered by the ill-timed announcement by Duncan Sandys on 20 August during a visit to Australia that Canberra bombers, which formed the major part of the UK's air-strike force in Malaya, were equipped to carry nuclear weapons. The defence minister's statement provoked outrage in Malaya; it threatened the conclusion of the Anglo-Malayan Defence Agreement and cast a shadow over the preparations for independence.[28] The episode did not, in the end, upset the timetable for Merdeka. It did, however, give an edge to Malayan self-determination with the result that signing the defence agreement was postponed until October.

---

[23] Letter and note from Sir Gilbert Laithwaite (permanent under-secretary, Commonwealth Relations Office) to Sir Harry Lintott (Commonwealth Relations Office), 6 March 1957, CO 967/312. Laithwaite was reporting from Kuala Lumpur on preparations for independence. Carcosa had been built in 1897–98 for the resident-general of the Federated Malay States during Sir Frank Swettenham's term as the first holder of this post.
[24] See PREM 11/1926; LCO 2/5829; Lynn (2001: I, xciii, note 133).
[25] See PREM 11/1926 and OD 19/109.
[26] The return of Carcosa was one in a series of moves by the British government to improve Anglo-Malaysian relations after their deterioration during the early years of Dr Mahathir's regime, *The Times*, 7 April 1984. Carcosa has since become a luxury hotel.
[27] See CO 1030/842 and DO 35/9747.
[28] See CO 1030/836 and DO 35/9785.

The celebrations on 31 August were 'most successful', reported Sir Geofroy Tory, Britain's first high commissioner to independent Malaya. 'Public enthusiasm was on the whole restrained and a quietly festive atmosphere prevailed.'[29] Whether it was the achievement of independence that was being celebrated or the fulfilment of an imperial mission or the birth of a Malayan nation or the triumph of Malay nationalism, it is clear that joy was largely confined to the capital. And even in the capital there was an air of lassitude. The crowd on the *padang* at midnight was small, well behaved and overwhelmingly Malay. 'Nor', observed US diplomatic staff, 'was there very much more spirit at Merdeka Stadium later in the morning.' They were not alone in attributing the restraint to, amongst other things, the lack of nationalist martyrs, the fact that 'the "British yoke" was easy to bear', 'the natural placidity of the Malays', and effective security measures.[30] These measures were necessary since the Emergency (1948–60) still gripped the land. On its guard against a flare-up of communist insurgency or communal conflict, the government instructed district officers to restrict commemorative activities to reading the proclamation and raising the flag. To its relief, the week passed without serious incident. In the kampongs Malays gathered round wireless sets to listen to proceedings broadcast from Kuala Lumpur. On rubber estates, 31 August was treated as a normal working-day. Some Malayans did not disguise their delight at seeing the back of the British, yet thousands of Chinese, Malays and Indians in Penang astonished European residents with a show of public grief on the waterfront (Shennan 2000: 343–44). Such grief is indeed astonishing in view of Britain's callous abandonment of the people of Penang to the Japanese in December 1941. The reason for their sorrow surely lay as much in the islanders' secessionist tendencies and premonitions regarding the centralism of the new regime as in any regret they may have felt at the passing of colonial rule.

In London a small ceremony took place outside Malaya House in Trafalgar Square, where the flag was broken and, in the presence of Lord Home (the Commonwealth secretary), Dato Nik Kamil (Malaya's first high commissioner to London) read out the proclamation of independence and inspected 50 Malayan Army cadets. Ten days later the Singapore Diocesan Association held a well-meant but somewhat incongruous thanksgiving service in St Martin's-in-the-Fields while Dato Nik Kamil, who as a Muslim did not participate, waited at the church door to greet worshippers as they filed out. The dawn of a new era excited Malayan students and their London base, Malaya Hall, was packed with visitors and seethed with activity. The Tunku's cries of 'Merdeka!' reached Malayan students as far afield as King's College in Newcastle (later Newcastle University) who to this day remember watching a film of the Kuala Lumpur celebrations at the Osborne Road Methodist International House. There was some disappointment that scant attention was paid to the event elsewhere in the world but Dr Ismail bin Haji Abdul Rahman Yassin (Malaya's ambassador to Washington and representative at the United Nations) soon brought the new state to international attention when he addressed the General Assembly proudly displaying a kris tucked into the waist of his national dress.[31]

---

[29] Sir Geofroy Tory to the Commonwealth Relations Office, 9 September 1957, CO 1030/845.

[30] 'Merdeka comes to the Federation of Malaya', RG 59: 797.00/9-1757.

[31] This paragraph is based on CO 1030/849 and DO 35/9491; *The Times*, 2 September 1957; Ooi (2006: 89–90); private communications.

Looking back on 31 August 1957, the Tunku recalled: 'I was a very happy man indeed.' His happiness was replete with goodwill towards the former colonial power. He declared:

> For many years past our fortunes have been linked with those of Great Britain. . . . We shall therefore always remember with gratitude the assistance which we have received from Great Britain down our long path to nationhood, an assistance which culminates to-day with the proclamation of Malaya's independence. But the long-standing friendship between our countries does not cease with independence.[32]

The British reciprocated. Although Macmillan refused to welcome Malayan independence with a prime ministerial broadcast on the BBC lest the British public thought he was celebrating the 'weakening of the United Kingdom',[33] he nonetheless sent a personal message to the Tunku in which he hailed Malayan independence as 'the culmination of the joint work of our two Governments over the past years'.[34] It has to be said that goodwill generally suffused the moment when power was eventually transferred, even in territories where the experience of decolonisation had been bitter and hard-fought. Kwame Nkrumah acknowledged that Britain was 'a great and ever-abiding friend' to Ghana and recognised its 'wise leadership and guidance' (Rathbone 1993: II, 417). Jomo Kenyatta of Kenya, who was detained by the British for years following a rigged trial, and Robert Mugabe, who fought a war for Zimbabwe's independence, paid similarly generous tributes to former colonial regimes at the moment when they terminated. Notwithstanding the almost universal exchange of courtesies at empire's end, the decolonisation of Malaya does appear to have been exceptionally good-natured in comparison with struggles elsewhere. To many at the time and since, the 'clockwork inevitability' of the independence process (Shennan 2000: 342) indicated measured planning and a high degree of Anglo-Malayan co-operation. The records reveal, however, that it was also accompanied by mutual mistrust and, at least on the British side, by mounting pessimism and a tendency 'to muddle through'.

A continuing Anglo-Malayan partnership?

What is striking about Malaya's advance to independence in the mid-1950s is its speed. Since 1948 the Malayan authorities had been locked in combat with communist guerillas and ministers had made it clear that independence could not be contemplated until the Emergency was over and a multi-racial, nationalist movement flourished. If the British did not envisage early independence, nor did most Malayans. Indeed, when the Tunku became president of UMNO in August 1951, its slogan was *Hidup Melayu!* (Long live Malays!) not *Merdeka!* Its aim was to advance Malay interests in a communally

---

[32]Tunku Abdul Rahman's speech in Merdeka Stadium on 31 August 1957, quoted in Miller (1959: 208–9).

[33]P. de Zulueta (private secretary to Macmillan), 15 August 1957, in Stockwell (1995: III, 412).

[34]PREM 11/1927. Macmillan's message was presented to the Tunku by Lord Kilmuir.

divided country, not to create an independent Malayan nation. At that time the people had yet to experience elections at any level. All members of the federal legislative and executive councils were either colonial officials or government nominees. Yet within six years the country had moved through municipal, state and federal elections to popular democracy and sovereign independence. Contrast this pace with that in Ceylon and Ghana. In Ceylon constitutional change was a long-drawn-out process. Elections based on universal suffrage were held as early as 1931 (it might be noted that universal suffrage had been introduced in the United Kingdom only two years before) and Ceylonese acquired ministerial responsibilities at the same time. Yet British rule continued for another 17 years. While political change accelerated in the Gold Coast/Ghana after 1948, nationalist claims were more thoroughly tested at the polls than they were in Malaya. Ghana, the first sub-Saharan African colony to achieve independence, went through three general elections before the British transferred power, whereas Malaya took the leap to freedom on the basis of only one, and even that was for a partially elected legislature.

The most remarkable aspect of the federal election of July 1955 was not the Alliance's victory but the size of its victory. That it would win had not been in doubt; that it would completely annihilate its opponents was, as Francis Carnell observed at the time, a great surprise (Carnell 1955: 315–30).[35] The Alliance gained 51 of the 52 electable seats and obtained approximately 80% of the votes cast, or ten times as many votes as its principal rival, Dato Onn's Party Negara.[36] The Tunku's appeal to the overwhelmingly Malay electorate lay in his commitment to Merdeka. Moreover, the fact that the Alliance also returned 17 non-Malay candidates appeared to vindicate his commitment to multi-racial politics. Although the Federation was granted limited self-government with the Tunku as chief minister, he was unwilling to wait on events. He had a popular mandate to make an immediate bid for more power. Whereas before the election he had aimed to achieve independence after four years, he now slashed the waiting time by half to bring forward the target date to 31 August 1957. Yet, instead of being rebuffed, as he had been on the previous Alliance mission to London,[37] the Tunku and his colleagues were promised all that they wanted on

---

[35] See also the telegram of 3 August and the despatch of 8 August 1957 from Sir Donald MacGillivray to Lennox-Boyd in which the high commissioner reported on the process and results of the general election, CO 1030/225.

[36] The general election was for 52 of the 98 seats in the new Federal Legislative Council. Although Malays amounted to just less than half the total population, they comprised over 84% of the electorate. This was because many adult non-Malays were not yet federal citizens or, if they were, had failed to register on the electoral roll. Chinese accounted for 37% of the population but only 11.2% of the electorate. The single electable seat not won by the Alliance was that which went to the Pan-Malayan Islamic Party. The 46 non-electable seats were filled by nominated members, five of whom were appointed by the high commissioner in consultation with the leader of the party winning the greatest number of elected seats, thereby reinforcing the Tunku's position.

[37] In May 1954 an Alliance delegation to London had failed to persuade the then secretary of state, Oliver Lyttelton, to accede to their demand for a larger proportion of elected seats on the Federal Legislative Council. Returning empty-handed, the Alliance leadership mounted a boycott of the public service and forthcoming elections. This forced the Malayan authorities to compromise over the composition of the legislative council.

'a golden platter' when they arrived in London for constitutional talks in January 1956 (Shaw 1976: 106).[38]

Why did the British so readily yield to the Tunku's demands? Could it have been that the Malayan Alliance had become irresistible? After all, 18 months earlier it had forced the high commissioner into concessions by threatening civil disobedience and a boycott of government.[39] Moreover, UMNO, which was the dominant party in the Alliance, had not lost that ability to mobilise Malays in mass protests which it had first demonstrated so effectively during the Malayan Union crisis in 1946. On the other hand, UMNO's Chinese and Indian partners hardly set their communities alight, while the Tunku himself was no nationalist firebrand. Temperamentally he was very different from Dato Onn bin Jaafar, the charismatic founder of UMNO, and, although he resembled Gandhi, Jinnah, Nkrumah, Kenyatta, Hastings Banda, Eric Williams and countless other nationalist leaders in having spent considerable time abroad, unlike them he did not return home to launch a popular anti-British campaign. He may occasionally have courted colonial displeasure in order to enhance his nationalist credentials but the British were never provoked into arresting him or inadvertently awarding him the nationalist's cachet of 'prison graduate'. It would seem, therefore, that the British government could have stood its ground – as several ministers in the Conservative Cabinet were inclined to do – when the Tunku arrived in London armed with a popular mandate for the achievement of independence no later than 31 August 1957. That it did not reject the Tunku's demand, was less because of the threat which he presented and more because of the values and interests which he shared with Britain.

Unlike many nationalist leaders who had bitter memories of living and studying in the United Kingdom, the Tunku had largely enjoyed the experience. Sometimes, indeed, the extent of his anglophilia embarrassed the British. For example, Whitehall recoiled from his suggestion that David Watherston, the colonial chief secretary, should stay on as Britain's high commissioner to independent Malaya. Such an appointment would give the impression of a phoney independence – an impression which they were anxious to conceal.[40] On most issues of major significance, however, the British saw eye to eye with the Tunku. His enemies were their enemies. Indeed, in due course he would erect a National Monument to commemorate, not the Malayan struggle against British colonialism, but those Malayans who had fallen alongside British and Commonwealth forces in two world wars and the Emergency.[41] He was also anxious to stem a post-Merdeka 'white flight' and hoped to convert colonial officials to public service in the new Malaya.

---

[38]This chance remark, made by Sir John Martin of the Colonial Office and overheard by the press, may have heartened the Malayan delegation when it arrived at London airport but it reinforced critics' suspicions of 'colonial stooges'.

[39]This episode, which began with an abortive mission by Alliance leaders to London in April-May 1954 and ended in July with a compromise over the proportion of elected to unelected seats in the federal legislature, is covered in Stockwell (1995: II, 21–68).

[40]See CO 967/313.

[41]The National Monument, *Tugu Negara*, was designed by Felix de Welden and inspired by the Iwo Jima memorial in Washington DC. It was completed in 1966 but annual ceremonies have been discontinued.

As independence approached, British ministers welcomed the Tunku's commitment to multi-racialism and anti-communism, and their anxieties were allayed by his readiness to join the Commonwealth, remain within the sterling area, employ expatriates in key positions, retain British forces for internal security and, finally, to conclude a defence treaty which would guarantee British use of military bases in the region. His very public statement on Merdeka Day, that 'the long-standing friendship between our countries does not cease with independence', suggested that hardly anything of substance was being transferred from the British to the Malayans and that neither side expected their relationship to alter in essentials. As regards the question of sovereignty, Britain had few rights to dispose of in any case. Its presence in the Malay states had always rested on treaties, whereas Crown jurisdiction had been confined to Penang and Malacca which the Duke of Gloucester made a point of visiting during Merdeka week as a gesture to the 'Queen's Chinese' who were British subjects by birth. With respect to the realities of power, on the other hand, Britain would keep a controlling interest in Malaya's economy, internal security and external defence. Seen in this light, it is difficult to conclude that 31 August 1957 marked the start of a mature relationship between autonomous states.

The thesis that Merdeka Day represented merely a shift from colonialism to neo-colonialism in which Tunku Abdul Rahman performed the role of Britain's stooge or running dog has been strongly argued over the years.[42] It presents, nonetheless, a misleadingly simplistic view of power and the limitations of power. A puppet would have been of little use to the British. What they needed was a leader who commanded authority in his country and who would stand by international agreements. Once dismissed as a playboy, 'the student prince', the Tunku had risen in esteem since he had assumed the leadership of UMNO in 1951. Although the Alliance which he negotiated between UMNO, the MCA and MIC had at first been regarded as a rickety exercise, it was vindicated in the federal elections. This landslide victory of 1955 enhanced his reputation as a non-communal nationalist. Five months later, his handling of Chin Peng, who failed at the Baling Talks to win political recognition for the Malayan communists, confirmed the Tunku as a statesman in British eyes. He had become a leader with whom they could do business.

When the Malayan delegation arrived in London in January 1956 and demanded independence by 31 August 1957, it was, therefore, pushing at a half-open door. But there were still some in Whitehall who tried to keep it on the chain. They were uneasy about what the future held for Malaya. They were, in any case, averse to issuing a deadline by which British rule would cease, arguing that a timetable might turn out to be unrealistically rigid or detrimental to the interests of both Britain and Malaya. After all, it was not so long ago that Malay leaders themselves had answered calls for independence with *belum layak* (not yet ready). Indeed, there was reason to doubt the Federation's readiness in 1957. First of all, notwithstanding its election victory, the Alliance's multi-racial claims fooled nobody; consisting of three communally exclusive parties, it institutionalised communal politics. Furthermore, although the communists appeared to be a spent force militarily, the authorities could not yet afford to risk lifting Emergency regulations. There was a nagging fear, apparently supported by intelligence, that the insurgents were lying low, regrouping and waiting to

---

[42]See, for example, Mohamed Amin and Caldwell (1977). For an examination of the limitations of the neo-colonial thesis when applied to post-colonial Malaya/Malaysia, see White (2004).

strike after the British had withdrawn. Left to themselves, federal forces would be no match for the guerillas. Another British concern was the fragmentation of their responsibilities in the region: since the late 1940s they had intended to group their Southeast Asian dependencies into a single and eventually self-governing dominion. In the mid-1950s, however, the prospects of territorial consolidation were bleak. If Malaya became independent on its own, planning the futures of Singapore and the Borneo territories would become even more problematic. In addition, the British worried about the Tunku's political survival. Observers questioned his skills to run a government and they weighed the odds of his being able to handle subversion, or racial tension, or economic slump. Other 'cankers' in 'the rose-garden of Merdeka' included administrative decay and incipient corruption.[43] Finally, in spite of the political advantages that royal blood and a popular mandate gave him, the Tunku was coming under pressure from UMNO ultras, and was showing signs of erratic behaviour. 'Time', it was noted, 'is thus not on the side of the Tunku'.[44]

In spite of the fact that aspects of the electoral result were unconvincing and that the Malayan experience of government was virtually untested, the secretary of state for the colonies reached the view that nothing would be gained from questioning the Tunku's legitimacy or rejecting his demands. Like elections in other 'emerging nations', as Justin Willis has written with respect to the Sudan, the 'democratic ritual' itself was seen as 'an assertion of political maturity' and a demonstration of 'readiness for membership of the international community'. It was something of a performance, and the impression it made on outsiders was crucial to success or failure (Willis 2007). In this, the electoral process resembled the independence celebrations. Lennox-Boyd, a key member of the audience, was convinced by the display. He informed his Cabinet colleagues that it was 'scarcely possible to exaggerate the strength of feeling in the Federation about self-government; and the Alliance could hardly be in a stronger position to pursue it'. Any attempt by the British to rein in the Malayan chief minister would undermine his reputation and encourage challenges to his authority. If he returned empty-handed from the London talks, he would be tempted to reopen negotiations with Chin Peng and seek a short-cut to freedom, or freedom of a kind. Lennox-Boyd therefore urged the Cabinet to 'be prepared to go a very long way with the delegation on the fundamental question of political advance'.[45] Since there was no alternative to whom they might turn – Dato Onn, once a man of destiny, was now a spent force – it made more sense to support the Tunku than to snub him. In short, respecting the verdict of the polls, the British government decided to comply with the Tunku's constitutional demands in order to keep him in the saddle and minimise the risk of his becoming a prisoner of hardliners within his own party or doing a deal with Chin Peng.

Independence day was announced on 8 February 1956. Although the date 31 August 1957 was qualified with the phrase 'if possible', it soon became imperative to meet this

---

[43] 'Future of the Alliance government', note by the Commissioner-General's Office, March 1957, CO 1030/440.

[44] 'The outlook in Malaya up to 1960', note by the commissioner-general's office, [May 1957], paragraph 11, FO 371/129342, no. 8. One official commented that the 'somewhat pessimistic analyses ... need not discourage us unduly' since similar forecasts had been made for India after partition.

[45] 'Conference on constitutional advance in the Federation of Malaya', memorandum by Lennox-Boyd for the Cabinet Colonial Policy Committee, 7 January 1956, CAB 134/1202, CA(56)3.

deadline. Politicians and their planners had been given little time in which to accomplish a great deal. Indeed, 18 months were scarcely enough even to perfect the rituals for the ceremonial handover. There was definitely no time to conclude the Emergency, or bring about regional consolidation, or improve the Alliance's attempts at racial integration – all of which had been regarded hitherto as essential prerequisites for independence. But they did manage to complete a defence agreement, arrangements for internal security, the independence constitution, Malaya's application to join the Commonwealth and a financial settlement (not that the Federation was eligible for much). Each of these tasks had immense significance for the shape of the new state and its position in the world. Not surprisingly, tempers frayed in the rush to complete on time. Race relations deteriorated as a result of disagreements over provisions in the independence constitution relating to citizenship and Malay rights. Some of his supporters rounded on the Tunku because of the concessions he made on defence, internal security and the retention of expatriates in senior government posts.

Although the Tunku was accused of being in thrall to Britain, the British by no means had it all their own way. They had been induced to move faster towards independence than many judged to be prudent and they failed to persuade the new Malaya to join what was for them the key defence pact of SEATO. By and large, however, in the years that immediately followed Merdeka, British and Malayans worked in concert to conclude the Emergency, develop the economy, integrate Britain's remaining Southeast Asian dependencies within the Federation and to contain Indonesia. Co-operation was assured not because the British manipulated the Tunku, though they did try, nor because the Tunku readily complied with British policies, though his bonhomie did help. Rather it derived from a congruence of national interests. Ten years after independence, however, these interests were diverging and a once special relationship was jostled by other international connections. Thus, recognising they could no longer afford a massive military presence east of Suez, Britain began to withdraw from the region, while Malaysia joined the exclusively Asian association of ASEAN. At the same time British business struggled to compete in Malaysian markets and Malaysian trade expanded far beyond the Commonwealth (White 2004). In May 1969 there occurred what was euphemistically called an 'incident' which would assume a significance in the modern history of Malaysia as great as that of Merdeka Day. Race riots almost destroyed the independence settlement and shattered the prime minister's dreams. By now an isolated figure, Tunku Abdul Rahman gave way to the next generation of leaders who openly blamed the inequalities of their society upon exploitation and divide and rule by the former colonial power. It would not be long before they would be buying British last.

References

Archival sources

The National Archives, Kew, UK

Files in the following series have been cited:

CAB 134	Cabinet: miscellaneous committees
CO 967	Colonial Office: Private Office

CO 1030	Colonial Office: Far Eastern Department
DO 35	Commonwealth Relations Office: Malaya Department
FO 371	Foreign Office: political (SE Asia)
LCO	Lord Chancellor's Office
OD	Department of Technical Co-operation
PREM	Prime Minister's Office, 1951–64

United States National Archives, College Park, Maryland

RG 59   Department of State Records

Newspapers
The Independent (London)
The Times (London)

Published sources

Abdul Rahman Putra, Tunku. 1977. *Looking back: Monday musings and memories*. Kuala Lumpur: Pustaka Antara.
Ashton, S.R. 2005. Mountbatten, the royal family, and British influence in post-independence India and Burma. *Journal of Imperial and Commonwealth History* 33 (1): 73–92.
Bayly, Christopher and Harper, Tim. 2007. *Forgotten wars: the end of Britain's Asian empire*. London: Allen Lane.
Brown, C.C. 1952. *Sejarah Melayu* or Malay Annals. *Journal of the Malayan Branch of the Royal Asiatic Society* 25 (2 & 3).
Cannadine, David. 2001. *Ornamentalism: how the British saw their empire*. London: Allen Lane.
Carnell, Francis G. 1955. The Malayan elections. *Pacific Affairs* 28 (4): 315–30.
Cowan, C.D. 1961. *Nineteenth-century Malaya: the origins of British political control*. London: Oxford University Press.
de Silva, K.M. (ed.). 1997. *Sri Lanka: British documents on the end of empire*. London: HMSO.
Devonshire, Andrew. 2004. *Accidents of fortune*. Norwich: Michael Russell.
Geertz, Clifford. 1983. Centers, kings, and charisma: reflections on the symbolics of power, in Geertz, *Local knowledge: further essays in interpretative anthropology*. New York: Basic Books, pp. 121–46.
Gullick, J.M. 1965. *Indigenous political systems of western Malaya*. London: Athlone Press.
Heine-Geldern, Robert. 1942. Conceptions of state and kingship in Southeast Asia. *Far Eastern Quarterly* 2 (1): 15–30.
Hennessy, Peter. 1993. *Never again: Britain 1945–1951*. London: Jonathan Cape.
Hyam, Ronald. 2006. *Britain's declining empire: the road to decolonisation, 1918–1968*. Cambridge: Cambridge University Press.
Jennings, Sir Ivor. 1956. Crown and Commonwealth in Asia. *International Affairs* 32 (2): 137–47.
Kartomi, Margaret J. 1997. The royal *nobat* ensemble of Indragiri in Riau, Sumatra, in colonial and post-colonial times. *The Galpin Society Journal* 50: 3–15.
Lee Kuan Yew. 1998. *The Singapore story*. Singapore: Times Editions.
Lynn, Martin (eds). 2001. *Nigeria: British documents on the end of empire*. London: The Stationery Office.

Maxwell Fyfe, David. 1964. *Political adventure: the memoirs of the Earl of Kilmuir.* London: Weidenfeld & Nicolson.

Miller, Harry. 1959. *Prince and premier: a biography of Tunku Abdul Rahman Putra Al-Haj first prime minister of the Federation of Malaya.* London: Harrap.

Milner, A.C. 1982. *Kerajaan: Malay political culture on the eve of colonial rule.* Tucson: University of Arizona Press.

Mohamed Amin and Caldwell, Malcolm (eds). 1977. *Malaya: the making of a neo-colony.* Nottingham: Spokesman Books.

Ooi Kee Beng. 2006. *The reluctant politician: Tun Dr Ismail and his time.* Singapore: Institute of Southeast Asian Studies.

Patten, Chris. 2006. *Not quite the diplomat.* London: Allen Lane.

Rathbone, Richard (ed.). 1993. *Ghana: British documents on the end of empire.* London: HMSO.

Sanger, Clyde. 1995. *Malcolm MacDonald: bringing an end to empire.* Liverpool: Liverpool University Press.

Shaw, William. 1976. *Tun Razak: his life and times.* Kuala Lumpur: Longman.

Shennan, Margaret. 2000. *Out in the midday sun: the British in Malaya 1880–1960.* London: John Murray.

Smith, Simon C. 1995. *British relations with the Malay rulers from decentralization to Malayan independence 1930–1957.* Kuala Lumpur: Oxford University Press.

Stockwell, A.J. (ed.). 1995. *Malaya: British documents on the end of empire.* London: HMSO.

Stockwell, A.J. (ed.). 2004. *Malaysia: British documents on the end of empire.* London: The Stationery Office.

Thornhill, Michael T. 2004. Trevelyan, Humphrey, Baron Trevelyan (1905–1985). *Oxford Dictionary of National Biography.* Oxford: Oxford University Press.

Tinker, Hugh (ed.). 1984. *Burma: the struggle for independence 1944–1948. Constitutional relations between Britain and Burma.* London: HMSO.

White, Nicholas J. 2004. *British business in post colonial Malaysia, 1957–1970: 'neo-colonialism' or 'disengagement'?* London: RoutledgeCurzon.

Willis, Justin. 2007. 'A model of its kind': representation and performance in the Sudan self-government election of 1953. *Journal of Imperial and Commonwealth History* 35 (3): 485–502.

Ziegler, Philip. 1986. *Mountbatten.* London: Fontana/Collins.

The Pattern of Independence: A Postwar Chronology[1]

State	Name before independence	Former colonial power	Date
Vietnam	Annam	France	2 September 1945
Pakistan	(India)	Britain	14 August 1947
India	India	Britain	15 August 1947
Union of Myanmar	Burma	Britain	4 January 1948
Sri Lanka (from 1972)	Ceylon	Britain	4 February 1948
Laos	Laos	France	19 July 1949
Indonesia	Dutch East Indies, Indonesia	Netherlands	Independence declared in August 1945; recognized on 27 December 1949
Cambodia	Cambodia	France	9 November 1953
Sudan	Anglo-Egyptian Sudan	Britain	1 January 1956
Morocco	Morocco	France	2 March 1956
Tunisia	Tunisia	France	20 March 1956
Ghana	Gold Coast	Britain	6 March 1957
Malaya (forming Malaysia, 1963)	Malaya	Britain	31 August 1957
Niger	Niger	France	3 August 1958
Guinea	French Guinea	France	2 October 1958
Cameroon	Cameroon	From French-administered UN trusteeship and part of UN trusteeship territory of British Cameroons	1 January 1960
Togo	Togo	from French-administered UN trusteeship	27 April 1960
Senegal	Senegal	France	Joined Federation of Mali in 20 June 1960; seceded on 20 August 1960
Mali	French Sudan	France	20 June 1960
Madagascar	Madagascar	France	26 June 1960
United Republic of Somalia	British Somaliland	Britain	26 June 1960

[1] Not including the Middle East mandates

Democratic Republic of Congo (Congo-Kinshasa)	Belgian Congo	Belgium	30 June 1960
United Republic of Somalia	Italian Somaliland	Italy	1 July 1960
Benin (from 1975)	Dahomey	France	1 August 1960
Burkina Faso (from 1984)	Upper Volta	France	5 August 1960
Côte d'Ivoire	Côte d'Ivoire	France	7 August 1960
Chad	Chad (France)	France	11 August 1960
Central African Republic	Ubangi-Shari	France	13 August 1960
Republic of Congo (Congo-Brazzaville)	Middle-Congo	France	15 August 1960
Cyprus	Cyprus	Britain	16 August 1960
Nigeria	Nigeria	Britain	1 October 1960
Tanzania	Tanganyika	Britain	26 April 1961; formed Tanzania with Zanzibar, 1964
Sierra Leone	Sierra Leone	Britain	27 April 1961
Kuwait	Kuwait	Britain	19 June 1961
Algeria	Algeria	France	3 July 1962
Jamaica	Jamaica	Britain	6 August 1962
Trinidad and Tobago	Trinidad and Tobago	Britain	31 August 1962
Uganda	Uganda	Britain	9 October 1962
Malaysia	North Borneo	Britain	31 August 1963
Malaysia	Sarawak	Britain	22 July 1963
Singapore	Singapore	Britain	Accession into Malaysia 31 August 1963; separation 9 August 1965
Kenya	Kenya	Britain	12 December 1963
Tanzania	Zanzibar	Britain	19 December 1963; formed Tanzania with Tanganyika, 1964
Malawi	Nyasaland	Britain	6 July 1964
Malta	Malta	Britain	21 September 1964
Zambia	Northern Rhodesia	Britain	24 October 1964
The Gambia	The Gambia	Britain	18 February 1965
Maldives	Maldive Islands	Britain	26 July 1965
Guyana	British Guiana	Britain	26 May 1966
Botswana	Bechuanaland	Britain	30 September 1966
Lesotho	Basutoland	Britain	4 October 1966
Barbados	Barbados	Britain	30 November 1966

The Pattern of Independence 133

Yemen	Aden	Britain	30 November 1967
Mauritius	Mauritius	Britain	12 March 1968
Swaziland	Swaziland	Britain	6 September 1968
Equatorial Guinea	Equatorial Guinea	Spain	12 October 1968
Tonga	Tonga	Britain	4 June 1970
Fiji	Fiji	Britain	10 October 1970
Bahrain	Bahrain	Britain	15 August 1971
Qatar	Qatar	Britain	3 September 1971
Bahamas	Bahamas	Britain	10 July 1973
Guinea-Bissau	Portuguese Guinea	Portugal	24 September 1973
Grenada	Grenada	Britain	7 February 1974
Mozambique	Portuguese East Africa, Mozambique	Portugal	25 June 1975
Cape Verde	Cape Verde	Portugal	5 July 1975
Sao Tome and Principe	Sao Tome and Principe	Portugal	12 July 1975
Angola	Angola	Portugal	11 November 1975
Suriname	Dutch Guiana	Netherlands	25 November 1975
Seychelles	Seychelles	Britain	29 June 1976
Djibouti	French Somaliland	French Territory of the Afars and the Issas (from 1967)	27 June 1977
Solomon Islands	Solomon Islands	Britain	7 July 1978
Tuvalu	Ellice Islands	Britain	1 October 1978
Dominica	Dominica	Britain	3 November 1978
St Lucia	St Lucia	Britain	22 February 1979
St Vincent and the Grenadines	St Vincent and the Grenadines	Britain	27 October 1979
Kiribati	Gilbert Islands	Britain	12 July 1979
Zimbabwe	Southern Rhodesia; Rhodesia after illegal UDI 1965	Britain	18 April 1980
Vanuatu	New Hebrides	Britain	30 July 1980
Belize	British Honduras	Britain	21 September 1981
Antigua and Barbuda	Antigua and Barbuda	Britain	1 November 1981
St. Kitts and Nevis	St. Kitts and Nevis	Britain	19 September 1983
Brunei	Brunei	Britain	1 January 1984
Namibia	South West Africa	Germany; occupation by South Africa from 1915	21 March 1990
(transferred to China)	Hong Kong	Britain	1 July 1997

Index

Aden 5, 118
Africa *see also* particular countries
  Belgium xvi
  French decolonization 99-103, 106-10
  Guyana, Africans in xiv, 72-4, 76, 79, 82-3, 86-7
Agong hereditary rulers 114-17, 121
Algeria 100, 101, 107
American Declaration of Independence 4
Angola xvi-xvii, xviii
anniversaries xvii-xviii, 58, 60-1
Arden-Clarke, Charles 62, 64-7
ASEAN 128
assassinations 9
Attlee, Clement 11, 32-3

Bahamas 21, 24
Banda, Hastings xvii
Bangladesh 54
Bao Dai solution in Vietnam xv, 103-6
BBC 40-1
Belgian Congo's independence from Belgium xvi
betrayal, sense of 9
Botswana xi, xvii
Brazzaville, discours de xv, 100-3, 106-7
British Empire, independence from the *see also* India's independence from United Kingdom; India's independence from United Kingdom, media and; Malaysia's independence from United Kingdom; royal family at Independence Day ceremonies, presence of Aden 5, 118
American Declaration of Independence 4
Bahamas 21, 24
Botswana xi, xvii
Burma 6, 118
colonial separation, stages of 4
Commonwealth 5, 10, 36, 91, 115, 126, 128
costs of ceremonials 6
dates of ceremonials 118
de-dominionization 4-5, 8
dominions, independence from 8
Egypt, independence of 4, 5
flag symbolism xii, xviii
French decolonization 101-2, 105, 109
Ghana xiii, xvii, 10, 19-20, 23, 57-70, 123
Guyana xiv, 21, 71-88
Hong Kong x-xi, xviii-xix, 3, 11, 25, 118-19
Ionian Islands x-xi
Irish Free State, creation of 4
Jamaica 20
Kenya xviii, 6, 10, 24, 118, 123
Malawi xvii

136 *Index*

Mauritius 22, 24-5
merger of countries 7
Middle East, departures from the 4-5, 118
New Hebrides xv-xvi
Nigeria 20
non-ceremonial paths to independence 4-5
observances in London 12
Palestine 5, 118
parliamentary democracy, legacy of 10-11
protocol and pageantry of imperial recessional 117-23
religious services in London 12
self-congratulation 32-3, 42
Sierra Leone 25
Sri Lanka 24, 114, 118, 124
successor state, UK as 11-13
Tanganyika 21-2
twice, countries gaining independence 8
British Guiana *see* Guyana's independence from United Kingdom
Burma 6, 118
Burnham, Forbes xiv, 71-87

Callaghan, James 90
Cameroun 99
Campbell-Johnson, Alan 37-41
Cannadine, David xi-xii, 101
Carrington, Peter 90-4
Carter, Jimmy 90, 91
cartoons 35-6, 38
Castro, Fidel xiv, 74-8
Central African Republic 99-101
Ceylon 24, 114, 118, 124
Chad 100
Charles, Prince of Wales 8, 11, 21, 24-5, 89, 95-6, 118-19
China xviii, 3, 11, 118
chronology of independence 131-3
Churchill, Winston xii, 42
CIA (Central Intelligence Agency) 78
citizenship 52, 55

class struggle in Guyana 72-3
Cold War 75, 77
Commonwealth
  goodwill 5, 10
  India 36
  Malaysia 115, 126, 128
  Zimbabwe 91
communism 71-7, 79, 86
comparative studies xvi
conflict *see* violence and conflict
Congo xvi, 100
constitutional conferences 79-80, 83
conventions, mix of xv-xvi
Côte d'Ivoire 107
Cuba xiv, 74-9, 84
Cyprus
  state of emergency 6-7

D'Aguiar, Peter 71, 78, 80-3
dates of ceremonials
  British Empire 118
  French decolonization 100
  Ghana 61-4
  Guyana 77, 80-1
  India ix-x, 118
  Malaysia 119, 121, 124, 127-8
de Gaulle, Charles xv, 100-2, 107-9
decolonization *see also* British Empire, independence from the; French decolonization
  Belgium xvi
de-dominionization 4-5, 8
Defferre, Gaston 106-7
disloyalty 49-55

Egypt, independence of 4, 5
elections
  Ghana 61-3, 124
  Guyana 72-4, 83, 86
  Malaysia 124, 126-7
  Sri Lanka 124
  Zimbabwe 90-6
Elizabeth II, presence of 19-20

Federation of French Equatorial Africa (AEF) 100, 106-7

flag symbolism
  British Empire xii, xviii
  Hong Kong xviii
  India 31-2, 47, 52-3, 117-18
  Pakistan 47, 52-3
Foccart, Jacques 100, 109
France *see* French decolonization
'freedom at midnight' ix-xii
  Angola xvi-xvii
  anniversaries xvii
  Botswana xi
  French decolonization xv, 101
  Hong Kong x, xviii-xix, 6
  India ix-x, xviii, 8-11, 31-2, 47-8, 118
  Malaysia 113-14
  Midnight's Children. Salman Rushdie ix-x
  Pakistan 47-8
  Zimbabwe 89-90, 93-5, 97
French decolonization 99-111
  Africa 99-103, 106-10
  Algeria 100, 101, 107
  Bao Dai solution in Vietnam xv, 103-6
  Brazzaville, discours de xv, 100-3, 106-7
  British models of celebrations 101-2, 105, 109
  Cameroun 99
  Central African Republic 99-101
  Chad 100
  Communauté 100-1, 107-9
  Congo 100
  Côte d'Ivoire 107
  date of ceremonies 100
  de Gaulle, Charles xv, 100-2, 107-9
  development funding 103
  empire-state, creation of 102-3
  federal membership of *Communauté*, proposal for 107-8
  Federation of French Equatorial Africa (AEF) 100, 106-7
  Framework Law (*Loi-Cadre*) 106-7
  'freedom at midnight' xv, 101
  French West Africa (AOF) 106-9

  Gabon 100, 107, 109
  Guinée 108-9
  Indochina 101, 103-6, 109-10
  Madagascar 99, 106-7
  Mali 109
  myth-making 102
  New Hebrides xv-xvi
  ornamentalism 101
  permanence, constitutional myth of xv
  referendum 107
  Senegal 109
  Soudan 109
  Sub-Saharan Africa xv, 99-100, 107-10
  transfer of power concept xv, 101-2
  Vietnam xv, 101, 103-6, 109-10
    Bao Dai solution in xv, 103-6
    Doc Lap 105
French West Africa (AOF) 106-9

Gabon 100, 107, 109
Gandhi, Mahatma 33, 50
Ghana's independence from United Kingdom 57-70
  50th anniversary celebrations xvii, 58, 60-1
  constitution 62, 64-6
  Convention People's Party (CPP) 59-63
  costs 65-6
  coup d'etat xiii, 59
  date of independence 61-4
  elections 61-3, 124
  fly-past 65-6, 67
  Ghana@50 xvii, 58, 60-1
  goodwill 123
  infrastructure 66
  Kent, Duchess of 66-7
  National Liberation Council 59
  National Liberation Movement 62-3
  Nkrumah, Kwame xiii, 10, 23, 58-61, 63-4, 67-8, 123
  northern Ghana 59
  oppositions 62-3

138 *Index*

royal family, presence of 19-20, 23, 66-7
southern Ghana 59
traditions, invented xiii, 66
violence and conflict 62
Gloucester, Duke and Duchess 7, 20-1, 23, 114, 120-1, 124, 126
Gold Coast *see* Ghana's independence from United Kingdom
goodwill towards colonial power
  Commonwealth 5, 10
  Ghana 123
  India 32, 38
  Malaya 123, 125-6
Great Britain *see* British Empire, independence from the
Guinée 108-9
Guyana's independence from United Kingdom 71-88
  Africans xiv, 72-4, 76, 79, 82-3, 86-7
  Booker 71, 76
  boycotts 83-4
  Burnham, Forbes xiv, 71-87
  Catholic Church 76-80
  CIA (Central Intelligence Agency) 78
  class struggle 72-3
  Cold War 75, 77
  communism 71-7, 79, 86
  constitutional conferences 79-80, 83
  Cuba, revolution in xiv, 74-9, 84
  D'Aguiar, Peter 71, 78, 80-3
  date of independence 77, 80-1
  elections 72-4, 83, 86
  emigration 86-7
  Indians xiv, 72-4, 76, 78-9, 82-3, 86-7
  Jagan, Cheddi xiv, 71-87
  Labour Relations Bill 78-9
  Marxism 72-6, 81-2, 84-5
  Marxism-Leninism 74-6
  People's National Congress (PNC) 71, 75-81, 84
  People's Progressive Party (PPP) 71-4, 80-1, 84-6
  population decline 86-7
  Portuguese 71, 77-8
  racial conflict xiv, 72-4, 76-9, 82-3, 86-7
  royal family, presence of 21
  socialism 71-2, 76
  state of emergency 84
  sugar industry 78-9, 82
  trade unions 78-9, 82
  Tri-continental conferences 84, 85
  United Force (UF) 71, 75-81, 84, 86
  United States xiv, 71, 76-80, 83, 86
  violence 71, 79, 81-2, 85

Hefford, Eric xii, 2-3, 6
Hindus 50-4
historical perspective of independence day celebrations 1-17
Ho Chi Minh 103-6
Hong Kong
  Charles, Prince 11, 25, 118-19
  China, return to xviii, 3, 11, 118
  Chinese flag xviii
  'freedom at midnight' x, xviii-xix
  rain xviii
  royal family 11, 25, 118-19
Houphouët-Boigny, Felix 107-8

national identity *see* nationalism and national identity
image and presentation 39-40
Indépendence cha cha cha xvi
India's independence from from United Kingdom 47-56 *see also* India's independence from United Kingdom, media and xii
  assassinations 9
  Bangladesh 54
  betrayal, sense of 9
  citizenship 52, 55
  Congress Party 48-9, 53
  continuities 54-5

date of independence ix-x, 118
disloyalty, suspicions of 49-50
flag symbolism 47, 52-3, 117-18
'freedom at midnight' ix-x, xviii, 8-11, 47-8, 118
Gandhi, Mahatma 33, 50
Hindus 50-4
Midnight's Children. Salman Rushdie ix-x
minorities 53
Mountbatten, Louis ix, 8-9, 12, 105, 117-18
Muslims 48, 49-54
national identity and loyalty 49-55
nationalism and nation statehood 54-5
Nehru, Jawarhalal ix, 47-8, 50-2, 55
Pakistan xiii, 33-6
partition xiii, 9, 49-50, 52
prisoners, release of 49
private homes, ceremonies in 51-2
rain xviii
refugees 51-2
religious rituals 50-1
swaraj (self-rule) 48-9
violence 118
India's independence from United Kingdom, media and xii-xiii, 29-45
Attlee, Clement 32-3
BBC 40-1
cartoons 35-6, 38
Commonwealth, role of 36
coverage 30-1
flag symbolism 31-2
'freedom at midnight' 30-1
freedom struggle, lack of discussion of Indian 33-4
geographical scope of coverage 30
goodwill 32, 38
headlines, examples of 311
image and presentation 39-40
Indian Civil Service (ICS) 32
massacres, reports of 34-5, 42-3
nationalism, lack of discussion of Indian 33

news agencies in Delhi 30
newspapers xii, 29-40
newsreels 40-1
Pakistan 33-6
partition 33-5
personalization of politics 32-3
princely states, dereliction of duty to 35, 114
public opinion 42-3
Raj, potted history of the 32
self-congratulation 32-3, 42
self-governance, questioning India's capacity for xii-xiii, 42
symbolism, explaining the 31-2
violence 34-5, 42-3
Indians in Guyana xiv, 72-4, 76, 78-9, 82-3, 86-7
Indochina xv, 2, 101, 103-6, 109-10
informal celebrations xvi
insurgents 10, 122, 126-7
Ionian Islands' independence from United Kingdom x-xi
Iraq, British withdrawal from 119
Irish Free State, creation of 4

Jagan, Cheddi xiv, 71-87
Jamaica 20
Jinnah, Muhammad Ali 34, 48, 53

Kambalu, Simon xvii
Kennedy, JF 71, 76-9, 81
Kent, Duke and Duchess of xi, 7, 20-1, 23-5, 66-7
Kenya xviii, 6, 10, 24, 118, 123
Kenyatta, Jomo 10, 123
Kilmuir, Lord 120-1
Kwayana, Eusi 73-4, 83

land restitution 91
Lennox-Boyd, Alan 63-6, 120, 127
Levin, Bernard 2
list of independence days and royal participation 16-17
London, observances in 12, 122
loyalty 49-55
Lumumba, Patrice xvi

MacGillivray, Donald 114, 120-1
Macleod, Ian 75-6
MacMillan, Harold 11, 12, 74, 78, 120-1, 123
Madagascar 99, 106-7
Malawi's independence from United Kingdom xvii
Malaya *see* Malaysia's independence from United Kingdom
Malaysia's independence from United Kingdom xiii-xiv, 113-30
  Agong hereditary rulers 114-17, 121
  Alliance 113, 114, 115, 124-8
  Anglo-Malayan Defence Agreement 121, 128
  ASEAN 128
  Commonwealth 115, 126, 128
  controversies 121
  date of independence 119, 121, 124, 127-8
  elections 124, 126-7
  'freedom at midnight' 113-14
  Gloucester, Duke of 23, 114, 120-1, 126
  goodwill 123, 125-6
  head of state 23
  installation of Agong 115-17
  insurgents 10, 122, 126-7
  Kilmuir, Lord 120-1
  London, ceremony in 122
  MacGillivray, Donald 114, 120-1
  Malayan Union crisis 1945-46 114
  Merdeka xiii-xiv, 113-15, 118, 119, 121-8
  monarchy 114-17, 121
  multi-racialism 10, 123-4, 126, 128
  nationalism 114-15, 122, 123, 125
  neo-colonialism 126
  protocol and pageantry 115-17, 118, 119-23
  Rahman, Tunku Abdul 113-14, 115-17, 119, 121-8
  royal family, presence of British 16-17, 114, 119-21, 126
  rulers, British connections with 114-15
  scholarship fund, gift of 121
  speed of advance to independence xiv, 123-6
  tradition 113-17
  UMNO 109, 123-5, 127
  Yang di-Pertuan Agong 115-16, 121
Mali 109
Malraux, André 99-101
Margaret, Princess 20, 22
Marley, Bob 95
Marxism 72-6, 81-2, 84-5
Marxism-Leninism 74-6
Mauritius 22, 24-5
Mbanga, Wilf 94-6
media *see* India's independence from United Kingdom, media and
Merdeka in Malaysia xiii-xiv, 113-15, 118, 119, 121-8
merged nations, royal family participation and 7
Messmer, Pierre 100, 108-9
Middle East, departures from the 4-5, 118
Midnight's Children. Salman Rushdie ix-x
monarchs and rulers *see also* royal family at Independence Day ceremonies, presence of
  Agong hereditary rulers 114-17, 121
  Malaysia 114-17, 121
  princely states of India, dereliction of duty towards 35, 114
  Sri Lanka 24, 114
Mountbatten, Louis ix, 8-9, 12, 105, 117-18
Mugabe, Robert xiv-xv, 10, 89-90, 92-7, 123
Muslims in India and Pakistan 48, 49-54
Muzorewa, Abel 90, 92-4

nationalism and national identity
  India 49-55
  loyalty 49-55

Malaysia 114-15, 122, 123, 125
Muslims 49-50
nation statehood 54-5
Pakistan 49-55
neo-colonialism 126
Nehru, Jawarhalal ix, 47-8, 50-2, 55
New Hebrides
  conventions, mix of xv-xvi
  France xv-xvi
  United Kingdom xv-xvi
  Vanuatu xv-xvi
newspapers, Indian independence and xii, 29-40
newsreels, Indian independence and 40-1
Nigeria 20
Nkomo, Joshua 10, 90, 92, 94, 96-7
Nkrumah, Kwame xiii, 10, 23, 58-61, 63-4, 67-8, 123
non-ceremonial paths to independence 4-5

Oliver, Brian 96
ornamentalism xi-xii, 101

pageantry 117-23 *see also* flag symbolism
Pakistan's independence from from United Kingdom 47-56
  assassinations 9
  Bangladesh 54
  citizenship 52, 55
  Congress Party 48-9, 53
  continuities 54-5
  disloyalty, suspicions of 49-50
  flag symbolism 47, 52-3
  'freedom at midnight' 47-8
  Hindus 50-4
  India, relationship with 9
  Jinnah, Muhammad Ali 34, 48, 53
  minorities 53
  Muslims 48, 49-54
  national identity and loyalty 49-55
  nationalism and nation statehood 54-5
  newspapers 33-6

partition xiii, 33-4, 49-50, 52
prisoners, release of 49
private homes, ceremonies in 51-2
refugees 51-2
religious rituals 50-1
swaraj (self-rule) 48-9
Palestine 5, 118
parliamentary democracy, legacy of 10-11
partition of Indian sub-continent xiii, 9, 33-5, 49-50, 52
Patten, Chris xviii-xix, 6, 11, 118-19
Pax Britannica xii-xiii
permanence, constitutional myth of xv
personalization of politics 32-3
Philip, Prince 20, 21-2, 24
Portugal
  Angola xvi-xvii, xviii
  Carnation Revolution xvi
  'freedom at midnight' xvi-xvii
  Guyana, Portuguese in 71, 77-8
presentation and image 39-40
princely states of India, dereliction of duty towards 35, 114
prisoners in India and Pakistan, release of 49
private homes in India and Pakistan, ceremonies in 51-2
protocol and pageantry 117-23

Queen Elizabeth II, presence of 19-20

race
  Guyana xiv, 72-4, 76-9, 82-3, 86-7
  Malaysia 123-4, 126, 128
Rahman, Tunku Abdul 113-14, 115-17, 119, 121-8
rain
  Angola xviii
  Hong Kong xviii
  India xviii
  Kenya xviii, 6, 118
Raj, potted history of the 32
Razak, Dato Abdul 119

refugees 51-2
religion
  Guyana 76-80
  Hindus 50-4
  India 48, 49-54
  London, religious services in 12
  Muslims in India and Pakistan 48, 49-54
  Pakistan 48, 49-54
restitution of land 91
Rhodesia *see* Zimbabwe's independence from United Kingdom
royal family at Independence Day ceremonies, presence of
  absence of royal family 6-7
  Bahamas 21, 24
  Botswana xi
  Burma 6
  Charles, Prince of Wales 8, 11, 21, 25, 89, 95-6, 118-19
  choice of representative 19-21
  elite royals 20-1
  gender 21, 24-5
  Ghana 19-20, 23, 66-7
  Gloucesters 7, 20-1, 23, 114, 120-1, 124, 126
  Guyana 21
  hierarchy, end of 19, 25
  Hong Kong 11, 25, 118-19
  Jamaica 20
  Kents xi, 7, 20-1, 23-5, 66-7
  Kenya 24
  list of independence days and royal participation 16-17
  Malaysia 19-20, 23, 114, 119-21, 126
  Margaret, Princess 20, 22
  Mauritius 22, 24-5
  merged nations 7
  Nigeria 20
  Philip, Prince 20, 21-2, 24
  public order 7
  Queen, presence of the 19-20
  role of xii, 6-8, 19-27
  Sierra Leone 25

Tanganyika 21-2
voluntary transfer of power, symbolism of 22-3
Zimbabwe 8, 89, 95-6
rulers *see* monarchs and rulers
Rushdie, Salman. *Midnight's Children* ix-x

sanctions 90
Sandys, Duncan 79-81, 84, 120, 121
scholarship fund to Malaysia, gift of 121
self-congratulation 32-3, 42
Senegal 109
Senghor, Léopold Sédar 107-8
Sierra Leone 25
Smith, Ian xiv, 83, 90, 93
Soames, Christopher 90, 91, 93-4
socialism 71-2, 76
Soudan 109
South Africa 90, 92-6
Southern Rhodesia *see* Zimbabwe's independence from United Kingdom
Sri Lanka's independence from United Kingdom 24, 114, 118, 124
swaraj (self-rule) 48-9

Tanganyika 21-2
territory, transfers of 3
Thatcher, Margaret 90-1
Touré, Sékou 108-9
Tory, Geofroy 122
trade unions in Guyana 78-9, 82
traditions xiii, 66, 113-17
transfer of power concept xv, 101-2
Tri-continental conferences 84, 85
twice, countries gaining independence 8

United Kingdom 119 *see also* British Empire, independence from the
United States
  American Declaration of Independence 4

CIA (Central Intelligence Agency) 78
Cold War 75, 77
communism 76
Cuba 76, 79, 84
Guyana xiv, 71, 76-80, 83, 86
Zimbabwe 90, 91

Vanuatu xv-xvi
variations in ceremonies 6-8
Vietnam
  Bao Dai solution in xv, 103-6
  French decolonization 101, 103-6, 109-10
  Doc Lap 105
  Vietnam War 2
violence and conflict
  assassinations 9
  Ghana 62
  Guyana 71, 79, 81-2, 85
  India 9, 34-5, 42-3, 118
  Kenya 10
  Malaysia 10, 122, 126-7
  Pakistan 9
  Zimbabwe xv, 10, 90-4, 96, 123
voluntary transfer of power, symbolism of 22-3

Wavell, Archibald 37

Yang di-Pertuan Agong 115-16, 121

Zimbabwe's independence from United Kingdom 89-98
  appearances 90-4
  Charles, Prince 89, 95-6
  civil war 90-2, 123
  Commonwealth Heads of Government Meeting (CHOGM) 91
  elections 90-6
  'freedom at midnight' 89-90, 93-5, 97
  goodwill 123
  Government of National Unity (GNU) 90-1
  Gukuruhundi campaign xv
  hopes and dreams 94-7
  land restitution 91
  Lusaka Conference 1979 91
  military forces, integration of 92-3
  Mugabe, Robert xiv-xv, 10, 89-90, 92-7, 123
  Muzorewa, Abel 90, 92-4
  NIBMAR (No Independence Before Majority Rule) xiv
  Nkomo, Joshua 10, 90, 92, 94, 96-7
  Patriotic Front 91
  Rhodesia Front 90, 96
  Rhodesian security forces 90-4, 96
  royal family at ceremony, presence of 8, 89, 95-6
  sanctions 90
  Smith, Ian xiv, 83, 90, 93
  Soames, Christopher 90, 91, 93-4
  South Africa 90, 92-6
  UANC (United African National Congress) 90
  Unilateral Declaration of Independence (UDI) xiv, 95
  United States 90, 91
  violence and turmoil xv, 10, 90-4, 96
  world leaders, attendance of 89
  ZANLA (Zimbabwe African National Liberation Army) 90, 91-2
  ZANU(PF) (Zimbabwe African National Union) 89-90, 92, 96
  ZAPU (Zimbabwe African People's Union) 90, 92
  Zimbabwean Fifth Brigade xv
  ZIPRA (Zimbabwe Independent People's Revolutionary Army) 90, 91

For Product Safety Concerns and Information please contact our EU
representative GPSR@taylorandfrancis.com
Taylor & Francis Verlag GmbH, Kaufingerstraße 24, 80331 München, Germany